The Pageant of
Early Tudor England

The Pageant of Early Tudor England 1485-1558

ELIZABETH BURTON

Illustrated by
FELIX KELLY

**CHARLES SCRIBNER'S SONS
NEW YORK**

1 3 5 7 9 11 13 15 17 19   c/c   20 18 16 14 12 10 8 6 4 2

Printed in the United States of America
Library of Congress Catalog Card Number 76-54554
ISBN 0-684-14917-6

'. . . If secret powers
Suggest but truth to my divining thoughts,
This pretty lad will prove our country's bliss.
His looks are full of peaceful majesty,
His head by nature fram'd to wear a crown,
His hand to wield a sceptre, and himself
Likely in time to bless a regal throne.'

W. Shakespeare (*Henry VI*, Pt 3, Act IV, sc. vi)

For

Robert Mather Russell
(1908–1973)

'Dyvers thy death doo dyverslye bemone'
Henry Howard, Earl of Surrey

Contents

Acknowledgements

I owe so much to so many historians and biographers of the Tudor period and the present day that it is impossible to name them other than in the bibliography and I hope that this seeming discourtesy will be understood and forgiven.

I am deeply grateful to the Librarian and staff of the Bodleian Library, and to those of the London Library, particularly the Deputy Librarian, Mr Douglas Matthews, B.A., F.L.A., who helped me solve a problem concerning Henry VII. I am indebted to the Witney Branch of the Oxfordshire County Library which went to endless trouble for me, as did Miss Katherine Watson of Watson's Bookshop, Burford.

Curators, archivists and staff of local museums, of houses, of castles all over the country have treated me with the utmost courtesy and I am most grateful. Mr Edward Ingram Watkin put his immense store of knowledge at my disposal and also assisted me greatly with his enthusiasm and encouragement.

To Dr Margaret B. Noble, M.R.C.O.G., my sincere thanks for reading Chapter 5, and to Miss L. D. Grotrian and many other friends my appreciation for their help with a variety of 'intangibles'. I wish also to thank Mrs J. Becker who accepted the no easy challenge of my handwriting and typed the MS.

For any errors of fact or judgement I am indebted to no one but myself.

E.B.

Hailey, Oxon., 1976

CHAPTER ONE

Of England – and a New Dynasty

'And my der Hert, y now beseche you of Pardon of my long
and tedyous Wrytyng, and pray almighty God to gyve you as
long, good and prosperous Lyfe as evyr had Prince, and as
herty Blessyngs as y can axe of God. At *Calais Town*, thys Day
of Seint *Annes*,* [Agnes] that y dyd bryng ynto thys World
my good and gracyous Prynce, Kynge, and only beloved
Son.

By
your humble Servant, Bede-woman, and Modyer
MARGARET R.'[1]

This letter, with its slightly biblical flavour, was written perhaps
in 1501 by the Lady Margaret Beaufort, Countess of Richmond,†
to her son, King Henry VII. He was born on 28 January 1457 at
Pembroke Castle and was a posthumous child, his father, Edmund
Tudor (1430?–56), Earl of Richmond, having died early the
previous November leaving his recently married wife, little more
than a girl of fourteen, to bear the 'only beloved Son' who was to

---

* Anne is an eighteenth-century misreading for Agnes; thus for centuries it
was thought that Henry VII was born on 26 July. St Agnes's day is 21 January
but there is a second, separate and minor commemoration falling on the
octave, 28 January. It is to this date modern historians assign the birth of the
first Tudor king.

† This is the official title given her by king and Parliament in 1485. She was
at this time, however, also Countess of Derby but I shall refer to her throughout by the name by which she is best known, the Lady Margaret Beaufort.

become future king and so fulfil the ancient prophecy that Wales would one day rule England.

Henry VII's claim to the throne was certainly shaky and there were other and rival claimants who had a better title. Henry's descent from John of Gaunt's legitimated child by Catherine Swynford was on the maternal side. His mother was Gaunt's great-granddaughter, while the old Lancastrian Duke himself had been the third son of Edward III. On his father's side Henry could claim to be half-nephew to Henry VI through that sad king's mother, Catherine of Valois, widow of Henry V. She had married – some say there was no marriage, but there was probably a canonical one – Owen Tudor, a Welsh gentleman whose descent, illustrious if a trifle obscure, he traced back to Cadwaladr. Of this marriage there were, probably, four children (half-siblings to Henry VI): Edmund, who married the Lady Margaret Beaufort; Jasper, Earl of Pembroke,* guardian to his nephew and a staunch supporter of his claim, and Owen, about whom very little is known. Polydore Vergil says he became a Benedictine monk and he may have died in 1502. There was also possibly a daughter who became a nun.

Although Henry's claim by blood was less than could be desired, he also won the throne 'by both steel and parchment . . . that is to say a conquest in the field, and an act of parliament'.[2] The field was Bosworth, where on 22 August 1485 he had defeated Richard III and where 'immediately after the victory, as one that had been bred under a devout mother, and was in his nature a great observer of religious forms, [he] caused *Te Deum laudamus* to be solemnly sung in the presence of the whole army'.[3] The army – Roman fashion – proclaimed king the twenty-six-year-old invader (for Henry had come from a long exile in Brittany and France) and Sir Thomas Stanley placed on his head Richard's crown, which had been found among the spoils. The army's proclamation was ratified by the new king's first parliament the following November.

The battle of Bosworth, although no one could have suspected

* Created Duke of Bedford by his nephew in 1485.

it at the time, was, if not the last, at least the decisive battle of the wearing and wearying Wars of the Roses which had commenced thirty years before, in 1455, just two years after the end of the intermittent Hundred Years' War. This century of a war had been begun by Edward III (1312–77) and it ended by leaving us bereft of all our conquests and possessions in France save Calais.

These Wars of the Roses, fought on home ground, were 'a factious fight between families allied to the royal house, contending for power and wealth and ultimately for possession of the crown'.⁴ But by practising neutrality and by giving presents of money to whichever king happened to be king, as well as to powerful nobles, London and other cities remained relatively unaffected by these ding-dong wars, and their citizens could carry on their trades much as usual.

This, however, was not true in the country – and England was predominantly rural; battles, although sporadic and wide apart in time and space, were nevertheless local battles, as great noblemen and landlords fought each other for each other's possessions. Ownership of land and overlordship of people spelled power and these wars gave many a great and noble landlord an excuse to settle, by arms, quarrels over the right of possession. Thus the small, private gentleman who wished to live safely and in peace could do so only under the patronage of some lord. The rural population was in the same boat; the people were not slaves but they too lived under patronage and owed allegiance to their lord for benefits received.

The wars, where a great lord might win, lose, change sides or be killed – and the Wars of the Roses were a great destroyer of ancient nobility – therefore caused intense discomfort, disorder and damage. What was needed was a strong king, peace and good government. Henry VII gave a tired and disillusioned country all three. Also, by marrying Elizabeth of York, daughter to Edward IV, to whom he had been contracted in marriage when in exile, he reconciled, at least symbolically, the warring factions of York and Lancaster.

Henry VII was a wise man. Bacon calls him 'one of the best of all wonders, a wonder for wise men'.[5] He saw what the country most needed and was strong enough to carry out this vision. What it did not need was a despotic king of the kind then so prevalent on the continent. It needed a strong king, but one who would build upon or, rather, re-animate the existing form of government which had been shattered and crippled during the wars: a king who would preserve the old institutions of King's Council, Parliament and Common Law. Henry's primary concern, then, was to maintain public peace, restore law and order, make the country economically sound, avoid war and make England respected by foreign powers. More personally, he wished to establish a dynasty.

The new king therefore made few changes. He built his government upon the structure existing in 1485. The nub of his Council had been formed during his last years of exile in Brittany when, on Christmas Day 1483, he had openly proclaimed his royal dignity in Rennes Cathedral. His close associates after the victory at Bosworth remained his confidential advisers – a sort of inner (or Privy) council to which other members were added to form the greater Council. The king, an excellent judge of character, also took as councillors those who had had experience under Edward IV and Richard III. Twenty-nine of the king's councillors had been councillors to one or other of the Yorkist kings, thirteen to both of them and nineteen to Richard III. Fifteen were near relatives of the councillors of Edward IV, whilst others had been administrators under the Yorkist régime. The first Tudor king was undoubtedly a great man, for he was big enough to employ the best men even if they were Yorkists; he was also wise enough to follow the York pattern of government and did not impose upon the country anything new and strange. Further, he kept his high officials. There were, during his reign of twenty-four years, only four Chancellors, two Treasurers and two Keepers of the Privy Seal. This made for stability, continuity and security.

Parliaments were held and Henry summoned his first on 7 November 1485, eight days after his coronation, which took place on 30 October. They were not held regularly – there were but seven during the reign – but there was not much interest in parliament at this time and little resentment if it did not meet for five or six years on end. However, law was restored throughout the country; the weak were protected from the strong – many of the strong, it is true, were in their graves – and the king, like all subsequent Tudors, was chary of creating new peers. Since a paid bureaucracy would have meant higher taxation – a thing most bitterly resented in those days – the king and his judicial councillors governed and maintained law through justices of the peace, an already well-established institution which dated back to 1361.

Justices of the peace were appointed annually, shire by shire, and the king not only re-animated but increased the duties of this commissioned body of men, so that 'it became a principle with Tudor Government to commit the carrying out of legislative reforms to the justices',[6] while 'as the justices took hold of the countryside, the gentry began to see in membership of the commission – work virtually unpaid and frequently tiresome – a necessary part of their lives and power'.[7] The number of justices increased greatly; so did the burden of their work. They dealt with a variety of felonies and offences, licensed ale-houses, fixed wages, enforced price regulations, poor laws and so on, and they were controlled by a watchful council which instructed them in their duties and could expel any justice for inefficiency or local opposition. By such means the king maintained law, order and good government which, since the justices were unpaid and independent gentlemen, had the immense advantage of being cheap.

The strong rule which began with Henry VII became the characteristic of the Tudor dynasty. The first Tudor was efficient, hardworking, paid off his debts as soon as possible, was one of the cleverest sovereigns we have ever had and was basically a splendid administrator. None of these qualities make for glamour but 'if there have been periods when the needs of "good government" prevailed over the demands of "free government"', the Tudor age 'was a time when men were ready to be governed, and when order and peace seemed more important than principles and rights'.[8] The first Tudor king provided good government, order and peace. A selfish and self-seeking aristocracy wanting power to enrich itself and its followers had proved the country's undoing in the past. It was not to happen again under the Tudors. No one man, no coterie, would be allowed to become stronger than the king.*

Yet in an essentially monarchical age, when the king was the source and fountainhead of all social and political activity and life, when kingship was semi-divine – a point the Tudors knew how to stress – this semi-divinity was still subject to the common law of the land. Therein lay the country's strength. Therein, too, were the king both wise and strong – as Henry VII was – lay the strength of the king.

Although the new king was strong he was neither bloodthirsty nor vindictive. It is true – and sad – that he did clap ten-year-old Edward, Earl of Warwick (1475–99), into the Tower immediately after Bosworth, because the young Earl, a direct descendant of Edward III and son of the late Duke of Clarence, had the best claim to the throne, but he did not indulge in the execution of his enemies. A number of leading Yorkist supporters of Richard III were attainted – their revenues and estates fell to the crown, which was useful – yet the king offered complete pardon to those who swore fealty to him. Many former adversaries took advantage of this; John de la Pole, Earl of Lincoln (1464?–87), son of Richard III's sister, Countess of Suffolk, and named by the dead Richard as his successor, was one of these. He was treated kindly and even became a member of the king's Council. Nevertheless, despite the king's desire to heal old wounds and unite the country, during the early years of his reign he was 'harassed by opponents . . . assaulted by enemies . . . troubled by insurrections'.[9]

Trouble began almost at once. In April 1486, Francis, Lord Lovell (1454–87?), ex-chamberlain to and friend of Richard III, broke sanctuary at Colchester and plotted to ambush the king who was on a royal progress to York. The plot failed; Lovell fled

* An exception was during the reign of Edward VI.

abroad and fetched up in Burgundy. At the same time Humphrey and Thomas Stafford also left sanctuary at Colchester and fomented a troublesome but abortive rising in Worcestershire. These two then fled to Abingdon for further sanctuary 'where they were soon arrested on the ground that even the protection of a holy place did not avail against high-treason'.[10] Here it is well to note that 'the court of the king's bench decided that sanctuary was a common-law [not a Canon-Law] matter in which the Pope could not interfere',[11] and Professor G. R. Elton points out that this was 'a striking instance of the growing resistance to ecclesiastical pretentions',[12] as the privilege of sanctuary 'did not cover treasonable offences'.[13] Humphrey Stafford paid the penalty for treason. He was hanged. But mercy was shown to his brother Thomas. Nevertheless, the king, having presented the Pope with a *fait accompli*, wisely and diplomatically wrote long letters to Rome 'explaining the abuses of sanctuary as a threat to peace and good order'.[14] Finally, in 1489, Pope Innocent VIII issued a bull limiting the privileges of sanctuary.

On 19 September in the year of the Lovell–Stafford attempts, the king's son was born. He was 'strong and able' and Henry 'in honour of the British race, of which himself was, named [him] Arthur, according to the name of that ancient worthy king of the Britains, in whose acts there is truth enough to make him famous, besides that which is fabulous'.[15] The heir to the throne had been born with unwonted celerity – he was an eight months' baby – and the succession, bar accidents, was secured more swiftly than nature generally allows.

But, again, all was not well. In November, following the birth of the heir, rumour ran that soon something would be heard of the imprisoned Earl of Warwick, and very early in the next year a reasonable facsimile of the Earl turned up in Ireland. Although in February 1487 the king, knowing this, had exhibited the Earl in London – he was taken to High Mass at St Paul's and allowed to speak to anyone who knew him – it made not a whit of difference. On 24 May in Christ Church, Dublin, the bogus Earl was enthusiastically crowned as Edward VI. This impostor was

Lambert Simnel (fl. 1487–1525?), a gentle, good-looking boy, the son of an obscure Oxford joiner* who, under the tutelage of a priest, William (or Richard) Symonds, was coached to play the part of the Earl. Who organized or who was behind this plot we still do not know, but it is fairly safe to assume that there must have been some very important Yorkist figures (after all, the Staffords had sought sanctuary near Oxford), particularly as John, Earl of Lincoln, repaid the king's leniency and kindness by joining Simnel in Ireland, possibly because he saw the boy as a cat's-paw and himself, ultimately, as king. We do know, however, that Margaret, Duchess of Burgundy (1446–1503), sister to Edward IV and aunt of the Earl, who hated the Tudor upstarts, had a hand in the plot (as did Lovell), although she did not organize it. The king's friends called this vindictive and meddlesome Duchess 'Juno because she was to him as Juno was to Aeneas, stirring both heaven and hell to do him mischief'.[16]

She supplied the impostor and her nephew with two thousand German mercenaries and, with these and some thousand Irish, Simnel crossed to England, where he was joined by not so many disgruntled English as he had hoped for. Further, the English liked neither the efficient Germans nor the wild Irish. Henry met the impostor's army and defeated it at the battle of Stoke on 16 June 1487. The Earl of Lincoln, who fought bravely, was killed. Lovell disappeared and was presumed dead. Henry, out of contempt or pity, gave young Simnel a job as turnspit in the royal kitchens. Symonds was imprisoned for life. The battle of Stoke was, however, the last battle of the Wars of the Roses.

Another impostor threatened the throne in 1491, but before that a number of things happened. Henry became involved, reluctantly, in a war with France – a country with which he had a peace treaty – and became an ally of Spain. The details of this war are 'extremely complicated and almost equally immaterial'.[17] Apart from the fact that Henry as king of England also claimed to be king of France, and that many people in England – but not the

---

* The father is variously described as being joiner, baker, shoe-maker, organ-maker.

king – still wanted back all the French possessions of Henry V, whose infant son had been crowned king in Paris, France wanted Brittany. But Brittany had helped Henry with men and money when he was in exile, while France had helped him to invade England. Henry was in a dilemma, but the Breton ports were very close to the ports of the western counties and to the east, Calais, our great foothold on the continent, could be cut off. France could then command the channel.

Spain, too, did not want Brittany to become a part of France, and Spain was a growing power on the continent. Henry, who wanted desperately to have his dynasty recognized by a strong continental power, became an ally of Spain (and also of the tricky Roman emperor, Maximilian I) and England's commercial, no less than her political, interests were served by the treaty of Medina del Campo (1489). This treaty gave us favourable commercial concessions, bound us to go to war on behalf of Spain if necessary and, further, opened negotiations for the marriage of the infant, Prince Arthur, with Catherine (1485–1536), daughter of Ferdinand of Aragon and Isabella of Castile, whose own marriage had united Spain and made her a rising power. The diplomatic intrigues of continental countries and the Papacy, plus the desire to curb the power of an over-mighty France, can be taken for granted. And in 1492, when Columbus crossed the Atlantic, Henry crossed the Channel (in October) to besiege Boulogne.

Little happened. France was unprepared and Henry kept the door open for a negotiated peace. After a few weeks the French king, Charles VIII, and Henry signed the treaty of Étaples, in which Henry agreed not to press the English claims on France and in return received from the French king 745,000 gold crowns, to be paid off at the rate of 50,000 crowns annually. For Henry it had been a lucrative war, and by the time the affair was over both France and Spain recognized the strength and ability of the first Tudor. Thus Henry 'who judged a diplomatic victory to be no less glorious to a commander than a military one'[18] achieved what he wanted with little bloodshed.

9

By now the dynasty boasted another two* children, a daughter, Margaret (1489–1541) and a son, Prince Henry, born 28 June 1491.

In the year of Prince Henry's birth, another and more serious impostor made his appearance – in Ireland: this time in Cork. He was a well-dressed, handsome youth of seventeen and was 'a finer counterfeit stone than Lambert Simnel'.[19] His name was Peterkin or Perkin Warbeck, and his parents lived in Tournai. Warbeck assumed the identity of Richard, Duke of York, younger son of Edward IV. As the king could produce neither this young prince nor his elder brother from the Tower, the false Richard was in a better position than Simnel had been, and his claim could be more strongly pressed. His first protector was Charles VIII, but Charles gave this up when the Treaty of Étaples was signed and Warbeck went to Burgundy, where the formidable Duchess took him up as her 'nephew'. It is hardly probable that she believed him to be Richard, but she was perfectly capable of taking up anyone as the rightful Yorkist heir. She undoubtedly coached Warbeck in his 'lineage' and in courtly manners and customs.

Warbeck, with these new accomplishments, then found a better protector in the Emperor Maximilian, who thought this an excellent opportunity of getting back at Henry for what he considered to be his double-dealing over the Treaty of Étaples. He recognized Warbeck as Richard IV and promised him every support in recovering the crown. Warbeck, grandly, made Maximilian his heir so that if he were killed in battle England would fall to the Roman emperor. That Warbeck could find so much support from foreign powers in itself signifies that there must have been great hopes of a Yorkist revival abroad as well as in England.

In England, Sir Robert Clifford fled to Flanders to join the impostor, thought better of it and returned to betray his English followers to the king – he may, of course, have been Henry's

* There were seven children of the marriage; only three survived to adulthood. Tudor babies did not live; Yorkist ones did.

man from the beginning. Heads rolled or necks were stretched, and among those executed for conspiracy was Sir William Stanley, who had come over to Henry of Richmond at Bosworth and had become chamberlain to the king's household. There seems small doubt that he was guilty of changing sides again. The fact that his elder brother, Thomas, first Earl of Derby (1435–1504), was the king's stepfather did not save him, which indicates how seriously he must have been involved, for it was never easy to persuade the king of anyone's treasonable intentions or acts.

The execution of the conspirators effectively killed the conspiracy in England but Warbeck, who had planned an invasion, was not wise enough to realize this. In July 1495 he began to land his forces off Deal; prudently, he did not land with them – his men were killed or captured without difficulty by loyal Kentishmen. Warbeck immediately set sail for Ireland and, having failed to take the loyal town of Waterford, made haste to Scotland and King James IV, who, although Scotland and England had a treaty, hated England. James welcomed Warbeck warmly and presented him with a wife, Lady Catherine Gordon, daughter of the first Earl of Huntly, and a Scottish army crossed the border to loot and burn with great savagery which, to be honest, distressed Warbeck. This distress occasioned some surprise to both the Scots and the English.

Henry, who preferred diplomacy and peace with honour to war as a settler of disputes, was not really disposed to make the border raid an issue, even though he had to gather his army together. He was encouraged in his peaceful intentions by Spain, which wanted his support against France, now growing too strong in Italy. Further, the heavy taxation needed to support a war had been so bitterly resented in Cornwall that in 1497, whilst the army prepared for a possible Scottish expedition, armed Cornishmen rose in their thousands and marched across England to London almost without hindrance. They encamped at Blackheath, where on 17 June they were easily surrounded by an army led by the king, and the rebellion collapsed. A good many were killed, many more, including the leaders, were taken prisoner, but only the leaders were executed; fines were exacted from others. The victory had been won by about two o'clock in the afternoon and the king, ever devout, gave thanks in St Paul's. On the next day the marriage treaty with Spain's elder princess was ratified.

After this Henry, urged on by Ferdinand and Isabella, suggested that James IV should hand Warbeck over to him and so avoid hostilities. James contented himself with dismissing Warbeck, but also showed that he wished to continue the war. Another attack by the Scots in August 1497 was easily repulsed and the English armies crossed the border; by the end of September an Anglo-Scottish truce was signed.

In the meantime the dismissed Warbeck, with some thirty followers, crossed to Ireland in a ship appositely named *Cuckoo*. His reception in Cork in June was so chilly that he determined to sail for Cornwall and profit by the discontent there. He arrived in September and, though joined by a number of malcontents, failed to take Exeter. He fled and was taken at Beaulieu; he then made a full confession, was sent to London and paraded through the streets, made a public confession, and was kept in light custody in Winchester Palace and provided for by the king. But Warbeck, still dreaming of grandeur and despite his confession, took to his heels and sought refuge in a Carthusian monastery at Sheen. He was taken, made yet another public confession in London and was sent to the Tower, where he was lodged next to the Earl of Warwick.

Early in 1499 another bogus Earl of Warwick appeared; this was Ralph Wulford (1479?–99), a tool of the Yorkists. He was put forward by yet another priest, Patrick, an Augustinian friar. The conspiracy was speedily detected and Wulford was hanged that February.

Meanwhile, Warbeck and the real Warwick were conspiring – or were said to be conspiring – in the Tower. No one knows quite how this happened: possibly through a corrupt gaoler or an *agent provocateur*. This conspiracy was uncovered in August; both young men were tried and found guilty of treason. Warbeck, the false Richard IV, was, reasonably enough, hanged on 3 November

1499. He had been a thorn in the king's flesh, a focal point for disruption and discontent, since 1491. The real Earl of Warwick, guilty probably of nothing more than Plantagenet blood, was executed on 29 November. It may be that Ferdinand and Isabella insisted on his execution, for they wished no rival claimant to the English throne now that their daughter was to marry Prince Arthur. Or perhaps Henry had decided that as long as Warwick lived he would continue to be impersonated and be a rallying point for Yorkist discontent. The second motive is just excusable; the first is not. Even so, the king was a good deal more merciful than most contemporary sovereigns.

So it was not until the turn of the century that the king could feel himself, his dynasty and the country secure. Much had happened in the fifteen years since Bosworth besides contention with impostors and Yorkist plots. Not the least important was that by 1492 the king was not only out of debt but had begun to build up his legendary fortune, so that when he died it was reported that he left 'near eighteen hundred thousand pounds' which, says his first biographer, writing in 1622, was 'a huge mass of money even for these times'.[20] What it would be today is beyond calculation. One way in which the king gathered money was by 'benevolences': that is, by gifts extorted from the rich, on the grounds that their wealth was so great they could afford it, and also from those who lived plainly and without ostentation, on the plea that thrift and economy must have made them rich too. Archbishop Morton apparently put this policy into action – it had also been used by Edward IV – but Bacon says of this that Bishop Morton, the Chancellor, used a '*dilemma* . . . to raise up the benevolence to higher rates; and some called it his fork and some his crutch'.[21] Polydore Vergil says this tax might equally well be called a 'malevolence', yet the king also reformed the antiquated machinery of the exchequer and made it function more efficiently by appointing trained administrators as under-treasurers.

Since wealth meant power and land meant wealth, the king, in order to be the most important man in the kingdom, also had to be the richest, which in turn meant he must be the greatest landowner. Thus, he also built up his fortune by increasing crown lands. These were, first, the lands belonging to the Tudors by inheritance, to which were added the spoils of the Wars of the Roses and lands forfeited by traitors or confiscated. When he created Prince Henry Duke of York at the age of three, the duchy of York came into the king's hands, as well as the earldom of March. The earldoms of Warwick and Beauchamp, acquired by Edward IV, were also his, as well as other properties with their rents and revenues. He began to live and dress with great magnificence, as befitted a powerful prince, and this impressed foreign ambassadors who reported back to their masters the king's power and splendour. He also began collecting jewels, for which he had a passion, and one foreign observer tells us that he spent more than £100,000 on them. Jewels were, of course, very useful as portable riches.

As important as sound finance and the respect with which Henry was regarded abroad was the fact that he now had a treaty with France and Scotland and that the Spanish marriage was now definitely arranged. Trade with Flanders, broken off in 1493 because the Flemish had refused to disown Warbeck, was most profitably resumed in 1496.

In May 1497 John Cabot with his sons, Lewis, Sebastian and Sancius, set sail from Bristol on their first voyage. They were commissioned by the king with 'full authority leave and power to saile to all parts, countreys, and seas of the East, of the West, and of the North under our banners and ensigns',[22] to discover the North-west Passage. Cabot returned convinced that the new-found land he had discovered belonged to the Great Khan. This, as we know, was erroneous. He also reported vast quantities of fish in the offshore waters. This was true and fishing later on became a profitable industry. There was great excitement on Cabot's return; he came to court dressed in silks and all London ran after the 'Great Admiral'. But no hint of this enthusiasm is found in the Privy Purse Expenses. 'To hym that founde the new Isle, £10',[23] is the dry entry. The king gave him an annual pension of twenty pounds, however, which seems to have been paid until 1499 when John Cabot disappears from historical records.*

It was also in 1497 that the betrothal of Prince Arthur and Catherine formally took place. In the following year negotiations for the marriage of the king's elder daughter, Margaret, to King James IV of Scotland were opened – the children of kings were valuable property for diplomatic, trade and martial alliances. A dispensation for this marriage, as the king and princess were fourth cousins via John of Gaunt, was granted by Pope Alexander VI in 1500. In this year the great Lord Chancellor, Cardinal Archbishop Morton, died.

But what was England like at the turn of the century, at peace, and under a strong and able ruler? Its population was probably around 3,000,000 (there are no exact figures) and the vast majority lived in rural areas. There were still wide stretches of land bare of all habitation, trackless and untroubled even by the casual traveller, where unbridged rivers and streams teemed with fish and harboured unfearing water fowl. Open moorland, wind-swept and lying long under snow, stretched for miles in the north up to the feet of high waste hills reft by valleys. The unbroken back of the Pennines bisected the land, which on one side stretched westward to the border of that wild country from which the new dynasty had sprung, and on the other, eastward through more fertile land to an icy sea rich in herring and other fish. Around York, the capital of the north, lay great farmlands cultivated by the monks and great estates belonging to the northern nobles. Here in the dales were many sheep walks. Fearful bogs and marshes trapped the unwary in parts of the Midlands and eastern counties, and in the more thickly populated south, where a greater area of land was cultivated, there were more towns and villages, more mixed agriculture and far fewer trees. In distant

---

* His second voyage, in 1498, was a failure, but neither the king nor the supporting merchants of Bristol were dismayed. Several voyages were made by others, and by 1506 these had led Bristol merchants to organize themselves into 'the Company Adventurers into the New Found Lands'.

Cornwall there were moors, mines and sheep. There was fine pasturage in Devon, a shire also noted for its apples.

But great forests still covered much of the countryside, and now there was more pasture land because of the great increase in sheep farming. This meant less arable and consequently less employment for agricultural workers. Agriculture, says an Italian visitor writing around the year 1500, was not practised beyond the extent necessary to feed the population, but this 'negligence' he feels was compensated for by the quantity of 'combustible', animals such as stags, goats, fallow deer, hares, rabbits and pigs. It is doubtful if stags and deer provided food for the ordinary country person unless he were a poacher. But we had, comments this visitor, innumerable sheep yielding the best quality wool and, ultimately, mutton, and an abundance of oxen which were much larger than those seen in Italy. There were fowl in abundance, the usual domestic kind plus pea-hens, partridge, pheasant and small birds. Nor, it seems, were we displeased with crows, but whether we ate crows I cannot say. We certainly ate sparrows.

This visitor also remarks that 'The number of people in this island do not seem to bear any proportion to its fertility and richness' and adds: 'I have ridd from Dover to London and from London to Oxford more than 200 miles and it seemed to me a great poverty of people . . . I asked those who rode north and it was the same.'[24] Similar reports were given to him by those who journeyed to Bristol or Cornwall.

The number of miles 'ridd' by this visitor was not great, and by his own account he rode through the more populated part of the country where roads must have been in fairly constant use. Had he fared farther afield he would have found roads – apart from a few main ones, chiefly Roman – infrequent; many were mere tracks and all were abominable – pot-holed, un-signposted (even King Henry lost his way between Bristol and Bath). They were either boggy and undrained – in winter largely impassable – or hard-baked and deep-rutted, depending on the weather. Of this last our Italian visitor has little good to say. He sets the hours of daylight at seven in the winter, but how long the sun really remained above the horizon he cannot tell because it appeared 'so seldom and only around mid-day'.[25]

In country districts people usually rose and went to bed with the sun and if and when they travelled from one hamlet to the next they did so on foot or horseback. There were no canals and goods were carried from one place to another by pack-horse – some bridges were wide enough only for a pack-horse – or by cumbersome four-wheeled wagons or two-wheeled carts with spiked iron wheels to keep them from slipping. Passengers were also

Baggage car with spiked wheels

carried in this way but the carter usually, and wisely, sat on one of the horses and not in the vehicle. Prosperous towns were generally sited on a navigable river, by the sea or on a travelled road. But roads were dangerous in another way too. Thieves and cut-throats were endemic. So were beggars, a motley crew of discharged soldiers, unemployed agricultural labourers, servants out of place, bands driven from the woodlands by the king's peace and just plain tramps.

Hordes of these roamed the countryside – the situation became even worse after the Dissolution – and were driven away by towns and villages not only because many beggars were thieves but because if they stayed they could become a charge on the rates.

> Hark, hark,
> The dogs do bark,
> The beggars are coming to town;
> Some in rags,
> Some in jags
> And one in a velvet gown.

This nursery rhyme, it has been suggested, reflects the state and wandering condition of the beggars in those days* who were becoming so numerous that they constituted a threat to society. G.M. Trevelyan makes this point when he writes: 'All through the Tudor reigns, the "beggars coming to town" preyed on the fears of dwellers in lonely farms and hamlets and exercised the minds of magistrates, Privy Councillors and Parliament.'[26]

With such a small total population and because of the lack of communication towns, hamlets, villages and farms existed in great isolation. Each small centre produced, generally speaking, what it needed for its own use. Although a village might lie near a manor house (also a world in itself), village life was centred round the church and the tavern – if it had a tavern. It was enlivened by market days – if it had a market – and by visits from wandering minstrels and pedlars who, since there were no newspapers, brought news of the great outside world with them and retailed it in song, verse, or just ordinary language. They told of the great fire in Bread Street, London, in which the priest of St Mildred's church had died; the discovery of the perfectly preserved and articulated body of Alice Hackney, dead these 175 years, which was dug up when the new foundations for the church of St Mary's Hill, London, were laid; the 'hayle-stones that were measured eighteen inches about' which fell at 'Saint

---

* During the reign of Henry VIII some large towns organized the administrative relief of the poor. By Queen Elizabeth's reign national legislation enforced this and it was paid for by compulsory poor rates.

Needs [Neots] in Bedfordshire'[27] on St Bartholomew's Day; the great fire which destroyed the king's palace at Sheen, and another which had all but wiped out Brabham, Norfolk. These and other similar items were told and retold long after they had happened. Such news undoubtedly grew in the telling, and Rumour with her big eyes must often have been as frightening as she was scurrilous or inaccurate. Yet after so many years of war and upheaval the Tudor peace must have brought, even to the most remote parts of the country, a greater sense of security just as, in the main, it brought greater prosperity to the nation as a whole.

The riches of England 'are greater than any other country in Europe'[28] our Italian visitor relates, and he claims that there was no one who did not have silver plate worth £100 sterling in his house – a patently absurd remark. But the riches displayed in churches impressed him even more. There was not a parish church without its crucifixes, candlesticks, patens and silver cups, whilst the monasteries were more like 'beautiful palaces' than religious houses.

At the beginning of the century London, as now, was the richest and largest city. With a population of some 70,000, it had become one of the great centres of world trade, a flourishing, busy port, overcrowded and expanding rapidly into suburbs along the waterfront east of the Tower to Wapping and Shadwell. Its streets were narrow and unpaved, while open kennels together with piles of rotting refuse made them stink abominably, particularly in summer. Ravens and kites were protected because they were natural scavengers and helped keep the streets free of filth. But there were patches of green still to be seen in the city where rich merchants' houses had large gardens not yet overbuilt.

The Thames, the great highway of London, was spanned only by London Bridge, so solid with houses on either side that it looked like a street. At the Southwark end was the towered gate where, above the arch, traitors' heads were pinned by iron spikes and left to rot away. All sorts of craft – beautiful barges of the livery companies, of royalty and the rich, pleasure boats, small vessels for hire, as well as sea-going ships, native and foreign –

plied the river, but despite the traffic 'it was a beautiful thing to see one or two thousand tame swans upon the Thames'.[29] It was often quicker to go from one part of London to another by river than by road because streets were so narrow that a horse could scarcely pass through many of them, while unlucky pedestrians, even in wider streets, went to the wall, thrust there by horsemen.

The spire of St Paul's, topped by a brazen eagle, dominated a horizon pierced by the lesser spires and towers of more than ninety parish churches. The cathedral was not only a church, it was a place where proclamations were read, penances performed and to which pilgrimages were made. It contained many sacred relics: a crystal phial containing some of the Virgin's milk, a fragment of the skull of St Thomas à Becket, a bit of St Mary Magdalen's hair, a bejewelled reliquary holding the blood of St Paul, an arm of St Mellitus, a hand of St John the Evangelist, and other lesser items. The king himself, pious and with a particular devotion to Our Lady, held as one of his chief treasures a leg of St George and, it is said, offered 1,500 ducats through Cardinal Morton to have St Anselm canonized, but 'Pope Julius was too dear'.[30]

London was full of open-fronted shops and stalls, taverns and markets. Everything could be bought, for we imported goods from all over the known world: 'Every luxury, every need and necessity abounds in London' – so did every vice and much misery in the squalid streets and alleys where the poor lived. In contrast to this was the richness 'of one street alone called the Strand, which leads to St Paul's' where there were '52 goldsmiths' shops, so rich and full of silver vessels . . . that in all the shops in Milan, Rome, Venice and Florence put together . . . there would [not] be found so many grand and magnificent pieces.'[31] The riches of London were not due to the fact that its inhabitants were all noblemen, the astonished Italian reports; on the contrary, people of low degree and artisans had come to the city from Flanders and elsewhere, while the citizens of London, themselves, were thought as highly of as the gentlemen of that other great sea-trading city, Venice.

Next to London in importance as a port came Bristol, with a

population of under 10,000. Here maritime trade made for prosperity. Norwich had a slightly larger population and its chief wealth – as with many other towns – came from cloth. Both Exeter and Salisbury had not yet reached 8,000 inhabitants, while Worcester, also a great cloth-making centre and situated on the Severn, its main highway, had less than 4,000. Other cities and towns were large at from 3,000 to 5,000 and most county towns were between 1,000 and 2,000, or even less than 1,000.* Villages were proportionately minute and many were shrinking because agricultural labour was leaving to seek a living in the towns. Even so, only about ten per cent of the population was urban.

And what were we like as a people? Our informative Italian, who cannot have known how the poor lived and did not travel far, says we wore fine clothes and always had. We were very 'polite' in our language – whatever that may mean. Our understanding he found good and we were quick at what we gave our minds to but few, bar the clergy, were given to the study of letters. Our dispositions, he says, might be 'licentious' but he noticed no one at court or amongst the lower orders in love, and from this he concludes that the English must be either the most discreet lovers in the world or incapable of love. This stricture, however, he applies to men only as women are 'violent in their passions'. Our attitude to foreigners hardly needs repeating but, in the words of our informant: 'They dislike foreigners and think none come to their island but to become its masters and to take over their goods.'³² Perhaps we had some grounds for this suspicion.

In 1500 Henry VII had nine more years to live, and he had already achieved, in the main, what he had set out to do for himself and for the country. Possibly he found this made for dullness; certainly the reign became quiet and safe with peace at home and abroad. There was only one more Yorkist incident to be coped with. Edmund de la Pole (1472?–1513), Earl of Suffolk, a brother of that Earl of Lincoln who had fallen at Stoke, fled the

---

* All figures can only be approximate. I have, perhaps, placed them a little on the high side.

country a second time in 1501 in the false hope that continental powers would gladly support one of Edward IV's blood. He was returned – no continental power wanted him – in 1506. He was en-Towered, but not executed until 1513. Sir James Tyrell, who is supposed to have murdered the little princes in the Tower (he confessed to it) and who was concerned in Suffolk's flight, was beheaded in 1502.

In April of that year the king suffered a heavy blow in the death of his elder son who was 'very studious and learned beyond his years, and beyond the custom of great Princes'.[33] The young Prince of Wales, who had married Catherine the previous November, died at Ludlow Castle on the borders of his own country and was magnificently buried in Worcester Cathedral. The following year the queen died on her birthday after giving birth to a princess who lived only a few days.

How much the king felt his wife's death is difficult to say. He was never a very confiding man, save to Archbishop Morton, and he, too, was recently dead. It is Sir Francis Bacon who seems to be responsible for the rumour that the king did not live on particularly amiable terms with his wife, for he writes that Henry 'showed himself no very indulgent husband toward her, though she was beautiful, gentle and fruitful. But his aversion towards the house of York was so predominant in him, as it found place not only in his wars and councils but in his chamber and bed.'

This I feel, possibly wrongly, maligns the king. His marriage to the daughter of Edward IV had been arranged not by 'divine intervention' as Polydore Vergil puts it, but by the Lady Margaret Beaufort, before her son left Brittany. It was, as such marriages were, politically advisable, and for Henry of Richmond dynastically advisable as well. The king, unlike his younger son, was not given to showing his emotions, but there is a touching story of how he rushed to comfort the queen when told of Prince Arthur's death, and she in turn comforted him by saying: 'God had left him yet a fair Prince and two fair Princesses; and that God is where he was, and that we are both young enough.'[34] They were young enough – she was thirty-eight – but she died in her next childbed. After her death the king shut himself up alone for days, and he did not attend her funeral.

In this same year, 1503, Prince Henry and his brother's widow were betrothed, at the wish of Ferdinand and Isabella – the king wished it too, but the first move came from her parents (the prince later made a formal protest against the marriage). Princess Margaret and James IV were married in Scotland, thus, it was hoped, ensuring a lasting peace between the two countries. It was a false hope but, in time, this marriage brought the Stuarts to the English throne.

Henry himself wished to marry again, presumably for diplomatic, financial or political reasons, and he seems first to have had the appalling thought of marrying his recently widowed daughter-in-law. It must have been a passing thought, but certainly he treated her badly, kept her short of money and bullied her into writing to her father to ask him to favour a match between the king and her own sister, the recently widowed Juana of Castile. Juana's sanity was very doubtful – she carried the body of her dead husband about with her – but she was mother of the boy (Charles V) who would, upon attaining his majority, rule all Spain and the Low Countries, and would in time be elected Holy Roman Emperor. Henry did not press his suit for Juana but instead sought the hand of the widowed Queen of Naples and gave his envoys minute instructions to find out everything about her vital and intimate statistics – which hardly sounds political or even diplomatic. This fell through and the king seems to have reconciled himself to remaining a widower.

By now Henry had become increasingly avaricious; fiscal extortion was the order of the day and from 1503 onwards Sir Richard Empson (d. 1510) and Edmund Dudley (1462?–1510), who were the king's instruments for implementing new fines and taxes, became the most hated men in the kingdom. Yet the king continued to entertain ambassadors and lesser foreign dignitaries with his usual prodigality and, as one foreigner observed, 'although noted for his excessive personal frugality, he does not change any of the ancient customs of England at his court, keeping a sumptuous table,'[35] – where at various functions he entertained 600 to 700 people at dinner. He was also very generous with civilities to foreign guests.

But, according to Polydore Vergil, he began to treat his people with more harshness and severity than usual, to teach them 'obedience'. The people, in turn, said they suffered from the king's greed and the historian, himself a friend of the king, remarks that at first it was not clear if it were greed, but admits that later on the king did 'sink into avariciousness'.

From about 1506 ambassadors and envoys began to notice, and to report home, that the king was failing. Perhaps he missed the stimulus of the early years of his reign which had called for all his great powers of courage, endurance, diplomatic skill, tact, prudence and quick-wittedness – or perhaps it was age. He was not quite fifty, but people began and ended earlier in those days. It was also noted that he was 'troubled with the Gout, but a Defluxion also taking into his Breast wasted his lungs'.[36] This would suggest consumption.

On 21 April 1509, after a three-months illness, the first Tudor king died at his palace of Richmond. He had reigned for twenty-four years and three months, and was buried in his magnificent chapel at Westminster. In his will, tidy as a lawyer, precise as an accountant, he ordered, among other things, 10,000 Masses to be said for his soul, stating the exact sum to be paid for each Mass. His alms were generous – as they had been throughout his life – and he offered redress to those he had injured by extortion. He left a peaceful, quiet, well-governed, united and economically sound kingdom, and a large fortune to his eighteen-year-old heir.*

As to the appearance and personality of this remarkable man there are various accounts. His portrait, painted in 1505 (probably by Michel Sittow) and now in the National Portrait Gallery,

---

* 'Henry VII's vast treasure is a myth,' Professor G. R. Elton writes, 'a legend quite possibly invented by Francis Bacon. At best he left a modest reserve in jewels and plate.'[37]

shows him thin-lipped, with a large nose, a strong chin and small eyes. His hands are beautiful; in the right one he holds a 'Tudor' rose. But the expression on his face is enigmatic and it almost seems as if the sitter were assessing the viewer, not the other way round.

According to Polydore Vergil, appointed as official historian (our first) by the king himself, the king had a remarkably attractive face and a cheerful one, especially when speaking. His eyes were small and blue, his teeth 'few, poor and blackish', his hair thin and his complexion sallow – which hardly sounds attractive or cheerful – but the king was not a young man when his portrait was painted or his description written. Bacon tells us he was a comley personage ... straight limbed but slender ... His countenance was reverend, and a little like a churchman ... it was neither winning nor pleasing but as the face of one well disposed. But it was to the disadvantage of the painter for it was best when he spake.' He adds, after chronicling the king's character, for which he has great admiration, that 'he had nothing in him of vainglory, but yet kept a state of majesty to the height, being sensible that majesty maketh people bow, but vainglory boweth to them'. As to what his subjects felt about him, this biographer says:' Of the three affections which tie the hearts of a subject to their sovereigns, love, fear and reverence: he had the last in height, the second in good measure, and so little of the first, as he was beholden to the other two.'[38]

The new king, proclaimed on 22 April as Henry eighth of that name since 'the king of the Normans',[39] was greeted with the greatest enthusiasm. Tall (six feet, two inches), handsome, with a beautifully proportioned body, auburn hair and pink and white complexion, and just a few months short of his eighteenth birthday, he was a youth 'upon whom Nature had showered apparently every gift'.[40] He excelled at all sports, was an accomplished musician, knew Latin, French, a bit of Italian and very possibly some Spanish, with a little Greek thrown in. He was a keen student of mathematics and later in his reign would take his great friend Sir Thomas More (1478–1535) 'into his travers [small anteroom] and there sometimes in matters of astronomy, geo-metry, divinity . . . and sometimes of his worldly affairs . . . sit and confer with him'; or he would take his friend upon the roof 'there for to consider with him the diversities, courses, motions and operations of the stars and planets'.[41]

The king also loved splendid clothes, jewels and dressing up. Hall, the untiring (and sometimes a trifle tiring) chronicler of his reign – for him the king could do no wrong – rarely leaves us for a moment unaware of what the king wore upon every occasion, bar intimate ones.

Henry was a good enough scholar though not, it appears, so good, nor so well taught, as his elder brother, but we have few details of his early life and education. As a second son much less is recorded about his early years than about those of the heir to the throne. There is, however, a story told by Lord Herbert of Cherbury in his *The life and raigne of King Henry the eighth* (1649) that Henry VII had intended his second son for the Church and ultimately for the See of Canterbury. Thus, with one son on the throne of England and the other on the episcopal throne of Canterbury, Church and state would be well served – and so would his two sons.

The thought that Henry VIII might have become Archbishop and even Cardinal Archbishop, is intriguing. There is, however, no supporting evidence for this, to us, astounding statement of Lord Herbert, but Henry does seem to have been well-tutored in theology and later, as we know, fancied himself as a theologian. He also heard Mass daily, sometimes thrice, and had a notably pious background; furthermore, theology was a subject much discussed by the intellectual élite of the day.

His first tutor was the poet laureate, John Skelton (1460?–1529), who took holy orders in 1498 and was appointed tutor to the then six-year-old Duke of York. It is said that Skelton was appointed to this post by the infant duke's grandmother, Lady Margaret Beaufort, who had by then (c. 1497) become, with her husband's permission, a religious recluse and who had charge of the boy's education (she died in June of the year he succeeded). In any event,

the fact that Skelton was his tutor seems to be borne out in one of
the poet's verses which runs in part:

> The honour of England I learnéd to spell
> In dignity royal at that doth excel.
> Note and mark well this parcél:
> I gave him drink of the sugared well
> Of Helicon's waters crystalline,
> Acquainting him with the muses nine.[42]

What else Skelton may have taught his apt pupil is a matter of
conjecture, but he remained the duke's tutor until the death of
Prince Arthur and was then rewarded by the Lady Margaret with
the gift of the living of Diss, Norfolk. Skelton, a considerable
poet, was cynical, contentious, bitter and conceited, with a weak-
ness for young girls and small use for his clerical vows of chastity
– but it is ridiculous to suppose, as certain Victorians did, that he
laid the foundation for his pupil's grossest crimes.

Yet here it is as well to walk warily. First, Henry as second son
had had no training whatsoever in kingship. He was never given
any responsibility, unlike his brother, and was forced to lead a
most restricted life. He was kept under strict supervision, never
allowed out save with some appointed person; nor was he allowed
to be approached or spoken to by anyone. Much of his time was
spent in his own rooms, which could be reached only through the
king's chamber. He must have been thoroughly frustrated and
inhibited by such treatment. Second, it should be remembered
that he was the grandson of that lusty king, Edward IV, and 'very
like him in general appearance'.[43] Small wonder, then, that this
hitherto repressed but vigorous young man should burst from the
submerged larva stage like a brightly marked, jewel-eyed dragonfly: swift, beautiful, graceful. Unlike the dragonfly he barely
paused to dry his glistening wings. Also, he was not harmless.

His very first act was to imprison his father's money-gatherers,
Empson and Dudley, in the Tower, which brought him immense
acclaim. Eighteen months later they were executed on a charge of
constructive treason. Their deaths were not merited, but tax

gatherers have never been popular. On 11 June 1509 he married Catherine. She was five years older than he, intelligent, courageous and obstinate. On 24 June their coronation took place in Westminster Abbey amid scenes of unparalleled splendour, with London decorated and shouting its joy. The ceremonies were concluded with a great feast and a tournament. Indeed, such festivities were to be almost endless during these early years. Court pageants, much music, dancing, tennis, archery, bowls, jousting, hunting, hawking, dicing, cards – every pleasure, every

Jousting

pastime was enjoyed to the full by the young and vigorous king. His father's ministers, still in power, could carry on with the usual routine of government business, for the new king was at first bored with it all. And after the chill, last years of the reign of that aloof monarch, Henry VII, this was a fairytale prince living, momentarily, in a self-created old romantic world of chivalry and knight errantry. He was prodigal of himself, his talents and his money. He was also our first Renaissance prince.

The Renaissance, born in Italy, began as the last phase of the Middle Ages: whereas Henry VII had accepted and to a certain extent absorbed what was called the 'new learning', he was essentially of a medieval cast of mind. His son, however, was brought up under humanist influences – and to the first humanists *humanitas* merely meant 'culture'.

This new culture sprang from a re-assessment, a rebirth, of the ancient Greek and Roman history and civilizations. This is not the place even to attempt to define how this fresh inquiry into the past came into being, but it does presuppose the existence of dissatisfied and, later, critical minds.

Medieval thought had held that this world was the centre of the universe and, with man, was God's highest achievement. A universal monarchy represented by the Holy Roman Empire, at whose head was the Emperor, and a universal church, at whose head was the Pope, represented indivisible Christendom. Within this whole everything fitted and was subordinate: nations, rulers, philosophy, ethics, morals, science – all had their described, fixed and unalterable places inside this larger, rigid framework.

The re-discovery, re-translation and new interpretation of the original works of classical antiquity showed that there had been other cultures to which the present civilization was heir, and this gave rise to a sense of continuity, a sense of history. Classical culture had produced men like Plato, Aristotle and Hippocrates whose works, now re-translated from original sources into elegant Latin, were, because of the new printing presses, now much more readily available to scholars and educated men. Such early authors, although pre-Christian, had thought deeply about politics, ethics, government, history, the state, philosophy, poetry, medicine, music and science. The discovery of this led to a 'new way' of thinking, which was brought to bear upon contemporary theories which were far removed from the actualities of the day. This critical spirit, first exercised on literature, soon began to operate in other fields. Man in fact began to react as an individual against the universal and was, ultimately, freed from the trammels of theological despotism.

As advances were made in Greek studies, scholastic thought fell into desuetude – but not without a fight. The new curiosity concerning nature, for example, led men like Leonardo da Vinci and others to reject the accepted, make experiments and attempt by trial and error to understand how physical forces worked; and to this end they had to invent scientific instruments.

The earth, as everyone knew, was stable: but Copernicus discovered its diurnal movement upon its own axis. The earth was also flat: but Columbus reached the West Indies; Cabot, Newfoundland; Vasco da Gama, India; while Magellan sailed around it. The science of anatomy had been long since perfected by Galen: Vesalius proved him wrong. Art's first concern was with sacred subjects, but side by side with this the artist could now draw upon the pagan myths and fables of antiquity. Secular princes began to see their own interests as the prime interest; nationhood and a new type of monarch developed. The Roman Catholic Church was supreme and could do no wrong. An heretical Augustinian friar was excommunicated for his long quarrel over the validity of this tenet, and there began the great split which ultimately was to wreck the Holy Roman Empire as well as Papal authority. Without the Renaissance and its spirit of critical inquiry there could have been no Reformation.

Henry VIII, that Renaissance prince, is probably best remembered by most of us for two things: the Reformation in England and what might be called sequential polygamy. Yet prior to the Reformation he was a staunch ally of four successive Popes and wrote – probably with some assistance – a treatise against Luther, *Assertio Septem Sacramentorum* (1521), for which in September of that year Pope Leo X conferred upon him the title of *Defensor Fidei*. He was also ready to stand for the Imperial election in 1519 which would have made him Holy Roman Emperor. As to his domestic life, apart from a few mistresses, he cohabited with his first wife, Catherine, until at least 1526 before embarking in 1533 on his subsequent and largely unsuccessful marital career, and by then he was forty-two, running to fat and given to violent temper tantrums.

Between the ages of twenty-one and forty-two he had done many things suitable to a Renaissance prince. He was spectacular, lived in the grand manner, was a patron of the 'new learning' and welcomed humanists, who were among other things anti-war, at court. For men such as Erasmus (1466-1536), Dean Colet (1467-1519) and Sir Thomas More he professed and probably felt, at least for a time, admiration or friendship. To be sure Erasmus received no bounty from the king who fobbed him off on Archbishop Warham. Colet, who re-founded St Paul's School, most unusually got into no trouble at all for preaching against the French war of 1513, but Sir Thomas More, a friend to both these men, was not deceived when high in the king's favour, for he remarked to his son-in-law: 'If my head could win him a castle in France . . . it should not fail to go.'[44]

Henry wanted much more than just a castle in France. He wanted to regain England's lost possessions there. He wanted prestige for himself and his country. He wanted to lead armies in person as befitted a king, a magnifico and the protagonist of the nostalgic cult of chivalry. He wanted to play an important if not leading rôle on the European stage. The adulation and flattery of courtiers, his belief in his own superiority, mental and physical – a belief which was, perhaps, the mainspring of his character – did nothing to curb a will which was already becoming over-imperious and would end by becoming despotic.

In 1511 the king joined the Holy League and plunged into tortuous European politics. Although at this time we had peace treaties with France and Scotland, we had intermittent wars with both countries from 1512 to 1544. The continental wars were chiefly with France, but in one England and France became allies against Charles V, who was Queen Catherine's nephew. All the wars cost too much money but the early ones brought 'a glory much to the taste both of the vain and eager young king and his equally vain but much more able minister' [Wolsey].[45] The king's international reputation probably reached its peak in 1520, when for a short time England held the balance of power between France and Spain. That was only eight years after the first war

New type warship with gunports

with France which began in 1512. The last one, a perfectly point-less war against the same enemy, began in 1544, when the king was fifty-three and had but three more years to live.

It would be absurd, however, to think that war was the only feature of Henry's reign. He embarked upon it early but even before this, in the very first year of his accession, he began to build up the navy. He did this brilliantly, instituting a new kind of battleship (known to the Italians) with guns mounted in the waist rather than on poop or fo'c'stle. These could fire broadside through gun ports, which revolutionized naval warfare. On 20 May 1514 a charter of incorporation was granted in the name of the Holy Trinity to a fraternity of seamen, and so Trinity House was founded to control pilotage and provide navigational aid for the Thames and its approaches. Thus the king laid the foundations of our naval supremacy, sadly lost in the following two reigns but regained by Queen Elizabeth in time to meet the Armada. The king's interest in the navy was 'no less than his interest in horses and arms'[46] but it was a good deal more useful.

In 1514 the king had what appeared to be a diplomatic triumph when, as a part of the Anglo-French treaty, he married his younger sister, Mary, to the ageing Louis XII. The French king survived this by only two months and his widow then secretly married Charles Brandon (d. 1545), first Duke of Suffolk, who already had a wife living. Henry was furious at this, but pardoned them when Mary's dowry from Louis was paid over to him and her jewels and plate returned. He also fined the couple £24,000 which they paid off in instalments and, as the validity of the marriage had already been secured by papal bull, the king also insisted on a public remarriage. The duchess ultimately became the grandmother of Lady Jane Grey and the duke★ stood high in the king's favour.

It is very likely that Wolsey arranged or helped to arrange the French marriage – and he certainly soothed the king's anger over the second marriage – for despite his over-weening ambition, his love of wealth, his arrogance, his enormous power, he was great

★ He captured Boulogne in 1544.

in the diplomatic field; at home, as Lord Chancellor, he reformed and improved much of the legal machinery of government and 'gave good justice to all men, many of them weak and poor'.[47] Wolsey was broken by his master in 1529 and providentially died in 1530; otherwise he would have been executed.

Sir Thomas More, who succeeded him as Lord Chancellor, was executed in 1535 and in 1536 Thomas Cromwell (1485?–1540) became Lord Privy Seal. A brilliant organizer but a more servile servant than his quondam master, Wolsey, he did much to reform the administrative side of government and also became quite indispensable to the king. He was dispensed with by way of the block in 1540. In fairness to both Wolsey and Cromwell, about whom diverse opinions are held, it must be said that they gave the country 'good governance'.

Among other events, good and bad, was the 'Evil May Day' of 1517 when angry apprentices in London rioted against foreigners whom they believed were attacking their commercial interests and taking work away from them. Of this, Hall says that 'the pore Englishe artificers could skarce get any living' and the foreigners were so proud that they 'disdained, mocked and oppressed Englishmen'.[48] This active xenophobia – part of the Englishness of the English – was shown by the rioters raging through the streets, throwing stones, sacking foreigners' houses, insulting foreign ambassadors and threatening the mayor, aldermen and Wolsey with death. By nightfall the riot was suppressed. Justice was swift; the ringleaders were quartered and about 400 others were imprisoned until the queen, on her knees (not for the last time) before the king, begged for their pardon.

By now the king had had several children; a boy, Prince Henry, born in 1510 amid tremendous rejoicing, had lived but seven weeks. After that there were several still-born babies and a girl, the Princess Mary (born 1516) who, although the queen had subsequent pregnancies and children, was the only child of the marriage to survive into adulthood.

In 1518 another event of consequence to the future took place when the king granted Thomas Linacre (1460–1524), his physician, one-time tutor to Prince Arthur, letters patent for the formation of an authoritative body of physicians – medicine was in an unhealthy state. This body later became the Royal College of Physicians. A small item of some interest today shows the king as what might be called an early anti-pollutionist: in the twenty-seventh year of his reign an Act of Parliament was passed for the 'Preservation of the Thames', since evil-disposed persons were casting dung and other filth into its waters. They were also digging and undermining its banks and carrying away piles and timber work. The fine for such misdemeanours was a thumping 100 shillings.

To return to the problem of the king's children or, rather, the lack of live ones. His natural son by Elizabeth Blount, Henry Fitzroy, was born in 1519 and in 1525 created Duke of Richmond, a significant title. The king, obviously despairing of a male heir – the country had not had a queen regnant since the Empress Matilda★ and, it was felt, would not take kindly to a queen – planned to leave the crown to his bastard son. But the boy died in 1536, very probably of consumption, although rumour had it that he was poisoned by Queen Anne (Boleyn) and her brother. It must have been a very slow-acting poison: the young duke died in July, while Queen Anne (1507–36) had been beheaded for adultery and incest nearly two months before, on 19 May. She had, however, produced a girl in September 1535 – probably the most unwanted daughter in history.

In January of the year in which Anne was beheaded, Queen Catherine died at Kimbolton. She had been a popular queen; her successor was not. And here we must touch very briefly on the matter of the king's 'divorce', which took six years to accomplish, during which time the whole outlook of the country was changed by the beginning of the Reformation.

It would be near nonsense, however, to think that the king's passion for Anne Boleyn was the sole reason for his wanting a

★ That is, if the Empress (1102–67) can be called 'Queen regnant'. Her brief acknowledgement in 1141 by the Council of Winchester as 'Lady of England and Normandy' hardly seems to put her in this category.

divorce, although undoubtedly it was a large factor. Henry, as we have seen, was after many years of marriage still without a legitimate son. There can be no doubt that he desperately desired one, and Catherine was past child-bearing. Thus he may at first have pretended to believe, and ended by really believing, that this lack of a male heir was God's judgement upon him for having married his brother's wife, an act forbidden by Leviticus but, unfortunately, enjoined by Deuteronomy.* The sad and cruel story of the king's treatment of Catherine and the wretched Princess Mary, and the complexities of the case, with its ensuing theological debates in England and Europe, are best read elsewhere,† but it was during this period that the break with Rome occurred. The king had warned (or threatened) Pope Clement VII that this might happen in England, as it was happening in certain Germanic countries, if a divorce or, more correctly, a decree of nullity were refused him but the Pope, now in the power of Catherine's nephew, Charles V, whose armies had sacked Rome in 1527, could not comply with this request, although there was certainly precedent for it.

At the same time and independent of this, the king felt, and had done for some years, that the Royal Supremacy, his own kingship, was not being fulfilled in a Christian community such as England as long as a foreign power could intervene in the country's affairs. As early as 1515 he had said that in the past the kings of England had never had any superior other than God. The divorce then, did not give birth to Caesaro-papism, but speeded up its growth.

By 1531 the king was recognized by Parliament as Supreme Head of the Church in England, the term 'Supreme Head' being primarily a legal one. It asked and answered the question: 'Has the Pope any jurisdiction in England?' – jurisdiction in the exact sense meaning 'the authority to declare what the law of the Church in England is, and to put that law into execution through the Pope's own courts'.[49] Henry denied this and further claimed

---

* See *Leviticus*, Ch. XVIII, v.6, and Ch. XX, v.21; *Deuteronomy*, Ch. XXX, v.5.

† Notably in Professor J. J. Scarisbrick's *Henry VIII* (1968).

that no foreign potentate had 'the authority to rule in England',[50] as this was treachery to the existing government. Therefore to refuse to declare Henry Supreme Head of the Church in his own country diminished his authority and was treason. The submission of the clergy came in 1532. Henry was excommunicated in 1533, and in 1534 Acts were passed forbidding the payment of annates (they had been confiscated by Henry in the previous year anyway) and Peter's Pence to Rome. The introduction of papal bulls and briefs was forbidden and a new Act of Supremacy, confirming those of the king's judicial and political powers in England which had formerly been held by the Pope, was also passed. For refusing to take the Oath of Supremacy the saintly Sir Thomas More and John Fisher (1469?–1535), Bishop of Rochester – whose patroness had been the Lady Margaret Beaufort – lost their heads.

They were the only two great men in the kingdom to do so, for there was very little opposition to the king. The new spirit of nationalism and, in a sense, of insularity had much to do with this; but there also seems to have been an underground tradition of Lollardy* through which the ideas of John Wycliffe (d. 1384), the religious reformer and first translator of the Bible into English, still lived. So many of the reformers believed they were carrying out what Wycliffe had begun. More important was that throughout the country there was a strong anti-clerical feeling.

The higher clergy, with notable exceptions, were not particularly concerned with their offices. Some bishops spent their lives in civil or administrative posts. Some were abroad as ambassadors. Some were Italian and absentees – for example, four Bishops of Worcester in a row were absentees and Cardinal Wolsey was Archbishop of York for sixteen years before visiting his diocese, and did so then as a fallen and dying man. Such men as these did not supervise their dioceses, where the lesser clergy, often badly educated and badly behaved, could not or did not carry out their duties. Further, there were too many clergy, perhaps one to every 100 laymen. This might not have mattered so much, for we were a devout enough people – even foreigners

---

* Lollardy was heresy and punishable by burning.

admitted that – had the clergy not been so rich. They controlled possibly ten per cent of the national income and, more importantly, about twenty to twenty-five per cent of the land. Theirs was a powerful and privileged class, nearly always exempt from the jurisdiction of the civil courts, yet in its own courts able to inflict penalties on laymen for various offences. These courts alone had power to deal with wills and testaments, and large mortuary fees were also exacted.

It would be wrong to say that all ecclesiastics of all ranks were guilty of such abuses of their spiritual office, but so many were that anti-clericalism had had a solid enough foundation for some time. But anti-clericalism also seems to have been largely a middle-class phenomenon and the government depended, in the main, upon middle-class support. It is also more than probable that papal power had come to be identified with Cardinal Legate Wolsey, with all his worldliness, arrogance and enormous riches. Wolsey was greatly hated, not the least by his own bishops. He too was an absentee and a pluralist, and he gave even greater offence when he presented his bastard schoolboy son with thirteen ecclesiastical offices. It was not the fact that the celibate Cardinal had a son (in fact he had several children) for 'a very different standard of morality then prevailed . . . and as the Popes themselves were in this respect by no means infallible, the frailties of a Cardinal were not considered an insuperable bar either to secular or spiritual preferment'.[51] No, it was the age of the boy and the preferments given him which constituted the outrage.

Nevertheless at this time the country was certainly not divided into two camps, Roman Catholic and Protestant. The clear division did not take place until the next reign, for the Reformation, like the Renaissance, was a process. At the time of the break with Rome honest as well as sequacious men kept on altering their opinions. There was, as yet, no consistent body of doctrine. Lutheran doctrines had, however, permeated England and there were a number of Lutheran princes with whom the king flirted from time to time for political reasons. These doctrines, as well as Erasmus's translation of the New Testament into Greek, unglossed, unadorned and uncommented-upon, plus Luther's translation of the Bible into German (and, later, the works of Calvin) had had a great effect upon many young men of the 'new learning'. Nowhere more so than at Cambridge, where the future makers of the English Bible, Tyndale, Coverdale and others gathered, along with Cranmer and Latimer, at the White Horse Tavern (nicknamed Germany and those who met there 'Germans') to discuss enthusiastically this new impulse which brought a fresh sense of joy, of life, of personal contact with God into religion. Late medieval religion had certainly been gloom-ridden and for most could probably be summed up in the following verse:

> Our plesance here is all vain glory,
> This fals world is but transitory
> The flesh is bruckle, the Feynd is slee:–
> *Timor mortis conturbat me.*'[52]

This is hardly calculated to make life on earth pleasant or life hereafter anything to look forward to.

In addition to the Cambridge men, 'the reforming doctrines whether of Erasmus or Luther had many secret sympathizers and open missionaries among the clergy: otherwise there could never have been a reformation in England'.[53] Further, there was now the printing press, and pamphlets and books on the new approach to religion were, although often banned, imported and secretly circulated. But the Church itself during these early years followed its old doctrine and Henry, as Supreme Head, could now appoint his own bishops. By the end of his reign he must have known that nearly half his bishops held Lutheran views, yet he protected Bishop Stephen Gardiner (1483?–1555) who, although he supported the Royal Supremacy, objected strongly to the religious doctrines of the Reformation. He also protected Thomas Cranmer (1489–1556) who had, indeed, been useful to him in his various marriages and had become, reluctantly, Archbishop of Canterbury, but who had risked the royal wrath and worse by pleading for More, Anne Boleyn, Thomas Cromwell and others with great courage and equal futility and who found himself, over the years, assisting in the shaping of the Church of England under a master who had no desire for change!

Henry was no Lutheran. He was conservative. He reformed the administration of the Church and became its Supreme Head, so that what had been the Church in England became the Church of England. The king, in fact, thought not of 'setting up a new church, but simply of reforming the existing English church'.[54] The Six Articles of 1539, passed to establish uniformity, were firmly Catholic and emphasized transubstantiation, Communion in one kind for the laity, a celibate priesthood, auricular confession, private Masses and charity. But the king did authorize a translation of the Bible into English and ordered it to be chained in every church (for a time) and thus made available to all who could read. And it was not until the next reign that Cranmer, who believed the Bible to be the word of God spoken to Everyman and that it came with its fullest power when not accompanied by gloss, exposition and comment, was able to supply the Church with a lectionary and in so doing 'made the Church of England in a day the greatest Bible-reading church in the world'.[55]

As for the king, he burned Lutherans for heresy and hanged Papists for treason with equal equanimity – although not in large numbers. But sometimes he had them executed together, which many found offensive. This, however, did not lose him the good will of the majority of his subjects; nor did the Dissolution of the Monasteries save in the north, far poorer than the south, where it was a contributory factor to the 'Pilgrimage of Grace' rebellion (1536–7). The king promised its leader, Robert Aske, pardon but had him executed at York in 1537. This uprising led to a reconstruction of the Council of the North in that same year.

The Lord Privy Seal and Vicar-General, Thomas Cromwell, and his agents, were largely responsible for the Dissolution. Certainly some monasteries deserved to be suppressed; others did not, and it is more than probable that Cromwell's agents in many cases reported on the 'scandalous lives' of the inmates largely as a pretext for dissolution. The suppression of lesser religious houses began in 1536. Many of the monks were pensioned off or were found employment, but many fared badly. Monastic land and property yielded great riches to the crown. The nobility and gentry, as well as lesser men, profited greatly as the king rewarded them with – or more often sold them – monastic lands. More land meant more power; in fact, most of the land slipped through the king's hands; but we still have the Royal Parks in London.

Shrines were also despoiled, notably the magnificent shrine of Thomas à Becket at Canterbury which provided the crown with 'two great chests of jewels "such as six or eight strong men could do no more than convey one of them" '[56] plus twenty-four wagon loads of other treasures.

An indirect result of the Dissolution was to give the laity a majority in the upper house (the 'nether house' nearly always bore goodwill to the king). Henry, it must be said – and considering how idle he had been about government in his youth this is surprising – was adroit and skilful in managing both houses. He was also 'the mainspring of the state-machine and under his hand he kept all the apparatus of an administrative despotism'.[57] But the money the king received through the Dissolution and the despoliation was not to any extent used by him for educational or charitable purposes, as had been done in similar circumstances by various German princes. Henry was chronically short of money, yet he did use some of the money thus gained for the navy and for coastal fortifications, and he founded Trinity College Cambridge with a lavish endowment in 1546.

Ten years before this, when Catherine had died and Anne Boleyn had been beheaded, the king married Jane Seymour (1509?–37) with indecent haste, and his daughters were declared illegitimate. In the following year, on 12 October, the longed-for male heir was born and christened Edward. Twelve days later his mother died leaving a robust child and a brace of powerful and ambitious brothers. The king, though not hastily, looked around for another wife and, it is said, the Dowager Duchess of Milan declined the invitation on the grounds that nature had not endowed her with two heads. In 1540, Henry married Anne of

Cleves (1515–57) to ally himself in a roundabout way* with the League of German Lutherans; he promptly had his marriage annulled, but Anne remained on sisterly terms with her ex-husband, settled in England and did her best, as Jane Seymour had done, to make life easier for the Princesses Mary and Elizabeth. Thomas Cromwell was, however, executed on a charge of treason brought by the Duke of Norfolk. The king did not intervene; the rôle Cromwell had played in arranging the marriage with the 'Flanders Mare' was not forgiven.

On the day of Cromwell's execution, 10 June 1540, the king married Catherine Howard. She was executed for treason (adultery) in 1542, which was the year in which Henry took the title of 'King' instead of 'Lord' of Ireland. The following year he reconciled Wales and England and established a Council for Wales and the Marches. Wales and Monmouth were 'shired', and petty kingdoms – and quarrels – were ended. English law and administration were superimposed on the country; the new shires and boroughs were to send twenty-four members to Parliament. This was good for England and also for Wales, but it is doubtful if enough attention was paid to the language and traditions of this ancient people. It is also doubtful whether anyone but a Tudor could have achieved this union.

In this same year Henry married his last queen, the ultra-Protestant, twice-widowed Catherine Parr (1512–46), who would have preferred to marry Sir Thomas Seymour and in whose household Lady Jane Grey (1537–54) had lived. She too showed great kindness to Prince Edward and his half-sisters, and in 1544, by the third Act of Succession, the princesses were de-bastardized and were recognized as heirs to the throne after their brother. In this year too a further, really disastrous, debasement of coinage took place, for the king's finances and those of the country were in a poor way. Out of this debasement the king himself made a profit of £363,000 but a desperate government was driven to

---

* The Duke of Cleves, her brother, was not a Lutheran but was allied by marriage and political interests to the House of Saxony and through it to the League of German Lutherans.

borrow money on a large scale from the Low Countries. By 1546 the king's health was rapidly deteriorating and he made his will. At two o'clock in the morning of 28 January 1547, at the age of fifty-seven and exactly ninety years to the day from his father's birth, he died holding Archbishop Cranmer's hand.

What he died of is not clear. He had been very ill in 1538 with, perhaps, a pulmonary embolus or a heart condition and he may have died of a recurrence of these, or from dropsy and uraemia. Certainly the slim, handsome, affable youth had changed into a gross, suspicious, treacherous despot. His waist, which had measured about thirty-five inches in 1514, measured fifty-four inches in 1541 and there was a proportionate increase in chest measurement. He had to be hauled upstairs by a mechanical device of some sort in later years because of excessive weight and ulcerated legs. Charles Dickens describes Henry VIII as 'a most intolerable ruffian, a disgrace to human nature, a blot of blood and grease upon the history of England'.[58] But Dickens was a great novelist, not a historian. We have learned to set the king within the framework of the time in which he lived; he was no more bloodthirsty or brutal than many a contemporary Renaissance prince. As for his own people, when he died they felt they had lost a great king.

Henry, among his non-personal effects, left immense debts, a debased coinage, continuing inflation, a theologically unsettled Church and a Council of Regency to govern during his son's minority. He had also provided in his will for the succession. Should he or his son die without heirs (and Henry might have had another male heir by Catherine Parr), the crown should go first to the Princess Mary and her heirs and next to the Princess Elizabeth and her heirs, always provided the princesses did not marry against their brother's or the Privy Council's wishes. Should they die without issue, then, passing over the claims of his elder sister, Margaret (the Stuart line), the crown should go to the heirs of his younger sister Mary, Duchess of Suffolk (d. 1533) who had two daughters: Frances, married to Henry Grey, Marquis of Dorset and later Duke of Suffolk, and Eleanor, married to the Earl of Cumberland, who had one girl. The more prolific Frances already had three, the Ladies Jane, Catherine and Mary Grey. Thus, when Henry died eight women were in line for the throne.

The immediate occupant, however, was a nine-year-old boy, Edward VI, and there was not much reason to suppose that he would not in due course marry and beget heirs. He had not been a delicate infant, and was an extremely fair child with white skin, faintly reddish hair and grey eyes. He was much admired for this lack of colour. An almost albino fairness of skin and hair was the Renaissance idea of beauty. Dark hair and a good healthy complexion were vulgar and low. From portraits of Edward as a very young child he looks rather like a fat little suet pudding waiting to be steamed in a bejewelled cloth.

His father had been very advanced for his time in the matter of hygienic household arrangements for his son, and what was then considered to be the strictest hygiene was enforced from the boy's birth to the age of one year. In addition to his own apartments at whatever palace he lived in, he had his own separate kitchen, buttery, pantry, ewery, cellars, wood yard, and so on. Floors were scrubbed, no dirty crockery was left about and dogs, save for ladies' pets, were confined to kennels; the usual custom of the household eating together in the hall was suspended. For fear of infections – or murder – no one was allowed to touch or come near anything used by the prince's attendants. When there was a plague scare not a member of the child's suite was allowed even to speak to anyone from London or the countryside. In addition to a wet-nurse and a dry-nurse he had four 'Rockers'. His physician was Dr George Owen (d. 1558), one of his father's physicians who had been with his mother on her death-bed.

All the precautions taken, together with his own constitution, meant that 'England's Treasure' (as he was called) was a robust and vigorous child, although he did have quartan fever at the age of four.

At his birth, London had gone mad with rejoicing; people laughed, wept and danced in the streets, bells pealed triumphantly, banners of every description were hung out, 2,000 salvoes sounded from the Tower, bonfires leapt up, conduits poured ale and wine, Masses were said and, as the news spread, the whole country went delirious with delight.

Even the Bishop of Worcester, Hugh Latimer (1485–1555) seems to have been swept away for, in a letter to Thomas Cromwell, written from Hartlebury on 19 October 1547 he says: '. . . Syr, here ys no lesse joynge and rejossynge in these parts for the byrth of our Prynce, hoom we hungurde for so longe; then [than] there was (I trow) *inter vicinos* att the byrth of St John Baptyste.'[59] He goes on to say that God, by granting a son, has after all shown himself to be an 'Inglysshe God' – which seems a slightly extravagant claim even for a bishop with extreme Protestant leanings.

The young king himself was a Protestant, the first king in our history to be born and bred so. His education began about the age of three. This was not unusual; when life is short, so is childhood; the education of children of the nobility and gentry began early. It was neither narrow nor specialized, embracing everything from sport to theology, from manners to music. Children embarked upon Greek and Latin at an early age and could speak the languages before they could write them – Latin was, after all, the *lingua franca* of the upper classes. Young Edward was no exception: he could speak both before he learned the alphabet. He was an intelligent, perhaps even a precocious, child though not so brilliant as his sister, Elizabeth, who was four years older than he. Training for the position he was to occupy began almost in infancy, so he could never have been unaware of his own importance.

He was brought up, he tells us, referring to himself in the third person, 'til he came to six yeeres old, among women'.[60] The women were those of his household, the chief of whom, Lady Bryan, had once been in charge of the Princess Elizabeth's household, and the prince and his sister spent some part of their young lives together. He was also fond of his elder sister and godmother, the Princess Mary, who was twenty-two years his senior, and of his stepmother, Catherine Parr, to whom he often wrote. Indeed, in 1546 he wrote to his 'most illustrious Queen and beloved Mother' asking her to 'preserve my dear sister Mary from all the wiles and enchantment of the evil one and beseech her to attend no longer to foreign dances and merriments which do not become a most Christian princess'.[61] Mary was then a woman of thirty – and fond of dancing; this sounds a remarkably priggish request from a boy of nine.

After the age of six the tutors took over and the boy was undoubtedly forced. He was put in the charge of Sir John Cheke (1514–57), a brilliant man who was a Greek scholar and a Cambridge professor. Among the lesser tutors were Roger Ascham (1515–68), a student of Cheke's who taught the prince penmanship, and Anthony Cooke (1500–76), one of whose daughters married young William Cecil. Cecil, too, had been Cheke's pupil. All the tutors were kind, able and devoted to their task, affectionate towards their charge and very conscious of his destiny. All, too, were extreme Protestants.

'Edward was naturally haughty and arrogant, like all the Tudors; also like all his family, he had marked intellectual ability which an appalling schooling had turned to a precocious passion for Protestant theology.'[62] And it was chiefly religious jockeying for power and economic disaster which characterized the young king's reign; it is called a reign by courtesy, for although in fact Edward was a real king both in theory and in his own opinion, he played no part in it. What was done was done by his advisers in his name.

His advisers consisted of the Council which his father had appointed and from which, to prevent trouble, he had excluded Catholic extremists such as Edmund Bonner (1500?–69), Bishop of London, who had once appealed to Pope Clement VII against Henry's excommunication and who, under Edward, spent four years in the Marshalsea prison,* and Stephen Gardiner, Bishop of

---

* Released, he later joined in the Marian persecutions with great severity but refused to take the Oath of Supremacy when Elizabeth succeeded. Died in the Marshalsea.

Winchester, who had inspired the Six Articles and who spent most of his time in the Tower during Edward's reign. Henry had also tried to stop any one man from becoming head of the Council by declaring all members to be equal. The Council, however, immediately chose the king's uncle, Edward Seymour (1506?–52), Earl of Hertford and soon to become Duke of Somerset, as Lord Protector of the realm. As Somerset had been careful to secure his nephew's person immediately upon Henry's death and also had the support of the Protestant and civil-service members of the Council, he could hardly not have been chosen; that a regent was necessary cannot be doubted.

The new Protector had a rival in John Dudley (1502–53), Viscount Lisle, Earl of Warwick and, later, Duke of Northumberland, who as Lord High Chamberlain was, in a sense, co-regent; but he also acquiesced to Somerset's sole protectorship. Both men had held high office under the late king and at the beginning of the new reign appeared to work together.

Somerset had much to tackle during the two years in which he was virtual ruler of the country. First, in November 1547, he forwarded the Protestant cause by repealing Henrician legislation. This included the abrogation of the laws of heresy and the non-enforcement of the Six Articles – these last were pretty much of a dead letter anyway. He immediately stopped the persecution of Protestants, so Protestant refugees from Europe flooded into the country; most of them were followers of Zwingli (1484–1531) or of Calvin (1509–64), whose doctrines, far more extreme than those of Luther, had been considered heretical while Henry lived and whose followers had been punished accordingly. (In spite of this persecution the number of extreme Protestants had continued to increase.) Somerset also engineered the fall of Lord Chancellor Wriothesley (1500–50) and thus removed the last notable Catholic from the Council, leaving it 'a council of Protestants and pliable indifferents'.[63]

It is the theological ferment of the period which is the background for most of the events of the reign. To put it briefly, there were no denominations, only religious positions. First, the Roman

Catholics, who wanted the abolition of the Royal Supremacy and the return of papal jurisdiction; they were considered traitors. Second, the Reforming party, which by now had split into two sections. The 'moderates' – often called Henricians – had as leaders Wriothesley (reinstated as Chancellor in 1548) and Bishops Bonner and Gardiner; they were, as Henry had been, Catholic in doctrine, supported the Royal Supremacy and called themselves Catholics. The other section consisted of extreme Protestants, and the most influential leaders after the death of Thomas Cromwell were Archbishop Cranmer and Bishops Latimer, Hooper and Ridley, who had gradually become impregnated with Zwinglianism and Calvinism. The Protector himself was an extreme Protestant but seems to have been much more liberal in his views than his fellow Councillors, for, in general, 'toleration was as little sanctioned by the followers of the Reformation as by the adherents to Papal supremacy . . . and the leaders of factions in the reign of Edward VI . . . were at all times disposed to accommodate their religious faith to personal interest'.[64]

This is a harsh statement but it was undoubtedly true of many in high and not-so-high office. In 1548 Somerset dissolved the chantries (a dissolution planned by Henry VIII in 1545). These were the numerous endowments made for religious, charitable and educational purposes and were usually connected with a chantry chapel or a parish church. Their main religious purpose was to offer Masses for the repose of the souls of the dead, but as the doctrine of purgatory had recently been removed this function was ended. Their lands and goods went to fill the almost empty royal coffers and were in turn immediately sold off to the nobility, gentry and others, many of whom had already increased their wealth and power by acquiring monastic lands and goods. The Protector profited greatly by this dissolution and spoliation. Although pensions were provided for dispossessed chantry priests, little of the money went for charitable or educational purposes. Some did, however, go to found about thirty grammar schools.

Somerset, it seems, thought the great religious questions of the time could be solved by discussion, and in 1547–8 the country was permitted to do as it pleased as far as church services were concerned – and some thought things went much too far. Experiments of all sorts were tried. The country became restless and involved in theological controversies, many of which were of a scurrilous nature. What was required was an Act of Uniformity, and this was passed in 1549 and imposed by the first *Book of Common Prayer*. It was in English and was a compromise between the old and the new. Its reception was mixed and in various places it caused rebellions, particularly amongst Cornishmen who knew little English but who had been brought up on the Latin Mass, which was familiar to them even though they did not know that language either. The rebellion was easily suppressed. The second Act of Uniformity, authorizing a second and more radical *Book of Common Prayer* – this contains the basis, with certain revisions, of the Communion Service known to most Anglicans – was passed by Parliament on 23 January 1552. The previous day Edward Seymour, Duke of Somerset, had been beheaded.

His nephew notes this event in his *Chronicle* briefly and without comment. 'The Duke of Somerset,' he writes, 'had his head cut off upon Towre hill between eight and nine a cloke in the morning.'[65]

Certainly Somerset had not won the boy's affection, had kept him on a tight rein, short of money, and had doubtless made him feel inferior. But for all his faults much can be said in Somerset's favour. He was far more liberal in outlook and more humane than many of the great men of his time.

When Edward succeeded, the country had an uneasy peace with France, where the ambitious Henry II had succeeded Francis I, but it had no treaty with Scotland. It is believed that upon his death-bed Henry VIII 'had charged Hertford [Somerset] to settle once and for all with the perfidious neighbour, still pledged, as he believed, to give her daughter in marriage to Edward of England'.[66] The proposed marriage had been a part of the treaty of Greenwich of July 1543, but the treaty and the betrothal had been repudiated by the Scots five months later. Small, retaliatory raids were made upon Scotland in 1545 and in 1547 Somerset invaded that country to enforce the marriage treaty. He hoped, unrealistically, for a peaceful union of the two countries, but saw no way of getting it save by war. He defeated the Scots at Pinkie Cleugh, and subsequently captured Edinburgh and other strong points which he garrisoned with English officers and men. However, the young Queen of Scots escaped being Edward's bride by becoming betrothed to the Dauphin and leaving for France in 1548.

Also in 1548 there was a rising in Norfolk in protest against enclosures and out-dated manorial rights. The rebellion was put down by Warwick; many were slain and its leader, Robert Kett, together with his brother Thomas, was hanged. As Somerset – known to many as the 'Good Duke' – had issued a proclamation to check enclosures, the wretched rebels believed him to be on their side – which he was – but rebellion of any kind obviously could not be tolerated.

Hidden forces working against Somerset were now in operation, taking the form of a conspiracy to bring about his fall. This was led by his brother, Thomas Seymour, a Privy Councillor and Lord High Admiral.

Thomas Seymour (1508?–49), Baron Seymour of Sudeley, had married the dowager queen, Catherine Parr, in 1547. He seems to have been a man of great personal charm (who treated his wife badly) but he was cunning, greedy, ambitious and jealous of his eldest brother.* He became intimate with his nephew, flattered the boy, gave him money when Edward was short, and promised him great power. He also made advances to Princess Elizabeth, whom he had known rather too familiarly when she had been in the care of her stepmother. He agreed with Henry Grey, Marquis of Dorset, that Edward should marry Dorset's eldest girl, Lady Jane Grey. He took illicit profits from the Bristol mint, and not only turned a blind eye upon piracy but connived at piratical enterprises which, as Lord High Admiral, he was supposed to suppress. It was, however, the illicit profits which were his undoing.

* A third brother, Henry, wisely kept out of affairs and lived quietly in the country.

Their discovery brought to light his other offences as well as his dishonesty. He refused private interrogation by his brother, or to answer the Council, on the grounds that he should have an open trial. This was not granted and in March 1549 he was beheaded.

This did not add to Somerset's popularity. He had not defended his brother, so was he capable of defending himself? Would a king who had made no effort to save his favourite uncle exert himself to save his more powerful one? Such questions were unsettling to say the least. A feeling of insecurity had been engendered by the agrarian rising in Norfolk and the religious ones in the West Country and in Oxfordshire, after which priests were hanged from the spires of their own churches, and by the fact that the French had declared war on us and begun the siege of Boulogne. By then it seemed to the Council that Somerset had failed to govern – thus had his 'liberalism' produced confusion and disorder; moreover he had haughtily ignored his fellow Councillors and behaved as if he were king.

Warwick was more authoritarian (and a good deal more dangerous); he and Wriothesley combined with those Catholic Councillors who were against the *Book of Common Prayer*, with those Protestant Councillors who felt Somerset's lenience was compromising with God's truth, and with the rich as a whole. Somerset was deprived of his Protectorship in August 1549 and sent to the Tower. Warwick, although he did not take the title of Protector, concentrated power and offices in his own hands, manoeuvred the Catholics out of the Council and tried to advance on Protestant lines. But he could hardly exclude both the Catholics and the Protestant Somerset so, in 1550, the ex-Protector was released, and for a brief time it seemed as if the two men would work together. Indeed Somerset married his daughter to Warwick's son, John Dudley.

The year 1550 also saw the attempt of the Princess Mary to escape to Flanders and seek the protection of her cousin the Emperor Charles V. It saw, too, the appointment of Sir William Cecil (1520–98) as principal secretary of state, and it brought the peace of Boulogne which ended the war with France and

Scotland. We returned Boulogne to the French on payment of 400,000 crowns. We still had our chief foothold, Calais.

In 1551 Edward was betrothed to Mme Elizabeth of France, but the marriage was deferred. Also in this year, Warwick was created Duke of Northumberland. He was a greedy, rapacious man with an insatiable thirst for power, an arch-intriguer and totally unscrupulous. Somerset, with all his faults, had tried in his muddled way to do some good; all Northumberland cared about was helping himself and those rich landowners who supported him and, like him, wanted to increase their own wealth and power. In fact it is difficult to find anything good to say of Northumberland other than that he recognized the evils consequent upon another debasement of the coinage and brought about a return (for a time) to good currency. By 1552, as we know, he and his colleagues had got rid of Somerset on the usual charge of treason and the more unusual one of felony. Edward did not intervene.

Northumberland had gradually packed the Council with his supporters until it became as good as impotent, and he used every means within his power to gain ascendancy over Edward's mind, with the object of freeing him from the swaddling of the royal minority. With Edward free from such trammels Northumberland would be the powerful puppet-master. He also pushed forward the Reformation with haste and energy, in contrast to the milder policy of Somerset. The differences between the first *Book of Common Prayer* and the second showed the doctrinal changes, and on a different level there were the further spoliation of shrines and images in churches, the banishing of crucifixes and rood screens, the whitewashing-over of beautiful wall paintings, the shattering of stained-glass windows and the removal of church plate and 'idolatrous pictures'. Even tombs were overturned and defaced and in many churches stone altars were replaced by wooden Communion tables by these early 'Puritans'. Most people acquiesced – there was not much else they could do – but not the Princess Mary, who resisted every effort of the Council to deprive her of the Mass.

But in 1552 – the year in which Walter Ralegh was born – Edward was ailing. 'I fell sike of the mesels and the small pokkes,'[67] he writes, and the onset of these diseases, acting upon what was probably a latent consumption, made it clear that the unfortunate, over-zealous and bigoted Protestant king was declining rapidly. His death would mean the accession of the Roman Catholic Princess Mary and the end of the Reformation in England. It would also mean the end of Northumberland's ambition.

Northumberland plotted well, however. In May 1553 he married his son Lord Guildford Dudley* to Lady Jane Grey whose father, now Duke of Suffolk, had to beat her into submission. Some time, we are not sure just when, Northumberland had persuaded Edward to change the provisions made in his father's will by making a new will of his own. In this he declared his two sisters to be bastards and therefore incapable of inheriting the crown, and he bestowed the succession upon his young cousin Lady Jane Grey. The crux of Edward's 'devise' for the succession – which he altered before it reached its final form – lay in the words 'to the Lady Jane and her heirs male'.† Originally it had read 'to the Lady Jane's heirs male'. The final document made Lady Jane his direct successor.

Back in February of that year Edward had developed a cold which turned to congestion of the lungs. By March it appeared to those around him that he was dying. Yet in that month he opened parliament with due splendour and ceremony, and in April he left the Palace of Westminster for the last time. By now he was coughing up huge gobbets of phlegm mixed with blood. He could not attend the marriage of Lady Jane on 1 May, but around the middle of this month people had been so terrified that he was dead that Northumberland had ordered the youth to be held up to a window so that the anxious crowd could see that their own

* Another son, Robert, the future favourite of Queen Elizabeth, had married Amy Robsart in 1550.

† Professor Bindoff, in a fascinating article (*History Today*, September 1950), points out that the final document was probably a forgery.

king was still alive. How the sight of this pale, emaciated boy could have reassured the crowd – if it did – is hard to understand.

His disastrous will was signed on 21 June by more than 100 people – bishops, peers, Councillors and aldermen – not without notable objections by some signators, including Sir William Cecil and Archbishop Cranmer. Cranmer could only be persuaded to sign at the personal request of his dying king. All Edward now had to do was die. His physicians, in a last-minute effort to save him, permitted an unknown woman to try her 'cure' on him. It probably contained arsenic, which acted as a tonic at first and then as a systemic poison. His hair fell out, his fingernails and toenails broke off, his skin peeled away. Numbness affected his hands (he may have had Raynaud's disease too). By 6 July the king was dead. He was a few months short of his sixteenth birthday. Rumour ran that he had been poisoned by Northumberland; 'he was poyssoned, as evere body says,'[68] Machyn notes, but wisely does not name the suspected poisoner. Northumberland had indeed poisoned the king – but not with any material toxic substance.

In the meantime, on 3 July, the Princess Mary, who was at Hunsdon, was summoned to the death-bed of her brother. What it seems she prudently did, although we don't know her exact movements, was to ride away to her house at Kenninghall, Norfolk, and from there on to Framlingham, in Suffolk. Here she was near the sea and could escape, if necessary, to Flanders and the protection of Charles V. Thus she delivered herself from Northumberland, who had planned to arrest her.

He, for his part, kept the king's death a secret for two days while he put into action his previously prepared *coup d'état*. On 8 July he summoned the Lord Mayor of London and other dignitaries, informed them of Edward's death and told them that, according to the late king's will, Lady Jane was the successor. On 10 July, amid great salvoes from the Tower, he had the unwilling but dutiful Lady Jane proclaimed queen.

This small, gentle, freckled, red-haired and learned girl of sixteen, who had also been tutored by Ascham, was the victim of a brutal, ambitious father and the lynch-pin in Northumberland's long-term objective. She cared no more for her unpleasant husband than he for her and she cared even less about wearing the crown. She wore it for nine days only.

Mary Tudor did not hear of her brother's death until 9 July. She immediately wrote to the Council demanding recognition as queen. The Council replied that she was a bastard, had no claim, and should therefore recognize Queen Jane. But in Norfolk and Suffolk, in Oxfordshire and Buckinghamshire, the gentry and people rallied to the princess and proclaimed her to be queen. The people of south-eastern England were firmly for her and – odd though it sounds – the uprisings which put Mary on the throne happened in the most Protestant parts of the realm: the Catholic north was too far away. Even that extreme Protestant Bishop of Gloucester and Worcester, John Hooper (d. 1555), urged his congregation to march to Framlingham and fight for Mary.

The fact that she was Roman Catholic did not weigh against her. It is even doubtful if people knew she planned to restore the Roman Catholic religion. What did matter was that she was Henry's daughter just as Edward had been his son. A deep sense of loyalty to the crown was probably the greatest force which moved people to fight for Mary, although there were other reasons too. Northumberland was hated as a corrupt and unscrupulous politician. Inflation, low wages, high rents, a falling off of the cloth trade, socio-economic distress, divisive religious issues, all played their parts. It should also be remembered that Northumberland (as Warwick) had put down Kett's rebellion and overthrown Somerset, and was deeply hated by the men of Norfolk. Latimer's sermon on Edward's accession had been based, rather inappositely, on the text, 'Woe to thee, O land, when thy king is a child'.* This must now have seemed a prophetic statement. And yet another 'child' had been proclaimed ruler, while her husband, Northumberland's son, would become king.

Northumberland, who had ordered the fleet to Yarmouth to

* Ecclesiastes, Ch. X, v.16.

prevent Mary's escape, quickly assembled an armed force; many of the soldiers were German and Spanish mercenaries, and on 14 July he led them out of a silent and sullen London. On the sixteenth he arrived at Cambridge, where he learned that the fleet had mutinied and declared for Mary; further, the mercenaries showed signs of disaffection: they believed Mary to be the favourite of their own Emperor Charles V. Northumberland's nerve seems to have failed. Instead of advancing on Framlingham he loitered at Cambridge for two days, then moved on to Bury St Edmunds, then back again to Cambridge.

Mary, however, had secret supporters in the Council and they too decided that the time had come for a *coup d'état*. London, it was clear, was for Mary, and her supporters were able to win over all but a few members of Queen Jane's Council.

On Wednesday, 19 July 1553, in the year of the world 5520, the Councillors saw the Lord Mayor and ordered him to proclaim Mary in the city. This was done between five and six o'clock in the evening. At the news there was a spontaneous outburst of wild enthusiasm all over London; nothing like it had been seen within living memory. Bells rang, bonfires blazed, crowds packed the streets, where tables of beer and wine were set out, and at 'Pawll's' the *Te Deum Laudamus* was heard with 'song and organes playhyng'.[69]

Upon hearing the news in Cambridge, Northumberland went into the market place and proclaimed Mary queen. This did not save him. He was arrested next day and so, subsequently, were his five sons. Lady Jane and her father were imprisoned in the Tower, but many nobles and officials who had supported her hurried to Framlingham to see Queen Mary and acknowledge their allegiance to her. She pardoned all but a few of them. On 3 August the queen, with her sister Elizabeth who had taken no part in the proceedings, accompanied by an escort and a vast concourse of people, rode in triumph into London.

And so this half-Spanish, thirty-seven-year-old daughter of Henry VIII and Catherine of Aragon became the first queen regnant in our history. She was a plain, very near-sighted woman of medium height with a deep voice, reddish hair and a flat-bridged nose. She suffered from frequent bad headaches and depression, possibly consequent upon severe amenorrhoea. History has dubbed her 'Bloody Mary',* but by nature she was gentle, merciful and kindly, and she loved children. She was also sensible – and obstinate. Her burning passion was to save the souls of her people from eternal damnation by a return to the Roman Catholic religion: the religion of her mother; the religion which had sustained her throughout a tragic life.

Within a few days of her entry into London, Northumberland and only two others were executed. The Council was shocked at the queen's lenience. Northumberland tried at the end to save himself by confessing the Catholic faith. He was not spared. But Lady Jane Grey and her husband were, while Stephen Gardiner was released from the Tower and reinstated as Bishop of Winchester, and a few days later became the queen's Lord Chancellor. She also released others who had been imprisoned for heresy or inconvenience during her brother's reign and imprisoned various Protestants, including Latimer and, a bit later, Archbishop Cranmer.

On 30 September, the day before her coronation – for which she had had to borrow £20,000 from her loyal London citizens, as there was not a groat left in the royal coffers – she went, as was customary, from the Tower to Whitehall, 'sitting in a chariot of cloth of tissue; drawn with six horses, all trapped with like cloth of tissue'. [70] Over the chariot was a rich canopy. The queen wore a gown of purple velvet furred with ermine, a caul of gold ornamented with pearls and other jewels, and a circlet of gold 'beset with precious stones'. [71] Caul and circlet were so heavy that she was 'fain to beare up hir head with hir hand'. [72] But she may have had one of her massive headaches due to nervous tension. In her retinue were seventy ladies, 500 noblemen, gentlemen and

---

* It should more fairly be 'Bloody Bonner'. Edmund Bonner (1500–1569), Bishop of London, was savage in the Marian persecutions; John, Lord Campbell in his *Lives of the Lord Chancellors* (Vol. II) calls him 'the most bloody persecutor who ever appeared in this island'.

ambassadors. Her own chariot was followed by another covered with red velvet; in this sat the Princess Elizabeth with her only surviving stepmother, Anne of Cleves.

There was certainly no lack of enthusiasm or pageantry. London had been preparing for the event for days. Streets were hung with banners; streamers – several flowed from St Paul's steeple – waved a welcome. Decorated stands where every craft was represented were set up and innumerable pageants were staged at strategic points along the route. Near Fenchurch Street the queen was greeted by four giants who made her 'goodly speeches'.[73] Conduits ran with wine, money was flung from windows, the streets were jammed and there was 'the blohyng of trumpet all the day longe'.[74] Next day, in Westminster Abbey, the queen was crowned by Bishop Gardiner. After the coronation ritual, Mass was said.

Four days later, after Mass in the Abbey, the queen opened her first parliament, which remained in session until December. During this sitting she had the act which had annulled the marriage of her mother and father and declared her illegitimate annulled. She repealed the Act of Uniformity – neither house protested at this – and we returned to the Henrician settlement. She also restored Mass throughout England, as from 21 December, and made it illegal to attend Protestant services. A bill of attainder was passed against Lady Jane Grey, her husband and Archbishop Cranmer; this was hardly fair to Cranmer, who had shown the utmost reluctance to sign Edward's will. He had been the last to do so, and then had signed only under pressure from the dying boy whom he loved. All three were sentenced to death at the queen's pleasure but, at that time, she seems to have had no intention of executing Lady Jane. The queen then announced her intention to marry her cousin Prince Philip of Spain, then Archduke of Burgundy.

Nothing could have been more unpopular. Mary's hand, which since childhood had been offered to and rejected by (chiefly because of her illegitimacy) kings and princes was, now that she had become queen of England, of great value. It was particularly valuable to the Emperor Charles V (once a suitor himself), for things were not going well with him at this point. He was at war with Henry II and had lost some territories and power to France. Henry II disliked the Spanish marriage; he had his own plans. Scotland was, he believed, already well within his grasp – and he also believed that in the young Queen of Scots, now betrothed to the Dauphin, he had a claimant to the English throne. An Anglo-Spanish match would interfere with this. Yet he could bide his time.

As for her own people, the idea of the Spanish marriage was anathema to them. For once Roman Catholics, Henricians and Protestants were united in fear and hatred. A long tradition of xenophobia, a fear of having a foreign king, the fear of the issue of such a marriage, a hatred of being involved on the continent, dragged in by a foreigner – all were strong. If the queen married she should marry an Englishman. Her distant cousin, Reginald Pole (1500–1558) was suggested. He was of the Plantagenet line through his mother, Margaret, Countess of Salisbury, whom Henry VIII had so shamefully executed in 1541. True, he lived abroad, and was a cardinal and therefore hardly to be trusted, but as he had only taken deacon's orders marriage was possible. But this future Archbishop of Canterbury, then fifty-three, declined and privately advised Mary not to marry at all – probably the wisest advice she ever received.

Another possible candidate was Edward Courtenay (1526?–56), Earl of Devon, weak, dissolute and an intriguer, but a descendant of Edward IV which made all the difference. Mary, however, was determined to marry a Spaniard. Gardiner was against it, most of the Council were against it. Simon Renard, the Spanish Ambassador and long Mary's confidant, pressed it carefully. The French Ambassador, Antoine de Noailles, did not. He made it abundantly clear that by such a marriage England would become a mere adjunct of the Spanish crown, like Naples and Sicily. We hardly needed to be told this.

In January 1554 the articles of marriage were announced. Among the provisions made were that Philip would be titled 'king'* and would assist the queen in government, but that all offices of Church and state were to be held by Englishmen. Our laws and customs were to remain intact and we would not go to war with France. Should the queen die without heir, Prince Philip was denied all further interest in England but, should she have issue, the child (or children) was to inherit, in addition to England, Burgundy and the Netherlands. Mary was also to have a jointure of £60,000 – which was useful. All this sounded far more advantageous to England than to Spain. But none of it was greeted with any enthusiasm. No one had any faith in the Emperor's promises.

Three weeks later several small and one serious insurrection broke out. The small ones came to nothing. The serious one was raised and led by Sir Thomas Wyatt (1521–54), son of the poet, a hot-headed Kentish gentleman; Kent was strongly Protestant and rallied to him. What his intentions were is still not clear. He detested the Spanish marriage, hated Spain, may have wanted to restore the Edwardian settlement and, as Courtenay (who betrayed Wyatt's plans to Gardiner) was a conspirator, he may have wanted to dethrone the queen in favour of her sister.

With a force of some 4,000 he set out for London; he was joined by others *en route*, but upon arrival found London Bridge held against him, so was forced to cross the Thames at Kingston. Marching via Knightsbridge and Fleet Street he reached Ludgate Hill, only to find the gate barred and fortified. His retreat cut off by troops at Temple Bar, he surrendered, and by late afternoon of 7 February he, with a number of his followers, was on his way to the Tower. His execution was delayed until 11 April in the hope that he would betray other conspirators. He never did. But more than 100 rebels were swiftly hanged and quartered in London and in Kent – many were ordinary folk – followers, not leaders. Their horrid deaths and exposed remains were meant to terrorize people. In March the Princess Elizabeth, suspected of complicity, was also sent to the Tower. She was released in May,

* The queen wished Philip to be crowned king. Parliament opposed this in 1555.

placed under 'house arrest' at Woodstock and drove her keeper, Sir Henry Bedingfield, nearly demented.

Wyatt's insurrection had the most unhappy immediate consequences. London and the government had been in a state of near panic – the capital threatened as never before! Only the queen exhibited real courage. She stayed at Whitehall but rode into the fortified city, made a stirring speech at the Guildhall, returned to Whitehall and was implored by her terror-stricken ministers and Councillors to take refuge in the Tower. This she refused to do, saying that she would set no example of cowardice. When the insurrection had collapsed she wished to show mercy, but a frightened and vengeful Council thought this an excellent opportunity to get rid of 'hurtful members' of the Commonwealth. Lady Jane Grey and her husband came into this category. They were executed on 12 February.* This gentle girl of sixteen and a half was 'as patient and mild as anie lambe at hir execution',[75] while the people cried out and lamented to see one so young and innocent put to death.

On the feast of St James, Spain's patron saint, Mary and Philip were married at Winchester by Bishop Gardiner. So that Prince Philip's rank should be equal to that of his wife, on the wedding day (25 July) his father made him king of Naples and of Jerusalem. Philip, at twenty-six, was a widower with a son, Don Carlos, and had been a reluctant and dilatory suitor. Mary, who had felt him to be too young, was reassured by being told that his previous marriage had made him much older – marriage aged a man! Her own attitude to marriage was that it was her duty to marry and provide an heir, but that it was also the first duty of a wife to love her husband, to be subservient to him in all ways and to bear him children. This was God's will. The wife's duty came before that of the queen.

The queen may have married out of a sense of duty to her country, but it seems clear that the woman fell wildly in love with her husband. Affectionate by nature, she had never had

* Lady Jane's father, the Duke of Suffolk, and her uncle were executed a few weeks later.

anyone of her own to love, other than her mother, from whom she had been so cruelly separated in 1532. The repressed and pent-up emotion of years was released on Philip. He, fair-haired, blue-eyed, handsome, with gallant manners and generous with public largesse, was also cold, calculating and a fanatic Roman Catholic. He did not love his wife; he cannot be blamed for this, his marriage was arranged by the Emperor to ensnare England into the Habsburg network. Further, Mary was too old, too thin, too plain. She dressed badly; that is, she did not dress in the Spanish fashion. Further still, it was rumoured he had other interests. He also hated England and its climate, and so did his retinue. They had been greeted upon their arrival at Southampton on 20 July by torrential rain. The omens were not good.

Rain or shine, the omens in England had been unpropitious for some time now. As Supreme Head of the Church – an embarrassing title for the queen – she had very early on sent Archbishop Cranmer to the Tower on a charge of treason – but he was to be reserved for 'heresy'. She also sent Bishops Latimer and Ridley to the Tower; Bishop Hooper went to the Fleet, the debtors' prison. In their room she appointed her own bishops; Mass was re-introduced and Protestant preaching forbidden, and Gardiner was given power to license all preachers. The Protestant refugees who had sought sanctuary here were allowed to leave the country and were soon followed by English clerics – John Knox, although not English, among them. By March of the year in which Prince Philip arrived, many priests had been deprived of their cures because they were married and 'it seems probable that throughout the realm one fifth of the clergy were removed'[76] and replaced by Roman Catholics. They were not compensated as many priests had been compensated at the Dissolution. Those churches stripped in Edward's day had to re-provide themselves with altars, cruci-fixes, chalices, patens, pyxes, holy-bread baskets, candlesticks, censers, images, holy-water pails and many other things which had been banished or destroyed by extreme Protestants. The queen also wanted to return Church lands. The ground was being prepared to save England from eternal damnation.

Two months after her marriage, in September 1554, the queen informed her Council that she was pregnant. Court physicians who had examined her agreed that she was. The chief midwife thought otherwise. She believed the doctors were either ignorant or had just said the queen was pregnant because they feared not to. Mary's desire for a child was intense.

On 29 November the act repealing Henry VIII's Act of Supremacy became law. Next day England was absolved from the sin of schism and the reconciliation with Rome was proclaimed. By Christmas a bill for the burning of heretics passed both houses. The salvation of England could now begin in earnest. It did.

The first Protestant martyr was John Rogers (b. 1500?), rector of Holy Trinity, London, a prebendary of St Paul's and editor of Tyndale's translations of the Bible, who had, on Mary's accession, preached against 'pestilential Popery'. He went to the stake at Smithfield on 4 February 1555. Bishop Hooper, an advanced reformer who nevertheless had urged his congregation to fight for Mary, was also burnt in February at Gloucester, his old diocese. In September Archbishop Cranmer and Bishops Ridley (b. 1500) and Latimer were tried; the last two were burnt at Oxford in October. Archbishop Cranmer, who had been almost alone in attempting to save Sir Thomas More and Bishop Fisher and had interceded for Mary's own life in 1536, recanted several times, but in his dying declaration repudiated his recantations. He was burnt the following March. He was succeeded as Archbishop of Canterbury by Cardinal Pole, who assumed the function of Papal Legate.

It is true that burning for heresy was neither new in England nor exclusive to the Tudor period, but the scale of the burnings was. Nearly 300 went to the stake in just under four years. Five bishops were made a burnt offering; so were about 100 priests. Many lay folk died, numbers of them of humble artisan class, and between fifty and sixty were women. It is also true that the queen's victims were fewer than those who perished in Roman Catholic countries on the continent, but the only thing she achieved by this holocaust was to make certain that Roman Catholicism would never again become England's faith.

Also in 1555, however, the real desire to discover new lands and new trade routes – something which Henry VIII had neglected – was implemented by the queen when Richard Chancellor returned from the first-ever journey to Russia. Shortly before Edward's death Sebastian Cabot, who had returned to Bristol from Spain in 1547 and was given a pension by the king, promoted a 'mystery and Company of Merchant Venturers' of London to seek the North-east passage to Cathay. Capital, provided by London merchants, was £6,000. Sir Hugh Willoughby (d. 1554) was admiral of the fleet of three ships, which left England in 1553. He and two ships were lost near the North Cape but Chancellor reached Archangel and went on to Moscow. When he returned Mary and Philip were on the throne, and on 1 May 1555 the articles of the Muscovy Company – the first of our great trading companies – were 'conceived and Determined for the Commission of the Merchants of this Company . . . for a second voyage, 1555'.[77] Richard Chancellor was 'grand Pilot of this fleete' and letters from 'the King [Philip] and Queen's Majesties'[78] were to be presented to the 'Emperor' of Russia and the desire expressed 'to continue in trafficke with his subjects'.[79] Chancellor did not return from this second voyage; he was wrecked off the coast of Aberdeenshire in 1556. The next year Anthony Jenkinson (d. 1611), captain-general and agent of the Company, set out on the fantastic journey which took him to Moscow, Astrakhan and Bokhara. He did not return until 1560. Mary was dead. But it was during her reign that the way was opened for the glorious expeditions and explorations of the next era.

But to go back to 1555. In April the Princess Elizabeth, owing to Philip's influence, was permitted to return to court and was reconciled with her sister. On the thirtieth of the month, rumour ran that the queen had been delivered of a prince. London celebrated with its usual bell-ringing, bonfires and processions. *Te Deums* were sung. The rumour was false. The date was then set for June. People waited but no news came. Nothing more was said publicly about the pregnancy.

Perhaps it was a pseudocyesis or perhaps, as the French Ambassador reported, Mary was delivered of a fleshy mole. Whichever was the case, it was Mary's own personal and terrible tragedy. She was very ill afterwards, but her health had never been good. In addition to gynaecological difficulties and severe headaches (migraine?), she had always had poor digestion, was frequently ill with unspecified maladies and was given to bouts of weeping.

In August Philip left England and in October Charles V abdicated and retired to a Spanish monastery. His brother, Ferdinand, became Holy Roman Emperor. Spain, the Netherlands and the rich American colonies went to Philip, who now became Philip II of Spain. It is only courteous to think that Philip, knowing in advance of his father's decision and the responsibilities involved, may have left England for these reasons and not because he could no longer bear the country – nor his wife.

His wife was, however, almost inconsolable. This is not to say that she did nothing but lament and mope. She concealed her misery as best she could but her ladies knew of it and tried to comfort her. Despite her failing health she continued to rise about six, took no breakfast, worked all morning with her secretaries, dined at one – which was late – and slept at night for perhaps three or four hours, since when she had finished with state business and what court pleasures there were she would sit up writing to Philip. She attended Mass regularly, often nine times a day, and on the great public occasions of the Church, such as the Good Friday ceremony of Creeping to the Cross, she displayed such emotion that foreign ambassadors, more accustomed to the restraint shown by their own Roman Catholic sovereigns, were embarrassed or at least disconcerted.

In March 1557 Philip returned to England to demand forced loans to support Spain's war against France and Scotland, and by 6 June England, despite the marriage articles, had declared war on France. Scotland promptly invaded. When Philip left in July the queen again believed she was pregnant. Everyone at court pretended to believe it too, for months, but again nothing came of it. It was obviously an hysterical pregnancy. July, too, saw the death of Anne of Cleves at the age of forty-one. She left 'to our most dearest and entirely beloved sovereign lady Mary . . . our best jewel' and to 'the lady Elizabeth's grace' her 'second best jewel' and requested her to take into her service 'one of our poor maids named Dorothy Curson'.[80] She was buried, by order of the queen, in Westminster Abbey near the High Altar, and was given a splendid funeral.

In January 1558 Calais, our last foothold on the continent, was lost. This was regarded as a national disaster by everyone. For the ailing queen it was the end. The Spanish blamed the English. The English blamed the Spanish, and whatever hopes Philip II may have entertained of becoming king of England in more than name were dashed to pieces. Hatred of Philip was intense, hatred of Mary only a little less so.

Once, towards the end of her life, Mary had told a lady-in-waiting that when she died and was opened 'Calais' would be found lying in her heart. It is more probable that 'Calais' lay in one half of that poor deluded and divided heart and 'Philip' in the other.

The queen died at four o'clock on the morning of 17 November 1558. She was forty-two.

CHAPTER TWO

Of Buildings – Great and Small

On 21 December 1498* fire ravaged the king's manor at Shene: 'A great part of the old building was burnt, with hangings, beds, apparrel, plate, and many jewels,' says Stow in his *Annals*. Some of the jewels were recovered, for on 1 January a reward of £20 was given to 'them that founde the Kings juels at Shene'.[1] The king, who had planned to spend Christmas there with his family, had to go elsewhere, but as Shene was a favourite spot he decided to rebuild. The new palace was a large Gothic building around a paved court. Although it was a big palace with embattled walls, a great tower, fourteen slim turrets, numerous windows, many state apartments and a chapel with, unusually, pews, it took only two years to build. When finished the king re-named it Richmond.

The finer details of the palace probably took longer than the actual building, as we find in the Privy Purse accounts on 21 June 1505 that one Thomas Bynkes was paid £8 6s. 8d. for 'the galorye and thorchard at Richemont', while Henry Smyth received £133 6s. 8d. for furnishing the new tower, leading it, paving both galleries and paying for the bricks and stone, as well as 'other diversse werkes'.[2] This, of course, does not necessarily mean the palace was not totally finished within the two years; it may merely mean that Bynkes and Smyth, who sound like small workmen, had had to wait for their money.

The palace of Richmond, of which next to nothing survives, was built by King Henry VII during the last phase of Gothic

* Both Holinshed and Polydore Vergil give the date as 1500.

67

Richmond Palace

architecture. Its irregular skyline, pierced by many turrets ornamented with painted and gilded vanes, and the massing of its buildings are typical of a Gothic which looks to a past. The slimness of its turrets, the thinness of walls and the great number of windows all suggest that it belonged, in part at any rate, to the terminal style of Gothic architecture.

If architecture is one of the chief forms in which a civilization expresses power, or what it regards as being powerful, then in medieval times the power of the Church, unquestioned and largely unquestionable, expressed itself in ecclesiastical building. Magnificent cathedrals, splendid abbeys, fine monasteries, cloisters and beautiful parish churches spanned and ornamented three centuries with Gothic architecture which is conveniently, if somewhat inaccurately, divided in this country into three periods, Early English, Decorated and Perpendicular.* But there was another

* These terms, which overlap, were not used until the nineteenth century.

68

power growing at this time: the power of princes, which meant princes of the Church no less than secular princes. The rising power of the Renaissance prince was also expressed in architecture. That prince of the Church, Cardinal Wolsey, built Hampton Court; that secular Renaissance prince, Henry VIII, who destroyed Wolsey and the power of the Pope, built among others the Palace of Nonsuch. The first still exists, greatly altered, the second was deliberately destroyed in the time of Charles II.

But when any style enters its final phase something new evolves or develops from the previous style. Our architecture during the early and middle medieval period had been closely linked with that of France. Yet, when it came to the final phase of Gothic, French and English architecture diverged completely. In France during the fifteenth and sixteenth centuries a style appeared which, with its over-emphasis on curves, carving and flame-like tracery, is now known as Flamboyant. In England the very opposite happened: 'We brushed away all the vagaries of Decorated and settled down to a long, none too adventurous development of plain-spoken idiom, sober and wide awake.'[3] In short, the Early English style had been dominant for about a century, the Decorated for perhaps fifty years, but the Perpendicular remained without essential alteration or modification for nearly two centuries. It dominated the whole of the fifteenth century and continued until the Dissolution of the monasteries. In fact what may be called Tudor-Gothic in the Perpendicular style persisted until about 1550, to be followed by the very different and more Italianate Elizabethan.

To recognize the Perpendicular Gothic is simple enough in ecclesiastical building, but what concerns us here, for the last fifty years of its existence, is its influence upon and adaptation to domestic architecture. Henry VII, for example, is responsible for the marvellous Lady Chapel★ in Westminster Abbey, which he built to house his bones and those of his descendants. But, as we

---

★ Henry III's Lady Chapel and the nearby White Rose tavern were pulled down to make room for Henry VII's chapel. The first stone was laid January 1502/3. The total cost was around £14,000, an enormous sum.

have seen, he also built Richmond Palace to house himself and his family, while many a rich merchant who gave a chapel to or otherwise embellished his parish church also built himself a new house. During the reign of the first four Tudors a good many new houses, great and small, were built all over England, while old ones were often enlarged and modernized.

A few, very few, castles were built. Among them was Hurstmonceux, Sussex,★ for which Sir Robert Fiennes had received a building licence in 1440. The external regularity of its imposing brickwork façade certainly shows a Perpendicular feeling, but Hurstmonceux is hardly a castle; it is more a fortified house, as the walls are thin and the windows are many and large. Hever Castle, Kent, although altered in Edwardian times, is another example. Small, rectangular and castellated, it was a late thirteenth-century moated castle before being brought up to date in the fifteenth century. Hever was the childhood home of Anne Boleyn.

Castles were by then changing in function and purpose. The invention of wrought-iron cannon or 'bombards' meant that castle walls did not need to be scaled, they could be breached safely from a distance, and this rendered the medieval castle obsolete. Castles were still constructed externally on medieval lines but as their function became less primarily a military one interiors were adapted more and more to home and family life – or perhaps, in view of the size, palace life is a more accurate phrase. As military importance declined, domestic comfort increased and the castle itself was transmuted into a great house, while subsidiary buildings were no longer required to house armed retainers, arms, horses, fodder and all the paraphernalia of war. Certain essential features remained, such as the great hall, now provided with large windows, and with kitchens at one end and private rooms at the other. In earlier houses neither hall nor door was central as they later became.

Externally, walls, gatehouse, moat and drawbridge still appeared much as usual, but were, particularly the gatehouse,

★ Now the home of the Royal Observatory.

chiefly decorative. Only on the border with Scotland and around the coast did castles retain their original function. Inland they slipped gently from the defensive to the domestic.

By mid sixteenth century when John Leland (1506?–52) made an antiquarian tour of England at the behest of Henry VIII and produced his *Itinerary*★ (1534–43), the number of ruined castles he notes is striking. Taking only a random few: Liskeard Castle, Cornwall, was in ruins and was being used as a pound for cattle. Leicester was a thing of 'smaul estimation'⁴ without walls or dykes and badly decayed; Rockingham, Northamptonshire, had a 'fair and strong'⁵ keep and the outside walls still stood but the rest of the castle buildings were in ruin. At Worksop, Nottinghamshire, the old castle was 'clene downe'⁶ and Doncaster, Yorkshire, was 'long sins clene decayid'.⁷ Redde Castle near Whitchurch, Shropshire, was 'now al ruinus'; it had once 'bene strong' but 'hath decayid many a day',⁸ while three miles away Middle Castle belonging to Lord Derby was in a similar state. At Netherby Castle, on the Cumberland border, the grass now grew on the ruined walls but this was exceptional, for in the north castles were plentiful and still defensive.

Belvoir Castle, Leicestershire (rebuilt by Wyatt in the nineteenth century) is perhaps an example of a castle which was now being transformed into a grand house. It had been much spoiled and defaced in the wars between Henry VI and Edward IV: 'Then,' says Leland, 'fell alle the castelle to ruine and the tymbre of the rofes onkevered rottid away, and the soile betwene the waules at the last grue ful of elders, and no habitation was there.'⁹ But in recent years the Earl of Rutland had rebuilt it and made it 'fairer than it ever was'. Significantly the dungeon, 'a fair rounde tour', was now 'turnid to pleasure, as a place to walk yn, and to se the countrey aboute'.¹⁰ There was also a garden within the walls.

Equally striking is the number of new houses he records as he jogs up and down the countryside. At Willington, Bedfordshire,

★ Not published until 1710. I have used the Centaur Press edition, edited by Lucy Toulmin Smith (1964).

a Mr Gostewicke had recently built himself 'a sumptuus new building of brike and tymbre *a fundamentis* in it, with a conduct of water derivid in leade pipes'.[11] At Chenies in Buckinghamshire, Lord Russell (1486?–1555) had 'translatid' the old house by rebuilding most of it in brick and timber with 'fair loggingse' [lodgings][12] in the garden. Lord Russell had also 'mad hym a fair place' of a house belonging to the Black Friars. It stood 'in the north side of the cemiterie of the cathedral church',[13] which sounds an odd site but Sir John, later Baron Russell of Chenies, had been a loyal henchman of Henry VIII who, in 1540, granted him the cemetery, part of the lands of the Abbey of Tavistock, and promised him still further largesse. This was forthcoming when Edward VI succeeded his father, created Baron Russell first Earl of Bedford* and granted him, among other lands, the area of Covent Garden and the reversion of the lease of Woburn Abbey which, completely rebuilt in the eighteenth century, is today a tourists' mecca.

With the Dissolution and the granting or selling of land and buildings to various nobles, a number of abbeys all over the country were turned into private houses. Lacock near Chippenham in Wiltshire, Newstead, Nottinghamshire, Lord Byron's family home, and Buckland Abbey, Tavistock, Devon, are three well-known examples still extant although now much changed by later alterations.

The entire cloister of the thirteenth- to fifteenth-century nunnery of Lacock was preserved by Sir William Sharington (1495?–1553), mint-master at Bristol, who in 1548/9 had been condemned to death 'for making fals coine'.[14] More fortunate than his friend, the plotter Lord Seymour of Sudeley, who the previous year had given his brother the Lord Protector such offence because he had secretly 'married the quene whos nam was Katarine',[15] and who was also condemned to death at the same time, Sir William kept his head and in 1550 began his work at

---

* Not to be confused with Jasper Tudor, Earl of Pembroke, created Duke of Bedford by Henry VII, 1485. The present dukes are descended from William, Fourth Earl and First Duke, second creation.

Lacock, aided no doubt by the 'fals coine'. He turned the Abbey into a house of great interest with certain early Italianate features such as flat-headed doorways with classical entablatures. He added the octagonal tower with flat-headed windows and round stone chimneys which look like twisted columns. The High Gothic Hall, however, is not original; it was designed in the mid eighteenth century as a suitable addition to the medieval and Tudor buildings. Sir William was also the first owner of Avebury Manor, Wilts., once part of a Benedictine community.

At Newstead only the west end of the thirteenth-century priory church survives, while the Tudor house itself was built by Sir John Byron around 1540. It included the cloister, the Great Vaulted Guest Chamber and the refectory; this last was re-done later and is now a saloon displaying much Jacobean plaster work. In the nineteenth century when the craze for a return to Gothic began, the house was reconstructed in the 'Gothick Style' by John Shaw.

Buckland Abbey, now a museum, was originally a Cistercian monastery and was granted by Henry VIII to Sir Richard Grenville, grandfather of the great Elizabethan naval commander, Sir Richard Grenville of the *Revenge*. He turned the nave of the monastery into a great hall with a splendid plaster ceiling. Few other alterations were made even by Sir Francis Drake (1540–96) who bought the house in 1581 after circumnavigating the globe. Today it looks much as it must have looked in Tudor times.

The Longleat estate, once a priory of the Augustinians, later a grange or manor belonging to the Carthusians, was bought in 1540 by Sir John Thynne (1515–80) for £53. He altered and rebuilt the old priory and turned it into a house. This is not the Longleat we know today, as the first house Sir John built burned down in 1567.

But none of these erstwhile religious houses is typical of Tudor architecture; they are medieval with Tudor touches. For typical Tudor one must look to the new great houses and the smaller houses which were built during the period.

The typical house, great or manor, was built in an H or E

shape, or on the hollow-square plan. Romantic tradition – and this sounds like a Victorian myth – has it that the H and E were products of the period, a Tudor invention to flatter the Tudor sovereigns. This is not so for, while no 'M's for Mary remain or are recorded, it is certain that both the H and E plans had been developing before the Tudor dynasty. Further, many large Tudor houses were until the end of the reign of Henry VIII – and later – still being built on the much older and still very popular hollow-square plan, which gave the house an enclosed and inward-looking central courtyard. The buildings, no matter which plan was used, were usually but one room thick with intercommunicating rooms, and in the hollow-square type of house the main windows faced the courtyard, whilst the exterior walls had smaller irregularly set windows and, often, boldly protruding chimney stacks which hugged the walls like spreadeagled buttresses. Two famous houses built on the hollow-square plan were Cowdray Park, Sussex, and Somerset House in the Strand.

Edward VI visited Cowdray Park in July 1552. He arrived on the twenty-fifth, having journeyed from Petworth, which had once been the southern mansion of the Percys, falling to the crown when Henry, Sixth Earl of Northumberland, had died without issue in the reign of Henry VIII. At Petworth the young king cut down his entourage to some 150 men, dismissing many retainers and about 4,000 horses, 'which,' as he writes in his journal on 21 July, 'ware inough to eat up the countrey; for there was little medow nor hay al the way as I went.' Doubtless the retainers were as difficult to keep in fodder as the horses. In any event the king proceeded to Cowdray, which was virtually a new house built on the old hollow-square plan. Plain and solid as to its exterior, it was splendidly decorated inside. The house had been built by William Fitzwilliam, later first Earl of Southampton (d. 1542), an intimate friend of Henry VIII and one-time treasurer to Cardinal Wolsey's household. Fitzwilliam had bought the estate in 1528, and in 1533 had been granted a licence by the king to enclose a park of 600 surrounding acres and call it Cowdray Park. He was also licensed to embattle the house. Southampton did not destroy what remained of the original house, a tall polygonal tower put up by the previous owners, the de Bohuns, but incorporated it into his new building as a kitchen.

The house, which covered nearly an acre, was built squarely about a quadrangle measuring 107 by 122 feet. It had a great, central four-turreted gateway, and at each of the four angles of the house stood a square tower with great projecting bay windows which looked out upon the park. Above, on the roof of the great hall, which resembled Wolsey's hall at Hampton Court, the louvre was ornamented by glittering, gilded vanes. At the time of the young king's visit this house was owned by Sir Anthony Browne⋆ whose father, of the same name, had been uterine brother to Southampton. Nothing of Cowdray Park, other than the gatehouse, now remains.

It was the king's uncle, the Lord Protector, who built for himself Somerset House in the Strand, begun about 1547. We, know very little about the original house, but it stood where the present Somerset House now stands on land where the Bishops of Worcester and Chester had had lodgings. In the late Middle Ages and right up until the Dissolution every bishop had a residence in London. With the Dissolution such places fell to the crown.

The south side of the Strand was now the most favoured and sought-after building site in London, as the land sloped to the river and this gave easy access to Westminster and Whitehall. As the monarch now lived more and more in London – the Tudors started this habit – at Whitehall palace, great noblemen who wished to remain at the very heart of affairs had to have London houses. The houses are now all gone but the names, Southampton, Essex, Norfolk, Howard, Exeter, all persist as street names in the Strand area.

Many small tenements were incontinently cleared away to make room for the Protector's house. What it looked like we cannot say, but some indication of the ground plan, together with the front elevation, is given by John Thorpe (1570?–1610) the great Elizabethan and Jacobean surveyor who, around 1603, was

⋆ Created Viscount Montague in 1554 by Queen Mary.

instructed to draw up plans for rebuilding the courtyard. The house was not completed before the Protector's execution in 1552 and 'how much Somerset achieved in these years is unknown but the Strand front as shown by Thorpe almost certainly belongs to this time'.[16] Who the original architect was remains a mystery. It is sometimes thought that it may have been a certain John of Padua, but few records of him survive. We know only that someone of this name was summoned out of Italy by Henry VIII and became deviser of his Majesty's buildings with a pension of two shillings a day, and that this pension was renewed in the time of Edward VI and the Protector. Nevertheless, it would be unwise to credit this near-mythological figure with the planning of the Protector's Somerset House.

The elevation shows a most interesting façade, obviously a transitional one, partly Tudor, partly classical in feeling. The main building around the courtyard rises two storeys, but the Strand front, of ashlar masonry, has a very curious three-storeyed gateway. At ground level this gateway is a triumphal arch; the storey above has a central projecting pier set between two windows which are flanked by columns and the top storey, which rises above the roof line, consists of double central columns which appear to be free-standing, with a pedimented window on each side. All the windows on the Strand front have triangular pediments and exhibit in this, and in their spacing, a classical regularity unusual for the time. At each end of the front, square bays extrude slightly and rise above the roof, each to terminate in a rectangular parapet with nascent open strapwork as a decorative feature. These bays are not thematically linked with the gateway. The roof is balustraded in classical fashion, but behind the balustrading appear typical Tudor brick chimneys. The whole building enclosed a central courtyard of 120 by 84 feet with, on the south side, the hall. A great chamber, a presence chamber and a gallery are also noted on the plan.

The Protector did not have to go far afield to fetch a part of his building materials: some of the stone he used was taken from the great cloister of St Paul's Cathedral and from the Privy

Church of the Knights Hospitallers at Clerkenwell. St Margaret's Westminster was spared, as its parishioners turned out with clubs and bows to defend it against the duke's workmen.

The destruction of the cloister took place, Stow tells us, 'in the year 1549 on the 10th of April' when 'the said chapel [it stood in Pardon churchyard and was founded by Gilbert Becket] by commandment of the Duke of Somerset, was begun to be pulled down, with the whole cloister, the Dance of Death, the tombs, the monuments; so that nothing was left but the bare plot of ground'.[17] The cloister had been famous because about it was 'artificially and richly painted the Dance of Machabray, or Dance of Death, commonly called the Dance of St Paul's . . . The meters or posey of this dance, were translated out of the French into English by John Lidgate [*sic*].'[18]

The Protector had destroyed this Dance of Death, if Stow's date is correct, just three years before he was to participate in one himself. The house 'should have been well finished and brought to a sumptuous end'[19] but it was the Protector who came to an 'untimely end' and the house, an Elizabethan commentator says, 'standeth as he left it'.[20] But the house, unfinished, passed to the crown. It was little used by Queen Mary, but Queen Elizabeth made use of it particularly as lodgings for courtiers or for officials attached to Whitehall.*

King Henry VIII 'the only Phoenix of his time for fine and curious masonry',[21] did a good deal of building. He, like his father, improved Eltham and modernized it and, as his father had done, improved Greenwich too. In addition to the fantastic palace of Nonsuch, he rebuilt or altered Wolsey's great palace at Hampton Court, acquired Oatlands in 1537 to add to the Hampton Court estate, took over Hatfield in the following year and, prior to this, had moved the royal residence from Westminster palace to Whitehall. About this time he also built St James's Palace.

When the Palace of Westminster was badly damaged by fire in 1512 (fortunately the Great Hall, with its magnificent hammer-

---

* It was granted to Anna of Denmark by James I, and was altered and used by her.

beam roof made for Richard II by Hugh Harland, survives), the king planned to rebuild it, but there was another great house close at hand upon which he had cast a green eye. This was York Place, the London residence of the archbishops of York which, under Cardinal Wolsey's tenure, had become a palace of such splendour and magnificence that it overshadowed every other palace in England, perhaps even in Europe. Wolsey had added to it a new great hall and chapel, and had spent vast sums in extending, improving and refurnishing the building. Henry VIII had often dined here, and enjoyed the luxury of York Place in contrast to the ramshackle Palace of Westminster, inconvenient and insanitary with its rushed floors, its tendency to flooding, its lack of heat (where there were no fireplaces charcoal braziers had to be used), its labyrinthine passages lit by flares and its courtyards haunted by dogs and beggars seeking something useful or edible in the piles of refuse which collected there.

With Wolsey's dismissal in 1529 the king decided not to rebuild Westminster but to move into York Place – he had been using the Whitehall already – and he also began to rebuild and add to it. He could and did better the Cardinal. New embankments were made on the river side with landing stages for the royal barges. A turreted gateway was built to overlook the entrance from the street. Land was acquired on the west side overlooking what is now St James's Park and on this side the king, predictably, built a tilt yard, a cock-pit and a bowling alley. Two gateways were built at each end – one erroneously called the Holbein Gate. Within a year the name York Place had disappeared and, as one gentleman says to another in describing the coronation of Queen Anne Boleyn,

> You must no more call it York-Place: that's past
> For, since the Cardinal fell, the title's lost:
> 'Tis now the King's, and called Whitehall.[22]

Whitehall Palace continued as the chief residence of the sovereign from the fall of Wolsey until its final destruction by fire in the time of William III. Its extent was enormous; it covered an area of twenty-six acres running from near Charing Cross to Westminster and from St James's Park to the Thames.

St James's Palace was originally a lazar house for leper maidens and remained as such until 1532. It stood isolated amid green fields and, as Henry VIII wanted more land to add to Whitehall, he dissolved the foundation, pensioned off all four inmates and then decided to 'make a fair mansion and a parke for his greater commoditie and pleasure'[23] where the lazar house had stood. The name St James's survives in the very different building which the king put up. It was built of brick, with a diapering of blue brick, around four courts of which three survive, although the buildings surrounding the courts are now greatly altered. The small Chapel Royal is possibly all that remains to show what the original interior work may have been like. But the great gateway must still look much as it did, with its small polygonal turrets and, over the arch, a Tudor rose bearing the initials H and A, for Anne's brief reign saw its completion. Later the palace became one of the favourite residences of Queen Mary I.

Much more simple than the hollow square are H- and E-plan houses. These are basically the same, in that the great hall is centrally placed. It occupies the cross stroke of the H or the back bar of the E, where a projecting porch, usually with a chamber over it, forms the shorter central stroke. Both plans have roots in traditional medieval designs, but differ from them in that, with the hall occupying the central position flanked by wings on either side, the entrance comes on the main axis of the house. Formerly the hall could have been off centre or in one of the wings. This centralization led to a greater symmetry of building, and greater symmetry is a feature of the transition from medieval to Tudor.

There were no architects as we know them – trained professionals who designed a building complete in every detail, and transferred the design to paper so that it could be translated into bricks, mortar, stone and wood by masons, carpenters and workmen. It is probable, however, that the master mason was the chief designer of a building and based his work on an idea suggested by the employer himself. Many a nobleman who had travelled abroad came home with new ideas and would incorporate them into his own new house. Henry VIII must have done some of his own designing, for we know that he certainly ordered a blockhouse to be built at Cowes 'according to a platte'[24] devised by himself. The function of the master mason (or masons – there might be more than one) was to estimate the cost of a building, to inspect the stone to be used, and probably even to draw a plan. We find Lord Bardolph telling Lord Hastings, when speaking of plucking down the kingdom 'to set up another':

> When we mean to build,
> We first survey the plot, then draw the model;
> And when we see the figure of the house,
> Then must we rate the cost of the erection;
> Which if we find outweighs ability,
> What do we do then but draw anew the model
> In fewer offices, or at last desist
> To build at all.[25]

This, it is true, was written about 1586 and so belongs to Elizabethan times, but surveying land, costing and drawing a 'platte' or plan were not new to that era. Although drawings of Tudor buildings are virtually non-existent, there is evidence in various manuscripts of payment ordered for drawing a 'platte' and that masons were expected to be able to draw at least a ground plan. In very simple buildings the ground plan was often drawn on the ground itself.

'Where a man should cytuate or sette his mansyon, place or howse'[26] for the sake of his health was also a question to be considered, whether the house was new or just an old one being altered into a 'commodyous and pleasaunt buyldynge'.[27] Ideally, the foundation should be on gravel mixed with clay, or on rock, or on a hillside. As 'elbowe-room' would be needed, quite an area of land was required and this should be wooded and watered, water being of more importance than wood. The outlook should be pleasant but the place should also be pleasant to look at from a distance. The air should be pure and good as 'contagious' air engendered many corrupt humours and bred diseases and infirmities. For this reason, and most important of all, a house should be so planned that the main rooms faced east and west. Especially recommended are north-east, south-east and south-west, because 'the merydyal wynde of all wyndes is the moste worste'.[28] In fact the south wind, says Andrew Boorde, 'doth corrupt and doth make evil vapours', whilst the north wind purged ill vapours; therefore it was much better to have main windows facing north than south.

Those conversant with the best situation for building therefore built facing north. The air may have been purer and, due to a sharp, cleansing east or north wind, such buildings doubtless escaped evil vapours, but the rooms must have been dark and cold in winter and rheumatism and chilblains chronic. Boorde further tells us that the hall should be central to the gatehouse across the quadrangle made by the house and its wings, while the door of the hall should be opposite but not directly opposite the gatehouse.

In houses great and small wings were gable-ended, and in many houses the apex of the gable was surmounted by a round ball. This particular type of ornament is said to have been derived from the skulls which primitive peoples placed on their roofs to ward off lightning. By Tudor times this piece of preventive magic had possibly been forgotten, as more often in great houses gables were topped by a vane or an heraldic beast painted and gilded.

The Great Hall which Henry VIII built after taking over Hampton Court from Cardinal Wolsey, probably in 1525, has octagonal turrets surmounted by the king's beasts, lions, leopards, and dragons, holding gilded vanes painted with the king's arms, while smaller beasts and gargoyles slide gently and gleefully down the coping stones.

The hall is built of brick, an important Tudor building material, and has a great and wonderful bay window which rises to just below the battlemented parapet. Both brick and bay window are Tudor characteristics. This is not to say that great houses were not also built in stone. For example, many houses were built of or faced with ashlar, a simple form of worked stone in rectangular blocks tooled on the outside face. It could be worked on a curve and was very handy for tower building. There were stone quarries all over England, in Kent, Surrey, Bedfordshire, Oxfordshire, Lincolnshire, East Anglia, Yorkshire, and Devon. And, of course, Portland stone and Purbeck marble were famous. But the most valued building stone was imported from Caen and one had to be very rich indeed to use this.

Bricks, once known as 'Flanders tiles', for we had imported them from Flanders as early as the thirteenth century for use in fireplaces, were now home-produced and used for building houses and walls as well. There is a curious item appertaining to Windsor Castle in 1537 'for makying of ij bolsters of bricke in the kitchen for to sette pannes on to seath the kynges brane'.[29] Undoubtedly the king's brain often seethed, but it hardly required this kind of outside assistance. Perhaps 'brawn' is the word.

But the king certainly used brick, as Wolsey before him had, at Hampton Court, and also in building St James's. And if brick was good enough for the king, it was good enough for less noble builders. Sir Thomas Lucy built his new big mansion of brick near Stratford-upon-Avon in 1558, at the very end of the period under review. It has a gabled front, a porch, wings, clusters of chimneys and a gatehouse★ with an oriel window. It was here, in the park of Charlecote Manor that, is it said, the young Shakespeare was arrested for poaching deer. True or not, Charlecote's builder, Sir Thomas Lucy, lives for ever caricatured as Justice Shallow – once of Clement's Inn – in the play *King Henry IV*.

Christ Church Mansion, Ipswich, now an art gallery and museum, is another brick house. It was built around 1550 and, although the interior of the house was gutted by fire in 1675 and replaced in late Stuart style, the brick exterior with its wings and curved gables remains, although the windows are not

★ This is probably the only completely original bit left. The house is now what might be called 'Elizabethan Revival', having been vastly altered in the nineteenth century.

Brick gatehouse

contemporary with the building. East Barsham Manor House, Fakenham, Norfolk (restored in this century), is of earlier date than these other two and is on a very different plan. It is grander, and has small turrets, a crenellated parapet, big windows and terracotta ornamentation, particularly on the string course.

Probably the greatest house of brick was built by a commoner, that son of a butcher and Prince of the Church, Cardinal Wolsey. Although greatly altered by Sir Christopher Wren, the architecture of much of Hampton Court still belongs to the earlier Tudor period. Originally a small manor house of a few buildings, it still belonged to the Knights Hospitallers of St John of Jerusalem when Queen Elizabeth of York went there in 1503 to pray for the safe delivery of a child. Her prayers were not answered. She died in childbed. Her husband, Henry VII, had also used the 'cell' as a subsidiary house when he was replacing the old, burned-down palace of Sheen with his new palace of Richmond. Wolsey acquired this manor in 1514 on a ninety-nine-year lease from the prior at a rental of £50 a year, as he needed a country house away from the smoke and fog of London and within easy reach, by river, of London and York Place. Nothing now remains of the original manor but the land, some 2,000 acres, was converted by the cardinal into two parks which he fenced partly with paling and partly with good, solid buttressed walls of a deep red brick chequered with black. Some of this wall can still be seen. The palace itself was also built of red brick, with stone used for coigns, window jambs, hood-moulds, coping of parapets, turrets, string courses and doorways. Stone and terracotta were also used for ornamental work.

The first building was probably the great west front which, with two wings, runs about 400 feet. Its two-storey façade is embellished at the angles of the building with towers, and has an embrasured parapet, twisted brick chimneys and various mullioned windows. Much of this remains, but the turrets no longer have leaden cupolas. Here stands the imposing central gatehouse with its fine oriel window and its parapet with quatrefoil perforations. Through this lies the First or Base Court, measuring 167

by 142 feet. In the buildings about this court servants and attendants lived. Windows faced on to the court on three sides; all of
these were of three lights, were set apart at regular distances from
each other and looked in upon several long galleries – these were
unusual at the time. On the fourth side of the court the buildings
rise in three storeys and the roof line runs gently to the Clock
Tower, which is eighty feet high. Through an archway in the
Tower was another court, the Clock Court, 160 by 91 feet, and
here lay the inner or chief part of Wolsey's palace. The east side
was almost entirely rebuilt by George II and the south side is
almost hidden by Wren's Ionic columns, but the Great Hall
remains. This, however, is not the cardinal's Great Hall; it was
built by Henry VIII between 1531 and 1533 and probably stands
on the same site as the original.

The king was so anxious to have the hall finished quickly that
workmen often worked at night, presumably in the interior by
candle- or torch-light. Bricks were brought in thousands from
nearby Taplow and a brick kiln was also set up in the park.
Stone, rough or cut, came from the quarries at Reigate and
Barrington, and some was imported from Caen; oak, the chief
wood, was brought from various places including St John's
Wood, London. The exterior length of the hall is 118 feet, and it
occupied the whole breadth of the Clock Court (now the Lunar
Court where the fountain stands). Its height from ground to gable
end is 92 feet. Small windows occupy the lower storey above
which the hall stands, and these look in on the old buttery and
cellars. In the right-hand corner a wonderful bay window rises
to just below the battlemented parapet, looking in upon the
raised dais. At the exterior angles of the building the octagonal
turrets rise to the height of the pitched roof. Inside is a late-
Perpendicular, single-hammer-beam roof, gorgeously painted and
gilded, with great bosses, pendants and spandrels exquisitely
carved with the arms of Henry VIII and Jane Seymour.* Queen
Jane gave birth to her son Edward at Hampton Court on Friday

* The roof was repainted in 1840 in what one hopes were the original
colours.

12 October 1537, which was the vigil of St Edward. Here she died thirteen days later.

After that the king, although he had obliterated almost all of Wolsey's work and continued to add to the palace himself, rarely visited Hampton Court, but the Royal Nursery for the baby prince was established there, in buildings on the north side of Chapel Court. And it was to Hampton Court that Queen Mary I and King Philip came on 23 August 1554 to spend their honeymoon. Poor Mary is unkindly described in a letter sent to Spain by a contemporary writer as 'ugly, small, lean, with a pink and white complexion, no eyebrows, *very pious and badly dressed*'.[30]

The enormous and beautiful bay window, with its forty-eight lights,* which illuminates the dais end of the Great Hall is typically Tudor, for one of the most notable characteristics of Tudor domestic architecture is the change which took place in windows. Ordinary windows became far more numerous and the bay, which had crept in tentatively at the end of the fourteenth century, became by the time of Henry VIII one of the most noticeable external features of a great house or manor; internally it added space and a new decorative interest to a room. Living rooms became so well-lit compared to medieval rooms that, later, Sir Francis Bacon grumbled about 'faire *Houses*, so full of Glasse, that one cannot tell, where to become, to be out of the Sunne or Cold'.[31]

Windows, bay or otherwise – and bay windows often rose the full height of the house – were set within a frame and divided vertically by stone mullions and horizontally by transoms. If they were arched, as they often were in the early part of the century, stone tracery usually filled in the arch. Stanchions and glazing bars were of iron, as were catches and stays. These were possibly painted. (Those in the Great Hall at Hampton Court were originally painted red.) Windows were also made with a 'leaning place', that is, a flat extension of the sill on which a person could rest elbows or crossed arms to look out. Ordinary

---

* The whole interior of the hall was restored in the nineteenth century and the windows re-glazed. Not a trace of original glass remains.

Oriel window

windows projected squarely from the wall; oriel windows projected like a small room and were supported on corbels.

Until Henry VIII's day glass in windows was comparatively rare, save in churches and in the houses of the very rich. Panes were small, square or diamond-shaped, and were diagonally set in lead cames – small grooved bars used for framing glass in latticed windows. Diamond-shaped panes were most favoured until the last quarter of the sixteenth century, and perforated lead quarrels or quarries – the name by which the diamond or square pane was known – were used for purposes of ventilation. The insertion of coloured glass was frequent. Sometimes this was arranged in a panel to display the arms and badges of a noble family. The Lady Margaret Beaufort's windows at Collyweston were glazed with her armorial bearings as early as 1505. Loyal or sycophantic subjects often inserted the royal arms with mantling and supporters in their windows. Mottoes and other inscriptions were also painted on glass – for what is a coat of arms without its motto? Painting on glass was done by using oxide of iron or copper mixed with water and gum arabic to make it stick; when dry, it was washed over with urine or vinegar which hardened the gum. Sometimes lattices made of wooden rods were used to protect the glass, although at the new tennis court which Henry VIII built for himself at Hampton Court, wire was used for this purpose. In the Privy Purse Accounts of Henry VIII we find an item 'to galien the glasier for glasing at York Place[32] £10 19s. 2d.'. We don't know what part Galien glazed but it can hardly have been the whole palace, even though the payment is a very large sum for the time.

Those who could not afford glass or who preferred to remain old-fashioned used linen or paper, waxed, greased or oiled and held in place by cross-bars. Horn was used too, polished thin and set, usually, in wood. All these alternatives to glass let in a rather joyless light, whereas in great houses with coloured glass in the new bays or oriels, on a bright day as the sun moved across the sky the glass would pattern the interior with shifting, elusive jewels of brilliant colour: this seems symbolic of the earlier Tudor era.

So far we have dealt only with palaces and large houses. These were vastly outnumbered by small houses and cottages – the dwellings of the majority of people – and the majority still lived in the country. Here villages clustered in a square about a green which held the church, the market place, the duck pond and, often, the stocks; but the term 'square' is loosely used to mean buildings arranged on two or more sides of an open space. Heighington, Co. Durham, not far from Stockton-upon-Tees, is an example of the four-square village. Or a village might straggle along a road with houses and cottages on either side but set back from the road itself. Weedon, Northamptonshire, was 'a praty thorough fare, sette on a playne ground'[33] and much frequented by carriers, as it stood 'hard by' the famous Watling Street. Because of this it was then known as Weedon-on-the-Street. Nevertheless, 'the tounlet itself' was 'very meane'. It had a horrid little church and no market. Some places were not then even designated as towns, townlets or villages, they were called merely 'street'. Thus Leland, travelling in Buckinghamshire, says: 'A mile and a halfe furthar toward London is a strete caulyd Litle Missendene.'[34]

But wherever the village lay, houses were nearly always built of local materials. Little or nothing was imported from foreign countries or from another area. Navigable waters were rare, roads rudimentary; therefore to attempt to bring building materials from another part of the country was as impossible as it would have been outrageously expensive to the majority. There was no need to do this anyway, as every village possessed its own building materials and its own skilled workmen – the village carpenter, mason, thatcher, tiler – to say nothing of the village folk themselves who, pioneer-like, could turn a hand to all kinds of work. It was the local geology which was, then, responsible for the kind of building material used in various parts of the country. The hard, dour, grey rock of the northern counties, the red and grey sandstone of Lancashire, Derbyshire and Nottinghamshire, the oolitic and liassic limestones of the Bristol area, the sandstone, marl and granite of the west country, the chalk and clay of part of the Chilterns, Norfolk, Berkshire, Hampshire and Kent – all these made for variety.

Where stone or chalk were not available, as in Norfolk, Suffolk, Essex and Middlesex, there was gravel, sand, clay and plenty of timber. Here wattle and daub and brick and timber houses predominated. And because of the differences of building material there were different methods of working stone and of placing timbers in relation to the brick or plaster. For example, most Northamptonshire towns and villages were of stone, Leland says, while the towns of Leicester and Loughborough were entirely of timber. 'Thacking' was done with stone, slate or tiles made of clay, or with straw or reed thatch, depending upon the availability of the materials.

If villages and towns had escaped the perpetual fire-hazard or had survived the depopulation, desolation and destruction which followed the Black Death, their architecture reflected several centuries in one small area from, say, Norman church and medieval market place to the modern Tudor house or inn with its new fireplaces and small glazed windows. Some windows, however, were long, set high in the room above the panelling and below the ceiling, frieze fashion.

Cottages were generally of one storey and of one room, with a beaten earth floor. When a cottage was enlarged this was done by 'offshoots' or 'offshuts', that is, an extra room, generally of the lean-to type, was added to any side of the main room or house place and used for sleeping or for cooking utensils. Cottages were often open to the roof, although now more frequently an upper floor was inserted below the roof to make a loft which was reached by a ladder.

Windows or 'wind-eyes' in all cottages or houses were open and had a drop shutter, or were filled in with a frame of plaited osiers. Richer men occasionally used a thick green bottle glass. Windows were, however, nearly always small, possibly because they were difficult to build or perhaps because houses or cottages were sufficiently ventilated by cracks in the structure or ill-fitting doors.

Probably the most outstanding and typical region in England for small villages of architectural perfection is the Cotswolds. Here three centuries of prosperity based on wool, the wonderful weathering quality of the oolitic limestone which lies just below the soil surface, the high standard of masons' work, and the fact that all buildings, from the smallest cottage to the grandest 'wool' church, were all built in the same style – and continued to be so built – produced a harmony of building hard to find anywhere else in the country.

In cities rather different conditions prevailed. Tudor cities – and London as we have seen was the only one of any size – still showed to a greater or lesser extent their medieval pattern. That is to say, houses had not been built along a line of pre-determined streets. Groups of artisans and tradesmen had long been settled in separate quarters which formed little islands and *peninsulae* within the larger confines of the city itself. In London different trades had for centuries occupied different small areas of the city (Westminster was a rich suburb separated from the city by green fields) and today some of the City streets (and some in Bristol) still indicate the sites of long vanished crafts or trades: Wood Street, Bread Street, Milk Street, Ironmongers Lane, Fish Street Hill, Sea Coal Lane. Lombard Street, the money centre, was so called because Italian bankers and money-lenders from Lombardy had settled there after the expulsion of the Jews in the time of Richard Coeur de Lion, better known to his contemporaries as Richard Piss-a-bed. The herb sellers were gathered in Bucklersbury, quite unaware that below them lay a great temple of Mithras; the butchers congregated in East Cheap. Smithfield (Smooth Field), once an open place for tilting, became in earlier Tudor times a market for horses and cattle, and a roasting-place for heretics under Queen Mary I.

Within each of these districts were 'footways' and the 'islands' were connected to each other by wider streets along which houses stood. But such streets were neither highways nor thoroughfares; they were largely unpaved, narrow and, unlike 'streets' in the country, were close-edged by buildings. Nothing wider than a cart passed through these streets and traffic – there was a good deal – consisted of pedestrians and innumerable horses. Still, between the fifteenth and eighteenth centuries the form of urban life was completely transformed. This was because in the Tudor century a new economy came into being in England, an economy based largely on manufactured cloth rather than on raw wool. London, the capital city, soon succeeded Antwerp and Venice as the largest multi-trading capital in the then known world. This meant a greater busy-ness, a greater prosperity. It also meant more overcrowding, expansion and new building. Even so there were still a few gardens and orchards left in this rich and ever-growing metropolis.

The ideal city was, perhaps, defined by Sir Thomas More in 1515; his traveller Raphael Hythloday describes Amaurot, the chief city of Utopia: 'There buildings are good,' he says, 'and so uniform that a whole side of a street looks like one house. The streets are twenty feet broad; there lie gardens behind all their houses: these are large but enclosed with buildings that on all hands face the streets; so that every home has a door to the garden.'[35] The reality was vastly different. In the footways and narrow streets new houses jostled medieval ones. In Wood Street, for example, not one medieval stone-built house was left; all had been pulled down and replaced by timber-framed houses. As timber-framing takes up less room than stone, the street was more closely built than before.

In 1498, which was a year of great drought, all the gardens 'which had been contained time out of mind, without Moor gate of London'[36] were destroyed and turned into a plain field where archers could practise. During the reign of Henry VIII three gun-founders were allowed to build and cast ordnance at Houndsditch, so that 'the poor bed-rid people were worn out'. The decibel-count must indeed have been very wearing, but, worse, 'in place of their homley cottages, such houses [were] built as do rather want room than rent',[37] and these houses were occupied by 'brokers, sellers of old apparel and such like'.[38] What happened to the 'bed-rid' people we do not know, but the remainder of the field became a market garden and later, in the reign of Edward VI, it was broken up into smaller plots and more houses – with small gardens – were built there. So change was rapid.

The timber-framed Tudor houses were nearly all built with jettied storeys which projected over the narrow streets. They were generally three or four storeys high, and those who occupied the upper floors could lean out of the windows and shake hands or hurl stones, imprecations or worse at each other with deadly accuracy. Slums did not arrive with the industrial revolution: the crowded, stinking alleys, the rotting, decayed old houses filled to bursting with rotting, decayed people were a commonplace in London and other cities. Grand old houses like Bucklersbury Manor, from which noble or rich owners had moved to the more salubrious air of Westminster or into the country at Chelsea were now divided up into squalid tenements. The same thing had happened to The Garland, the big house in East Cheap.

Conversely, and more on the lines of Amaurot, there was newly built Goldsmiths' Row, which lay between Bread Street and the cross at Cheap. This was built in 1491 by Thomas Wood, a goldsmith, and consisted of ten houses and fourteen shops in a uniform row which presented a dazzling front embellished with the goldsmiths' arms and woodmen riding on great beasts, all brightly painted and gilded. The houses on London Bridge were occupied by merchants, mercers and haberdashers. The old, fortified Baynard's Castle near the Tower had been torn down in 1501 by 'that peaceable politic and rich prince King Henry VII'[39] and replaced by an unfortified and unembattled house which was 'far more beautiful and commodious for the entertaining of any prince of great estate'.[40] Henry VIII took over St Bride's and built there the beautiful house of Bridewell, especially, it is said, for the second visit of the Emperor Charles V in 1522, but it swiftly fell to ruin and was given by his son Edward VI to the citizens of London, together with Savoy House, for the idle and the poor.

Great discomfort was caused to many Londoners when Sir

William Paulet★ (1485?–1572) built his new house. He enclosed the north side of his garden with a long, high wall. Formerly this land had belonged to the Augustinian friars and had consisted of many little gardens through which a footway with a gate at either end had run. Now the wall cut off and hid the garden, and Sir William had the gateways blocked up with stone so that the footway could no longer be used. He did not pull down the friars' church, however, but in 1550 closed off its west end, which was given to the Dutch community in London as a place of worship. The steeple end with the choir and side aisles he reserved for himself – as a storehouse for corn, coal and wood.

Throckmorton Street had once been built up with many small tenements, but these were torn down to make room for the new great house which Thomas Cromwell, Earl of Essex, one-time secretary to Wolsey and Lord Great Chamberlain of England, built for himself. When his new mansion was finished it had 'some reasonable plot of ground left for a garden'[41] but this was not reasonable enough for Thomas Cromwell, who, without warning, suddenly ordered all the pales of the gardens adjoining his on the north side to be removed and twenty-two feet measured off from each one of the gardens. He then ordered foundations to be laid on this new line and a high wall built, thus enlarging his own garden. 'My father,' John Stow tells us with remarkably little bitterness, 'had a garden there and a house standing close to the south pale; this house they loosed from the ground, and bare upon rollers into my father's garden twenty-two feet, ere my father heard thereof.' He was not warned beforehand and when he complained to the surveyor about it the only answer he received was that it was done by order of the master. There was no redress and no man dared protest or argue about this forcible seizure. All lost twenty-two feet of land. Stow's father even had to pay his whole year's rental, 6s. 6d., for the half of the land left to him.

★ First Marquis of Winchester, First Earl of Wiltshire and First Baron St John. Held various high offices under Henry VIII and Edward VI. He helped overthrow the Protector and proclaimed Queen Mary at Baynard's Castle in 1553.

After Cromwell was attainted the Drapers' Company acquired the house and it became their Hall.★

Yet Stow's father, a tallow chandler, was in a way fortunate, as had that house standing by the south pale of his garden been of stone it would in all probability have been torn down. The fact that it was 'loosed from the ground' and moved on rollers suggests that it must have been a timber-framed or 'timber-cage' house. These were built in town and country alike and could be large, like Little Morton Hall, Cheshire, with wood used decoratively as well as constructionally, or small and simple like many a cottage or modest house still to be seen in the country today; or, again, for city building they could be narrow and high, as London houses then were.

The wooden framework was often built at a distance and erected in pre-built sections on the site. Each piece of timber or section bore a carpenter's mark to show exactly where it should be fitted into the next piece or next sections. On the site itself posts were morticed into a wooden ground sill, the ground having first been flattened and beaten level. For large houses the ground sill was usually set in a low wall of brick or stone to stop rot and damp. The tops of the principal posts were then morticed into upper horizontal beams or wall plates but, if the house were of more than one storey, 'summers' (bessumers) were morticed horizontally into the principal posts. Studs, that is, shorter lighter posts running from sill to wall plate or, if the house were storeyed, from sill to the parallel summers above and then from there up to the wall plate, made strong vertical bars to support the horizontals; between the studs lighter framing was set. In small houses the joists of the upper floor which lay just below the roof ran from wall plate to wall plate. In houses of more than one storey they protruded over the summers to provide jettied floors. With this basic wooden cage much could be done. The interstices between wooden members could be filled with small, pliable woven branches, with clay, mortar or plaster rammed into them from both sides. This is the traditional wattle and daub; but by Tudor

★ Destroyed by fire in 1774 and rebuilt on the same site.

times in sophisticated areas laths were more commonly used to hold the mortar or plaster, which was further strengthened by the addition of cow's hair.

Such houses often had the exterior plastering moulded in designs: simple curves or more elaborate vine and leaves, scrolls and even figures. The plaster was always whitewashed. The interstices of the wooden cage could be filled instead with brick, often patterned by setting it with headers so placed as to form diamonds, squares, rectangles or a herring-bone pattern; or the frame could be weatherboarded.

Timber-framed houses were not new to the period; they dated back centuries, although methods of framing changed with the passage of time. Such houses were particularly common outside stone areas, and a very fine example of a large house still extant is Giffords Hall, near Bury St Edmunds, North Suffolk. The house, which has its studs closely spaced, Suffolk-style – for style varied according to locality – was probably built in the second half of the fifteenth century and was added to later, possibly in Elizabethan or Jacobean times. But John Stow's father's house was not a grand one, and to pull up a small timber-framed house, sill and all, and remove it on rollers twenty-two feet would present small difficulty to Tudor workmen and craftsmen.

Removable habitations for special occasions were also built, usually by royalty. On 28 July 1551, Marshal de Saint André, the French Ambassador, before taking his departure dined with King Edward VI at 'Hide Park, where ther was a fair hous made for him' and saw the 'cursing there'.[42] Hyde Park was then in the country and this was a temporary banqueting house especially erected for the purpose of speeding the parting envoy. It was fifty-seven feet long by twenty-one wide, complete with dais and a turret. Another such house was put up in 'Mary bone' park; both of them had light timber frames. A certain amount of bricks and mortar were also used in their building, although the chief material must have been canvas. In addition six 'standings' were built, that is, stands from which the spectators could watch the coursing. There were three in each park, ten feet long by eight wide, and these were decked with boughs and flowers, as were the banqueting houses. Being only temporary buildings, the houses took twenty-two days to build; the workmen worked 'at all hours, a space to eat and dryncke excepted'.[43] Carpenters and bricklayers received 1d. an hour, labourers $\frac{1}{2}$d., plasterers 11d. a day and painters 6s. 7d. a day. The cost of the house in Hyde Park came to £169 7s. 8d.

Possibly the grandest and most costly temporary building ever was that erected by command of Henry VIII on a dull plain in Picardy between the towns of Guines and Ardres. Here, in June 1520, the king with his entourage, which included the Lord Legate Wolsey, many nobles and gentlemen – one was Sir Edward Boleyn with his elder daughter Mary, who later became the king's mistress – plus retainers and servants to make a total of 4,544 people, met the French king, Francis I, for the purpose of forming the sixteenth-century equivalent of the *entente cordiale*. The *entente*, like the buildings, was purely temporary.

Nothing like this meeting had ever been seen before: the two kings with their queens – Henry VIII's at that time was Catherine of Aragon – met in a scene of unparalleled magnificence, and the building put up by the English king is described by Hall in his *Chronicle* as 'the most noble and royall lodgying before sene, for it was a palays'.[44] This palace was completely equipped with all the necessary offices for the Lord Chamberlain, the Lord Steward, Lord Treasurer of the Household, the Comptroller, the officer of the Green Cloth; wardrobe, jewel house and all other services appertaining to the royal household. There was a pantry, a 'seller', buttery, spicery, 'pitcher-house' (ewery), larder, 'poulterie' and various other domestic offices, 'large and fair'. All these together produced miracles of cooking and baking.

The great impermanent building which housed all this had taken 2,000 French and English artisans to erect its main structure. This was a framework of stone, brick and wood covered with cloth and wood painted to represent bricks. It was, in appearance, an imitation Gothic castle of four equal quadrangles and was 328 feet square. It had an impressive gatehouse with a curved,

The Field of the Cloth of Gold

shell-like pediment overtopping the battlemented walls. Four towers with arrow-slits ornamented the corners, but the rest of the front façade had eight great round-topped windows, four on each side of the gatehouse. There was also a secret passage which ran from this sham palace to the nearby fortified palace of Guines – just in case.

Outside the gatehouse a pillar bore four large golden lions, and above them hovered a winged and naked cupid symbolizing the love between England and France – an imp would have done just as well. On a nearby green, Bacchus presided over a tiered fountain which bore the inscription *Faicte – bonne chere quy bouldra*. Beneath Bacchus hidden conduits spouted red and white wine for the benefit of the poorer people.

Inside, the castle was brilliantly coloured and decorated in Renaissance style. The cornices were gilded, rich tapestries hung from the temporary walls, the arms of France and England were lavishly displayed and the Tudor colours, white and green, were everywhere, as was the English rose. The chapel had a gold shrine and contained gold images, the organ was of silver and the whole was freely garnished with quantities of jewels. The decor was done by John Brown, the King's Serjeant Painter, assisted by John Rastell (Sir Thomas More's brother-in-law) and Clement Urmystone, the great designer of pageants. The castle was called by contemporaries, perhaps a trifle sardonically, 'The Palace of Illusion' and it absolutely stunned the French. Large though it was it could not hold the overflow of retainers and these camped in the surrounding field in twenty-eight brilliantly coloured tents, many of them painted with stripes so that they looked like fluted shells.

The French had, for their part, constructed a small town of gay tents on the Ardres side of the field; as these were chiefly of cloth of gold or silver it was literally a *Camp du drape d'or*. The royal marquee, sixty feet square, stood in the middle of this glittering tented town. Its roof, lined a heavenly blue, was spangled with stars of gold and, under a gilded statue of St Michael, King Francis entertained his royal brother – and the Lord Legate. All went well in this comparatively modest little structure until one day a strong wind – a Picardy wind – rose and blew it down. The French king moved to Ardres, where they managed to provide new halls, a pavilion and a Roman theatre. Certainly, in pageantry, the English had won the day – we were always good at pageants. But it cost both kings a fortune and it cost many of those who attended upon them all they possessed. Everybody who was anybody – or who hoped to become somebody – from each country was present. It was the command performance of all time:

> . . . Each following day
> Became the next day's master, till the last
> Made former wonders its. Today the French
> All clinquant, all in gold, like heathen gods,
> Shone down the English; and tomorrow they
> Made Britain India: every man that stood
> Show'd like a mine. Their dwarfish pages were
> As Cherubins, all gilt.[45]

Richmond, Whitehall, Nonsuch, many a permanent palace and too many great houses have long since vanished as completely as the Field of the Cloth of Gold. But the splendour and pageantry of that meeting between the two kings – the glitter, the rich colour, the gold, the sound of trumpets, the feasting and jousting – which so transformed that dull Picardy plain nearly five hundred years ago still stir the romantic imagination and delight the inward eye.

Yet at the time, and by the end of the festivities, dark mutterings were heard that all this magnificence and show was merely a portent or a preliminary to the surrender of Calais. 'And for a trueth,' says Hall, 'the Frenchmen so spake and said, wherewith many English men were grived.'[46]

They were wrong. The loss of Calais was delayed by thirty-eight years.

CHAPTER THREE

Of Rooms and Their Furniture

We do not know why Andrew Smythe should have taken the alias 'Cocke'. We do not know the exact date of his birth or of his death or anything much about him. We do know, however, that he lived at Great Milton, Oxfordshire, where the fine church of St Mary the Virgin, with its work of Early English and Perpendicular periods, together with traces of Norman architecture, still stands, and that he must have died in the spring of 1557. For on 29 May in that year an inventory of his effects was taken by John Phelps, John Wener, John Est and John Wylmond. This inventory suggests that Andrew Smythe must have been a small farmer who went in for mixed rather than sheep farming. We can reasonably assume this because the winter corn standing in a field of seven acres was valued at £2 6s. 8d., while twenty-five acres of barley was worth, as it stood, £6 5s. Furthermore, he had three cows, a bullock, two calves, two hogs, a gelding, a horse, a cart, a pair of plough wheels, a grindstone and, among miscellaneous farm equipment, a 'mucke pott'.

The catalogue of household effects tells us a trifle more, chiefly by omission. All goods are listed as being 'in the hall', which sounds rather grand but probably means he had a small house or cottage, possibly of two rooms since two bedsteads are listed in the hall, one with 'a coverlett, a quylt, a bolster' valued at ten shillings and another of the same value with a 'flock bed',[1] that is, a mattress stuffed with flock, a coverlet and also a bolster. Two beds suggest that Andrew Smythe, alias Cocke, may have been married and had children – or perhaps he was young, single and lived with a widowed mother. Certainly he was not a peasant, he was too well supplied with worldly goods for that.

Unusually, there were '8 pere of sheets', listed at 12s. Sheets were not all that common and eight pairs for two beds is a large number. But the rest of the household furniture is what we would call scanty, although it was not so for the mid sixteenth century. There were '2 tabulls 2 trestelles on [one] forme', total value 3s. 4d., and 'on wolde [old] Coburde' 5s.; 'on pane 2 Kettelles A Chaffyngdyshe' 12s.; '3 pottes & a possnet' 10s.; '15 peces of pewter' 10s.; '5 Candylstyckes' 1s.;[2] also one round table and three coffers at 4s.; three tablecloths and one towel at 1s. 8d.; and three dishes, six trenchers, six lead spoons and a ladle, worth 4d. the lot. These items constitute the sole furnishings of the house. His clothing was valued at £1 3s. 4d., and at the time the inventory was made there were also '2 fleeches of baken', at 4s., which had perhaps been left over from the winter. The grand total of his effects, including cattle, farm implements and household goods, came to £30 11s., which again means he must have been quite prosperous, whilst the number of candlesticks, trenchers and spoons seems to indicate that he did not live alone.

What we can also learn from this inventory is that the beds must have been the small, stump bedsteads common at the time, for no valances nor side curtains of even the simplest kind are mentioned. There are no chairs. Andrew sat on a form and also upon the coffers – 'coffer' is a term often used for chest. He seems to have been well supplied with tables – trestle tables with removable tops, and one round table, which is rather unusual for a farmer at this period. The cupboard is interesting because of the qualifying adjective 'old'; it had probably been handed down in his family for years. What is not probable is that it was a grand cupboard. Grand cupboards – also called 'dressoirs' – had a flat top for the display of plate, a carved back and a canopy of wood. The lower half was enclosed by doors and below this was a shelf for the display of ewers and jugs. Simple cupboards were merely flat-topped stands with, possibly, a shelf, and the top covered by a cloth on which plate was displayed. There was also the food

Chair, table, oak chest, box chair and food cupboard

cupboard, entirely enclosed by doors. This cupboard was perforated, often in a Gothic design, to allow the air to enter.

Andrew Smythe's cupboard, provided it was not an aumbrey or even the earlier 'food hutch', was probably the place where he kept his five candlesticks, three dishes, six trenchers (these were probably of wood), his lead spoons and ladle and those fifteen pieces of pewter. English pewter was the admiration of the world, and foreigners were surprised to find that humble folk often had a piece or two. 'The English,' a visiting Venetian says, 'use for eating that splendid tin [*nobile stagno*] which differs little in beauty from silver.'[3] It is obvious that pewter must be meant by *nobile stagno*, and it is probable that some of Andrew Smythe's fifteen pieces of sad ware and hollow ware must have been inherited. In any event they would be given pride of place upon the cupboard.

The sheets, the three tablecloths and that single towel, as well as his clothing, must have been kept in the coffers. The fact that the cooking utensils included in addition to the pans, kettles and chafing dish already mentioned, a spit and a gridiron – that is, a square or circular iron grating with a long handle and short legs used for broiling food over an open fire – to say nothing of a fire shovel, pot angles, pot hooks and a 'frang pane', assure us that cooking was done in the hall or house place, though whether over a central fire or at a wall fire-place one cannot say. Neither can one say just what 'on Cocke 5 hennes 3 duckes'[4] were doing in that room,* unless they were gorging themselves on the half quarter of wheat and the six bushels of 'mastelin' which lay there among the barrels, the wooden tubs, the buckets, the hatchet, axe and bill, the chisel, and other miscellaneous bits of iron. Altogether the hall was, as always in cottages and very small houses, living room, kitchen, workshop, store room and possibly bedroom combined.

When this particular inventory was made, Calais, the last of our French possessions, was still ours. Mary Tudor had but a year

---

* In many cottages, however, fowl and small domestic animals were housed in the hall.

to live and it was nearly three-quarters of a century since her grandfather, the first of the Tudor dynasty, had won his title to the crown. If much had happened politically and economically in those years, much too had happened in the development of furniture. First, there was more of it; second, it had changed in style, although not so rapidly as it was to change in the succeeding reign. When Henry VII came to the English throne furniture was, generally speaking, still medieval; it was 'stout and serviceable but never clumsy'[5] and was relatively untouched by Renaissance influences. Since the Renaissance in all its aspects affected only court circles, the nobility, the rich and scholars, its influence took many years to seep down to the level of the average person. The average man lived much as his forebears had lived, surrounded by many of the same things his forebears had used. This means he had few possessions and what he had were more medieval than modern.

Even when we come to royalty and the nobility, we find that their palaces and great houses were not over-furnished. Films and television dramas showing the Tudor period have done domestic history a disservice in portraying lavishly furnished, brilliantly lit, and spotlessly clean rooms. The furniture of the court and nobility was certainly handsome and costly but there was very little of it. Rooms, apart from their wall-hangings, looked bare by our standards. For example, when the Emperor Charles V, with his retinue, came to England on his first visit in 1520, he was met at Dover by King Henry VIII and stayed at Dover Castle before going on to London. Furniture at the castle was so inadequate that beds had to be carted down from various other places, among them the king's palaces at Richmond and Baynard's Castle, and the Tower of London. Doubtless chairs had to be borrowed and brought down too, as there were very few of them and in late medieval and Tudor times they were reserved for royalty and statesmen – there were not many to spare for guests. Chairs were 'for state occasions only',[6] but the Lord Chancellor could be sure of sitting comfortably away from home when he executed his office because he sat upon the 'woolsack'; but this, at bottom, was not designed for comfort – it symbolized the wealth of England. Lesser folk used forms, stools and chests to sit upon, their hard surfaces sometimes tempered by a cushion or a piece of cloth.

Originally, the chair had been a seat occupied by the bishop in a cathedral and this 'throne', together with choir stalls, had provided a marvellous opportunity for English wood carvers to show their great skill. This medieval bishop's throne or ecclesiastical chair had at some point slipped out of the cathedral and fathered secular progeny, but its children were few and far between and did not go forth and multiply, to any great extent, until the seventeenth century. Very few examples of carved chairs prior to 1500 are extant but we do know that the art of the turner, a late development in northern Europe, was employed in making chairs at an early date. The Turners' Guild seems to have been established in England as early as 1478, which indicates that the trade, as such, must have existed for many years before becoming a guild.★

Whether the turned chair existed outside of monasteries – many monasteries were rich and well-furnished, often serving as chains of guest houses for high church dignitaries and travelling secular potentates – prior to the sixteenth century is difficult to say. An example of a very early turned chair can be seen in a twelfth-century stone carving at Chartres Cathedral in which a monk sits at a desk on a low chair which has four round turned legs and, presumably, a wooden seat. The two back legs run straight up above the chair arms, also turned, to form back posts. The front legs rise above the seat to support the arms and terminate in balls. The chair is strengthened not by stretchers but by an apron piece shaped like a cusped arch which is attached underneath the seat and stretched between the legs. Similar chairs, some with back posts topped by what looks like pine-cone finials, can also be seen in illuminated manuscripts.

As we had had such a close association with France over so long a period, there is no reason to suppose that such chairs were not

★ The charter was granted to the Worshipful Company of Turners of the City of London by James I in 1604.

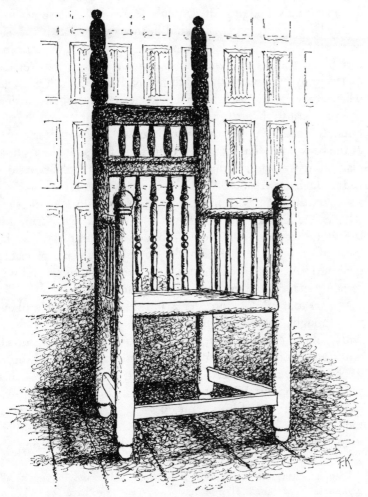

Erasmus chair

in use in English monasteries and, possibly, outside; but none has survived. What has survived is the descendant of this turned monastic chair known as the 'Erasmus Chair', still to be seen in the President's Lodging of Queen's College, Cambridge, and reputedly the only one of its kind in the country.* It is a well-proportioned chair made of pine, but looks horridly uncomfortable; the seat is trapezoid and the back is divided transversely by two rails set between the tall turned back posts. The lower and taller section of the back has five fairly elaborate spindles rising from the seat to the first rail. Above this, five simpler and shorter spindles rise to the upper rail, which is set well below the terminals of the back posts. The chair has round arms and stretchers. These plain stretchers set fairly high strengthen the legs at the two sides and in the front. Tradition – and we have no reason to doubt it – associates the chair with the great scholar Erasmus (1446?–1536) who visited England in 1449, 1505 and 1509. It was during his last visit that he moved to Cambridge University, where he lectured on Greek and the Epistles of St Jerome† and probably used the chair. Even if he did not, the chair is still unique and was certainly made some time around the year 1500.

We are told by Polydore Vergil in 1514 that Cardinal Wolsey, who thought himself 'the peer of kings',[7] used a 'golden chair' with golden cushions. But Vergil, who loathed the cardinal, unfortunately gives no details of what this chair was like. It may, of course, have been an ecclesiastical chair. But we do know that at Hampton Court Wolsey had five chairs of state for his own use and for the use of important guests, as well as several others, high- and low-backed. Some were covered in black velvet, others in red leather. Velvet seems to have been a popular covering for

---

* Similar chairs are in the Boston Museum and in the Pilgrims' Hall, Plymouth, Massachusetts. The second of these is said to have been taken to America by Elder Brewster, but it may possibly have been made in the colony, which would mean that it is of a much later date than the Erasmus chair at Cambridge.

† Archbishop Warham gave him the benefice of Aldington in Kent, but Erasmus commuted this to a pension of £20. He left England for good in 1514.

important chairs. On 1 January 1556, among other New Year's gifts received by Queen Mary was 'a faire cheire of ebonett, covered with crymson vellat, and frenged with silke and golde'.[8] The donor, one Jacob Rogoson, is described as being an Italian, although his name makes this seem most unlikely; but then we always tended to anglicize foreign names anyway.

Another type of chair in infrequent use was the bobbin-frame chair. Just how this almost frenzied example of the turner's art developed or where it originated is a matter of conjecture. According to one authority it is 'an archaic type from Scandinavia probably of Byzantine origin'.[9] According to another authority it is 'as English in conception as it is in material (most examples are of ash, elm or yew)'.[10] There is a splendid example of a most ornate chair of this type in the Victoria and Albert Museum, but it dates from the early seventeenth century. It is wonderfully be-bobbined at every possible point and one cannot believe that it, or its more simple earlier forms, were comfortable. Yet such chairs had the advantage of being draught-proof, provided a piece of cloth were flung over the triangular superstructure – and the Tudors flung cloth of one sort or another over nearly everything. From such a primitive beginning the comfortable, draught-proof, wing chair of some three hundred years later probably developed.

More structurally draught-proof, and well-nigh immoveable, was the box-chair, a development from the box used for storage and as a seat. This chair was made by joiners, not turners. One panel of the box was elongated vertically to make a high, solid back, the two side panels growing up to make equally solid supports for arms. The result was a rudimentary, ponderous box or close-chair which took several strong men to shift about. This rather throne-like chair was the really important chair used by the owner of a house, or occupied by some very important guest as a sign of respect. In fact a guest, so honoured, literally 'took the chair', although the meeting may have been a purely social or treasonable occasion. Naturally, the plain back, arms and en-closed seat characteristic of medieval times did not long remain unornamented, as they offered wood carvers ample opportunity to exhibit their skills. At first, early sixteenth-century box-chairs were plain with beautiful linenfold carving ornamenting the back, but soon other more intricate motifs appeared: chip-carved roundels on the box, mythological figures entwined with flowers or the favourite vine pattern, birds, beasts and heads in low relief on back and arms. Sometimes the front panel of the box seat was a door, which made the seat into a handy storage space, and at some time – around mid century – the side and back panels of the box itself disappeared, leaving only the front panel and the lower rails of the other panels as stretchers. Arms began to slope downwards from back to front and had rectangular hand-holes in them to make for easier lifting; but this kind of chair is not, strictly speaking, a box-chair. It is transitional, and is on the way to becoming the early very heavy armchair of late Elizabethan and early Jacobean times.

A much lighter chair, the *caquetoire** or *chaire de femme*, was, as the name implies, a conversation piece and is believed to have originated in France. One such chair found at Colyton, South Devon, about the turn of the present century, is now in the Victoria and Albert Museum. It is of carved oak with a semi-circular seat and a high, narrow, single-panelled back carved with a woman's head set within a lozenge and other devices such as flowers and leaf-tailed *amorini*. These are Renaissance in feeling. The arms are semi-circular; the two back legs, set close together, rise to support the carved back, while the two front legs are set at the widest points of the semi-circular seat, which has a scalloped apron-piece below. The chair is English and was probably made around 1540.

In 1524/5, thirty-odd years before Andrew Smythe quitted the pleasant village of Great Milton for ever, John Port of London died. He was obviously a much richer man than the Oxfordshire small farmer, for his funeral expenses came to £73 6s. 8d., a large sum for those days, and he was possessed of a fair amount of gilt plate and a few jewels valued at £117 7s. 6½d. He was probably a widower, for 'the wyffes raiment' now mostly 'old and broken'

* *Caqueter* means 'to chatter'.

as well as 'her bonnets' and 'Jewels for her body'[11] are included in the inventory of his own effects. He kept some sort of shop – and a muddle of a shop it sounds too. But shops were few and largely unspecialized. Here we find, amongst various negligible things, wood, coal, several swords and daggers, a primer* with a silver clasp and printed on parchment, another one illuminated and decorated with gold, a mother-of-pearl image of the Virgin, a silver bead, a standish and one gold button, plus various remnants of cloth. The total value of the contents of the shop was £74 15s. 1d., which would just pay for the funeral, so it is fairly safe to assume that the late John Port, whose house was large for its type, must have had business interests outside of shop-keeping. He obviously lived over the shop, as all tradesmen did, and his house consisted of at least six named rooms, among them a hall, a parlour, a napery, a great chamber and two garrets, one situated 'over the Great Chamber' and the other described as being 'next the street'.[12] These were possibly servants' rooms and were scantily furnished.

But what makes one really think that John Port was a man of substance – and mystery – is that he had six chairs! Four of these, the two 'turned chairs' valued at 4d., the close-chair at 10d. (this was probably his own special chair) and, most expensive of all, an imported chair 'of Spanish make' valued at 1s. 4d., stood in the hall. This leads one to suspect that it may have been here that John Port carried on his real business; perhaps he was a money-lender in a small way – the various unrelated articles in his small shop also suggest this. For private use he had his own parlour; for 'in the Payrlor' among thirty-seven yards of green say hangings at 2d. a yard, the joined forms, the books and six cushions – John sat softly – are two more 'turned chairs with a jake'[13] at 4d., jake included. No chairs appear in any of the other rooms, but forms, stools and chests do, so these must have served as chairs. When one

---

* These primers cannot have been medieval school books. The decoration suggests that they were primers for devotional purposes. This type of primer was in use before the Reformation and continued in use for some time afterwards.

considers the date and remembers that Henry VIII had to borrow furniture for Dover Castle, John Port was certainly well supplied with chairs, both for his ostensible profession and for his time. It is just possible that the turned chairs were of the late medieval kind, bound with cane and with a solid wooden seat. One, the close-chair, was made by a joiner and may or may not have been carved. The Spanish chair makes one wonder again how the owner came by it; for an imported Spanish chair to be valued at only 1s. 4d. seems sheer nonsense, even for those days.

John Port's house must have been a typical London dwelling: a three-storey town house, probably in a row of similar houses. On the ground floor it had a hall, then a parlour, a buttery, then the shop, which may have been formed by a partition across the hall. On the first floor was a great chamber over the hall with 'a lytyll chamber next', also a room designated as 'His Chamber'[14] with the two garrets above. Like all houses of the period, from cottage to manor, the interior plan sprang from a central nucleus, the hall. This was often the only room in a cottage. In large houses, during late medieval and early Tudor times, it was the chief room, rising two or three storeys to the hammer-beam roof* and dividing the house into two separate parts. At one end – the screens end – were the offices: buttery, pantry, napery and kitchen, although the kitchen, like the brewhouse and bakehouse, was often in a separate but adjoining building. At the other end – the dais end – were the private, family rooms which included a bower (a withdrawing room for ladies), another private room and, on the first floor above, a solar, or sunny room, whose chief feature was its oriel window. There is a beautiful solar still to be seen at Stokesay Castle, Shropshire.

By the mid sixteenth century, however, new houses were being built in which the hall, although still the central feature of the house, rose only one storey, whilst in old houses great halls were often re-beamed and ceiled over, thus providing a greater area for rooms on the first floor. The solar was partitioned off to make

* Simple roofs were supported by tie-beams, collar-beams and king or queen posts.

more bedrooms, one of which, the great chamber – although this might have been placed directly over the hall – was used as a withdrawing room. On the ground floor the bower gave way to the parlour, a private, family room used frequently for dining – though it was a long way from the kitchen. 'Make the hall of such a fashion that the parlour be annexed to the head of the hall, and the buttrye and pantrye at the lower end.'[15] Andrew Boorde thus advises prospective house-builders in 1547. So by that date the parlour had already become a room of importance and the decline of the great hall as the principal room had begun. Unusually, at Ewelme Manor, Oxfordshire, the hall had 'great barres of iren overthaurt it instead of crosse beames' and, says Leland, 'the parler by is exceeding fair and lightsum.'[16] He adds that most of the good building of the manor was done during the reign of Henry VIII.

A passage on one side of the dais led to the new family room or rooms. This passage held a staircase, and just beyond this was the parlour. Beyond this again (all rooms were interconnecting) were one or two smaller rooms. Off one of these, if the house were a great house, lay the chapel. In one of the smaller rooms estate business was carried on. Here tenants paid rent, aired grievances and had disputes settled, and here accounts of estate or household affairs were rendered. This room can have contained little furniture but there is one piece we can be sure of, a counting table with a chequered top (hence, exchequer). On this the jettons or counters were moved about and accounts 'cast'. If the table top was not chequered, a cloth with an embroidered chequer pattern was used. For small accounts a slate did service. Very few examples of exchequer or counter tables survive. One, in the R. T. Gwynne Collection, took the form of a chest on a stand: 'The top was marked out with lines to assist calculations and could be slid over laterally to reach the interior, in which money was kept.'[17]

The other small room was where the lady of the house carried on all the business connected with the household. Here she saw to the servants and to the countless tasks involved in running an establishment where such things as baking, brewing, distilling sweet waters, supplying medicines and providing one's own meat were all a part of the routine.

The parlour was, of course, larger and better furnished. A large table was necessary, as the room was used for family meals or for entertaining intimate friends informally. There was, undoubtedly, one chair for the master of the house (and possibly two), several stools, a bench and a cupboard of some sort. Another table was provided for games such as chess or backgammon; once, 'for a par of tables and dise'[18] King Henry VII paid 1s. 4d., which is what John Port's Spanish chair was worth. So either the chair was cheap or the backgammon board expensive.

Walls, as in other rooms, were often wainscoted. Small panels were formed by plain stiles and uprights and were sometimes brightly painted. Larger panels held linenfold carving. Tapestries, arras-work and painted cloths were also much favoured for walls; they enriched a room with colour and also made it warmer. Painted cloths must have been cheap, as we find in the accounts of Henry VII that, on 1 March 1503, 2s. 3d. was paid 'for 10 painted clothes'.[19] A curious item appears in the Household Books of John, Duke of Norfolk, where it is noted that 'my lord paid to the assectory of webys for ix peces of hangynges with lyons xls'.[20] Webs are cloth or fine hangings and these must have been especially woven for the duke, as the lion was his crest.

Cardinal Wolsey possessed such tapestries and such furniture and plate that foreigners were astounded and thought there was nothing like Hampton Court outside Rome. In December 1522 the cardinal bought at one sale alone twenty-one complete sets of tapestries consisting of 132 pieces, which were to furnish rooms in the great Gate House at the centre of the west front. The subject matter of most of them was biblical. In the larger room on the first floor, six pieces told the story of Esther. A further six in another room repeated the story of Samuel. Our Lady, David, Jacob, Susannah, Judith and Holofernes, Solomon and Samson ornamented other rooms in the palace, *en suite*, while single tapestries showed David harping, Christ casting the tradesmen from the temple, and St George. More secular, more pagan, were the mythological subjects – Jupiter, Pluto, Ceres, Paris and Achilles, Priam, Herakles, Jason, Hannibal, Dame Pleasaunce, *The Romaunt of the Rose* – and also pieces known as *ouvrages de verdure*, because they depicted woods, gardens, birds, beasts, flowers and sports such as hawking and shooting.

The Venetian Ambassador reported home that the cardinal had so many tapestries they were changed every week, and John Skelton, in *Colyn Cloute*, refers to the more secular ones in the lines:

> Hanging about the wallés
> Cloth of gold and pallés,
> Arras of rich array,
> Fresh as flowers in May;
> With Dame Diana naked;
> How lusty Venus quakéd.
> And how Cupid shakéd
> His dart, and bent his bow.

Here Skelton is aiming a poisoned dart at the cardinal, whom he intensely disliked.

Doors were, in the early part of the century, small, narrow and wainscoted, let into the wainscot wall so that when closed a door, bar its hinges and latches, looked like a part of the panelling. Later on, doors became a decorative feature flanked by pilasters or columns and supporting an entablature, but this decorative importance was not much seen until Elizabethan times.

Walls, when plastered, were often covered with murals. The painted decorations, of which few survive, consisted usually of a pattern or running design of some sort – often leaves, animals and human figures formed a part of it. When a row of old cottages was being repaired at Picott's End, near Hemel Hempstead, Hertfordshire, in 1953, some splendid wall paintings were discovered[*] under layers of old wallpaper. Further investigation of the ground plan showed that these cottages must once have been a single

* The cleaning and preservation of these rare murals was carried out in 1958–9.

house of some importance, with the hall running to the roof beams and twin doors at one end presumably leading to the offices. It is thought that the building may have been originally a pilgrims' hostel; this seems likely, as the wall paintings depict scenes from the life of Christ and from the lives of saints. St Catherine and St Margaret of Antioch help date the paintings, as both wear gable head-dresses such as were worn in the days of Henry VII. The colours are still clear, although not so bright as they must have been when the mural was first painted – decoration in bright simple colours was used for all plaster work and for ceiling ribs.

At Cowdray Park, Sussex, the walls were remarkable for their painted frescoes. These showed Sir Anthony Browne's services to Henry VIII and also the coronation procession of King Edward VI. The paintings must have been in mint condition when the young king visited the house in 1552. We do not know what colours were used, as the house was almost completely destroyed by fire in 1793, but we do know that colours were brilliant at that period: greens, reds, vermilions, bice (cobalt blue), indigo and all shades of yellow. Gilding was lavish, and so was silvering. Colour was a characteristic of the times; it was the Renaissance which introduced the fashion for whiteness.

Although, as we have seen, the great hall was declining in importance, no house was without one and in those houses where halls rose to the roof and so divided the house in two, two staircases were needed to reach the upper floors. These rose from narrow openings at each end of the hall and were, as they had been for centuries, of the spiral, newel kind. Made of oak or stone, they were narrow, badly lit and easy to defend. The potentialities of a staircase as a structure of beauty and ornament were not generally realized until the time of Queen Elizabeth, and then we lagged far behind the continent.

The hall in cottages and small houses was often called the house room. In typical cottages this house room or house place had merely a partition across one end, behind which the domestic animals were kept. In old houses, and there were many

The great hall with centre hearth

of these, the hearth was in the centre of the hall and the smoke wandered about, blackening beams and choking and blinding the occupants of the house place until it found its way out through a rough wooden funnel or a barrel with both ends knocked out set in the thatched, fire-hazardous roof. In great houses where the hall rose two or three storeys the draught was greater and the occupants were less likely to be smoked out, particularly when louvres were used. Sometimes an iron fire-back was placed against a wall of earth, brick or stone and the fire built here, protected by a hood supported by angle stones. The smoke was carried out through the roof by a flue on the inner face of the wall. Harrison speaks of making a fire 'against a reredos in the hall', where people dined and 'dressed their meat'.[21]

Fortunately at some point the usefulness of chimneys for domestic purposes was discovered. Chimneys, with their projecting stacks, were a Tudor innovation. The stack, projecting beyond the outside wall, took the width of the hearth and it was this discovery which removed the fire from the centre of the hall and meant that the hall itself need no longer rise to roof height. In old houses the hall could now be floored halfway up to make an upper storey, level with the existent upper storeys. This was done, for example, at Stoneacre, Otham, Kent, where during the first half of the sixteenth century the hall of the timber-framed house, built somewhere around 1480 by a yeoman, John Ellys, was ceiled over, the central fireplace moved to a hearth and a new brick chimney built against a wall.* It may be that the use of coal had something to do with moving the fire to an outside wall. Wood smoke in a large hall is bearable, coal smoke is not. In time it was also discovered that with the flue taken up vertically a fireplace need no longer be placed on an outside wall but could be built into an interior wall, which made more fireplaces possible. One thing John Leland noted in the hall of Bolton Castle, Yorkshire, was 'how chimeneys were conveyed by tunnells made on the syds of the wauls bytwixt the lights in the haull; and

---

* The house has now been restored to its original plan and belongs to the National Trust.

by this meanes, and by no lovers [louvres] is the smoke of the harthe in the hawle wonder strangely convayed'.[22] When great halls were floored halfway up, thus doubling the floor space, the floor – or ceiling – was at first left bare to show the floor beams, which were often carved and painted. Later, ceilings were plastered and richly ornamented.

In small houses and cottages this removal of the central hearth introduced the fitted cooking crane or plain iron bar from which the adjustable pot crane was suspended. In addition, a baking oven was often built, its rounded end curving outside the house wall. In large new houses fireplaces built into a wall were, of course, not used for cooking but became a central feature of the hall and, more sparingly, of other rooms too. Wall fireplaces at first had a simple stone Perpendicular arch with, perhaps, a chimney beam of carved oak. Logs for burning were supported on relatively plain iron dogs. Later on, fireplaces became much larger and had a slightly raised hearth, and bigger logs lay across heavier and very bow-legged dogs. These fireplaces had a brick interior and a simple, flattened, four-centred arch of stone, ornamented with restrained carving. It was not until Elizabethan times that fireplaces became rectangular, and then their chimney breasts provided such a field for ornamentation that in the end they looked like 'the front elevation of a fantastic gatehouse or a riotous Sicilian tomb'.[23] Unusual for the period is the fireplace at Lacock in what is now the Stone Gallery. The chimney piece is of stone, with Doric pilasters and a correct entablature which is most delicately and exquisitely carved. It is purely classical and slightly French in feeling, and much in advance of the usual fireplaces of the time. The mason employed to do this work was probably John Chapman, who worked on some of Henry VIII's buildings.

Even though the hall was declining from its medieval importance it was still the main room of a great house for the more conservative families, where they still dined and where retainers slept, but those who moved with the times now lived a more private life and tended to use the great hall chiefly for special occasions such as feasting and, of course, for dancing, as well as for Christmas and other occasions for revels. Screened at one end and with a dais at the other, the hall was entered on the long side via a porch, sometimes an interior one, which led into a long narrow passage formed by the space between the end wall and the screen. The screen, of carved and wainscoted wood, was usually pierced by two openings or doors which led off the passage – known as 'the screens' – into the hall. Doors on the wall side led to the domestic offices and, sometimes, a stair.

A screen could be relatively plain or very magnificent; the one at Cowdray Park must have been of the magnificent variety. It was carved with the emblems of the Southampton family, scrolls, trefoils and the initials 'W.H.', plus the motto *Loiaultie s'approvera*, while eleven life-size stags carved in oak and holding banners pranced or stood about the cornice. The hall itself was sixty by eighty feet in area and rose fifty-two feet from the floor to the top of the open louvre.

Screens were fixed to a sill into which uprights were set which were then carried to a horizontal beam above. Between the uprights were cross rails and the spaces so made were infilled with panelling or wainscoting. It was not usual for a screen to reach the roof, and at the point where it stopped – that is, where the uprights joined the cross beams – there was often a minstrels' gallery.

At the opposite end of the hall and on the dais stood the top table, a permanent fixture. Such tables had carved oak supports at each end and in the middle, but the fixed top was often of elm. Some top tables were more than twenty feet long and three feet wide. Or the table might be the new type, a framed table with four or six solid legs and very solid low-set stretchers or underpinning to hold down the rushes and keep the heavy legs steady.

Below the dais, at mealtimes, trestle tables were placed at right angles to the top table. These had removable tops and when not in use were dismantled and stood against the walls.

At the top table sat the host or master in his own chair which was rarely moved and, if he was important enough, he probably had a cloth of estate, upon which his arms were displayed, behind him. An item in the accounts of Henry VII tells us that he paid 'To Anthony Crosse for a cloth of an estate, contayning 47½ yerds. £11 the yerd, £522 10s.'.[24] This was a good deal of money, and of course one does not know if this particular cloth was used for dining. Beside the host sat his wife, possibly in a lower chair, but – save for the queen – more likely on a stool. On the other side of the host, if this was a feast, sat the most important guest, whilst other guests were allotted places according to rank and importance and sat on forms, chests or stools.

Dispensing with precedent was not unknown, however, at a jolly gathering of friends. Shakespeare's Timon, when he gives that Barmecide's feast to his 'mouth-friends', cries with false affability: 'Each man to his stool ... your diet shall be in all places alike. Make not a city feast of it, to let the meat cool ere we can agree upon the first place to sit.'[25] Where these guests sat did not matter, but they certainly sat upon stools in this rich man's house, and this play, written about 1608, shows that even at this late date stools were customary seats at table. Solid, flat-seated and plain in the early years of the sixteenth century, they had a solid carved support at each side and a simply-carved apron-piece back and front. By mid century four-legged joined stools with a very low underframing became much more common; the legs of these were turned and carved. Forms, which were narrow, also had solid end supports, while ogee arches often decorated the apron-piece. With a back added the form became a settle. Settles sometimes had reversible backs, so that they could be used either for sitting in front of the fire or, with the back reversed, for sitting at table.

Box chests with chip-carved or linenfold front panels gave way to framed chests with shaped and grooved stiles which at the extremities were prolonged into feet. Sometimes the grooving made the stiles look like minute pilasters without capitals. These chests were often carved with arcading or inlaid with geometric or floral patterns. Others displayed front panels carved with structural and decorative forms of Perpendicular Gothic architecture; many were imported from Flanders. Still other chests, imported by the rich from Italy, were dower chests or *cassoni*; they were gessoed, elaborately ornamented, painted and gilded, but were not for everyday use in the hall, unlike the more simple chests, forms and stools.

Hall furniture included aumbreys, buffets and sideboard tables, though not necessarily all of these at the same time. There is an item in the accounts of Henry VIII which shows that a joiner was paid 44s. for eight cupboards 'some with Ambreys and some withoute'.[26] That would come to 5s. 6d. apiece; these must have been for use in the inferior regions of the royal household. Buffets had three tiers, on each of which plate or food for use at the table was displayed. Buffets stood on four legs which were usually carved but did not yet suffer from the severe oedema which afflicted furniture in Elizabethan times. The court cupboard, so dear to the Elizabethans, was rarely seen before the last half of the century.

Indifferent lighting was provided by candles of beeswax or tallow – these last smelled vilely and dripped curtains of fat into and over the rims of large grease pans. Candles were set in wood or iron supports, sometimes in a cross-beam, sometimes in a wheel-shaped structure, and these were known as candle beams. They were suspended from the ceiling beams and were operated by a pulley. Individual candlesticks were of iron, brass or latten and were of the pricket or shallow-socket type. They stood on a tripod or a solid round base. Flares were also used, but chiefly in passageways. The poor used rush dips, often not even these. They rose and went to bed with the sun in summer, and in winter had only the firelight to see by.

Upstairs in great houses and manor houses were the bedrooms, many with anterooms, but both bedroom and anteroom were usually small and narrow and, as all rooms were inter-communicating, they also served, most inconveniently, as passages leading from one larger room to another. The largest room was the great chamber, usually situated over the hall, and this was a bedroom and reception room occupied by the master of the house. In the attics servants slept, a dozen or so to a room, which was insanitary if snug, and a good deal better than sleeping among the stinking rushes of the hall.

Bedrooms by this time had small fireplaces, while walls and ceilings were treated in much the same way as those of the parlour. If plastered they were gaily painted. If wainscoted they were often painted too or, equally often, hung with arras or painted cloths. Windows were small and here, as elsewhere in the house, made up of small square or diamond-shaped panes of glass, sometimes stained. But glass was so expensive that only the rich could afford glazed windows. The sum of 5s. 4d. was paid 'For glaysing the King's chambre'[27] in 1493, and in a house with many windows, including that new favourite the oriel window, it is probable that only the chief windows were glazed.

Bedroom furniture included, perhaps, a chair, certainly a stool or two, chests for linen and clothing and a cupboard for toilet requisites – ewer, basin, cosmetic jars and a chamber-pot. If there was a looking-glass it was a hand-glass of polished metal. Dressing tables, wardrobes and chests of drawers had not yet developed. But the chief article of furniture was the bed. The great bedstead was vast, and when closed off at night with hangings became a small, raised, more or less draught-proof room within the room. Edward VI had a huge bed standing on a dais, painted and gilded and hung with cloth of silver and gold upon which were embroidered crowns, roses and fleurs-de-lis.

Beds were, however, in a transitional state. The older late medieval type of bed – a heavy rectangular frame on four short legs – had wooden boards upon which the mattress was supported and a canopy or tester suspended over it by cords attached to the roof beams. Hangings or bed curtains were hung on rails fixed to the wall behind. By day the curtains enclosing the top of the bed were drawn aside, turned up and folded in upon themselves, hanging like great puffed-out bags from the rails. Hangings and coverlets could be very expensive, made of silk, velvet or damask, and some coverlets were of fur. A bolster and pillows completed the furnishings of the bed.

Suspended canopy bed

But a new type of bed began to come in during the first quarter of the sixteenth century and must have been much more comfortable, as the boards which supported the mattress or feather bed were replaced by rope mesh. Support holes bored in the sides and ends of the frame held the rope-ends and were concealed by the coverlet, which came well down over the frame. The bed itself now sprouted two heavy foot-posts – in addition to the existing short foot-posts – to match the tall head-posts.

Posts were straight-sided and elaborately carved. The tester was freed from suspense and came to rest firmly on top of the four posts and also upon the head-board which had stretched up from the once slightly raised head. This now became a wonderful surface for carving and, as the century progressed, the carving of the head-board became more and more elaborate and intricate. Architectural and floral designs, figures in bas-relief, armorial bearings, medallion heads, entwined initials – all were used lavishly and a place in which to stand a candle or two was also introduced. For example, some bed-heads had, amidst the carving, a small arched recess; at the top of this recess and completely hidden by the arch was a hole to let out the candle-smoke, which streaked the wall with soot or even charred the back of the bed.

In most houses of any size there was at least one four-poster for the master and his wife and in great houses there were a number of them. Cardinal Wolsey had 280 beds at Hampton Court, scores of them with testers and full backs. He loved to lie softly and his own bed had eight mattresses, each stuffed with thirteen pounds of carded wool. The 'Great Rich Bedstead' may have been his. It had four gilt posts and four 'boulles' bearing cardinals' hats, gilded. The 'ceiler' of red satin was embroidered with roses, garters and portcullises; these, however, are all badges of the Tudors, and the valance and fringe were of white and green, also Tudor colours, so it is probable that Henry VIII refurbished this bed for his own use.

The larger and more elaborate the bed and its furnishings the greater the status symbol. Beds such as these were so valuable and so durable that they were left in wills and handed down from father to son. When John Pynnok[*] died in 1486 he left £1,000 to his son, Thomas, with a good deal of plate and 'two feather beds with bolsters, four blankets and four pairs of sheets with coverlets with figures of lions "de la Tapestry"' and 'one bed-stead with hangings and a tester, six pillows and a "banker"'.[†][28]

---

[*] The chapel of Holy Trinity adjoining Burford church was built at his cost and he is buried there.

[†] A covering usually of tapestry, more generally used on chairs.

As the tester is mentioned separately, one may reasonably suppose that this was one of the older kinds of bed where the tester was hung from the roof beams.

Less grand beds were for lesser personages. The boarded bed was the most usual type and was made like a shallow wooden box, standing upon four short legs. In this a straw mattress was placed. In some farms and a few cottages the boarded bed was the best bed, and the better ones had a narrow shelf at the head on which to stand a candle. A lighted candle and a straw mattress in such close proximity in a draughty room gives rise to some uneasiness.

Then there was the trestle bed and also the truckle bed, low and running upon truckles (solid wheels), which could be rolled under the great four-poster when not needed. It was generally used by a page or maid who slept in the bedroom or anteroom of master or mistress and was not much used in ordinary manor houses, although common in great houses and royal palaces.

And the poor? They slept upon a straw pallet or on a rough mat 'covered only with a sheet, under coverlets made of dagswain or hop-harlot . . . and a good round log under their heads instead of bolster or pillow' and if 'the goodman of the house had within seven years of his marriage a mattress or a flock bed, and thereto a stack of chaff to rest his head upon, he thought himself to be as well lodged as the lord of the town'.[29]

Although the lord of the town or country may have lived in comfort, nevertheless he had no water closet. There was the very occasional privy, and Andrew Boorde wisely recommends that this 'the common house of easement' should be over some water or else 'elongated from the house'.[30] He also urges one to beware just where 'pysse-pottes' are emptied and to be even more wary of 'pyssing in chiminies'. By being cautious rather than careless with excrement 'the air of a house is kept clean and unputrified'.[31] Boorde was, however, well ahead of his time.

The privy (a misleading name) was also called a garderobe, originally a place where clothes were kept – the parallel modern euphemism is 'cloak-room'. It was also known as a latrine, a seat house, or a jakes or jaques. Jakes, apparently, could also refer to close-stools, according to John Port's inventory. The close-stool, a box-like affair, holed and lidded, was a most necessary article of furniture and could handily be moved from room to room on demand, as it were; it could also be taken when travelling. One made in 1547 'For the Kings mageste'[32] was covered in black velvet, ornamented with ribbon and fringe and 2,000 gilt nails. It had a leather cover and could be transported from palace to palace with his 'mageste', who was, at this time, Henry VIII.

When Henry VIII's mother was about to give birth to her first child, his paternal grandmother, the Lady Margaret Beaufort, drew up a special set of ordinances for the kind of apartment to be made ready at the royal palace of Winchester in anticipation of this event. 'Her Highnesses Pleasure being understood,' the ordinances begin and, with a fine disregard for capital letters, continue, 'in what Chamber she will be delivered in, the same must be hanged with rich Cloth of Arras, Sides roof, Windows and all, except One Window must be hanged so she may have Light when it pleases her.'[33] She might also have needed a little air, but no mention is made of this – air was suspect.

Next, the private chapel was to be 'worshipfully arrayed' and the great chamber also had to be hung with rich arras and was to contain 'a Cloth and Chair of Estate and Quishions thereto', so that when the queen came from chapel with her lords and ladies she might 'either standing or sitting at her pleasure' receive 'Spices and Wine'.[34]

Between the great chamber and the bedchamber, which contained a royal bed and had the floor 'laid over' with carpets and a cupboard covered with the same stuff which was hung over walls and windows, was an anteroom also 'well worshipfully hanged'.[35]

The child was born on 20 September 1486 and was laid in a wooden cradle one and three-quarter yards long and twenty-two inches wide, within a frame 'fair set forth by the Painters craft',[36] ornamented with silver gilt and tongueless buckles on either side 'for the swathing bands'. When shown off to foreign ambassadors the baby was put into 'a great Cradle of Estate'.[37] This was five and a half feet long and two and a half feet wide, all garnished with gold, fringe and crimson. This magnificent cradle bore the king's arms on 'the middlemost stulpe' (post) at the head.

The little prince, born into such splendour and magnificence, died, a married man, at the age of fifteen and thus England came to be ruled by an eighth Henry rather than a second Arthur.

CHAPTER FOUR

Of Food and Drink

On 25 November 1487, 'La tres hault, tres puissant, tres excellent Princesse, La tres noble Reigne d'Engleter, et de France, et Dame d'Irland',[1] Elizabeth, wife of King Henry VII, was finally crowned queen in Westminster Hall where, at one end, a high stage had been built to hold trumpeters and minstrels, 'whiche when the first Course was sett forwarde began to blowe'.[2]

The first course, thus trumpeted in and preceded by a 'warner', consisted of twenty-four dishes; among them were shields of brawn, frumenty with venison, a rich bruet (stew or sauce), salted hart, pheasant, swan, capons, lampreys, crane, pike, heron, carp, kid, perch, rabbit, mutton, baked custard, tart fruit and a 'Soteltie'. The second course was even larger. Also preceded by a warner, it was made up of twenty-nine different dishes. In this course appeared the inevitable festal peacock, as well as egrets, cocks, partridge, plover, red shanks, snipe, quail, larks, venison pasties, baked quinces, marchpane and 'Castells of Jelly in Temple wise made'.[3]

This was, of course, a very splendid feast to mark a royal occasion. Even so, lesser men, that is the rich ones, were given to feasting whenever an excuse arose and the length of their menus far exceeded those of great Victorian banquets. It will be noted that only two courses are listed for the coronation feast – and two courses was customary – but each course contained a vast number of dishes and was preceded by a 'warner' and concluded with a 'subtlety'. Warners and subtleties were usual at feasts, but were made not to please the palate but to delight the eye. Confected of sugar, plaster and pasteboard, the warner was carried in first to warn guests – as did the blast on the trumpets – that the real business of eating was about to begin. The subtlety ended each course. These ornamental devices were made to rise two or three feet above the table and were gaily coloured and gilded set-pieces in miniature, often depicting fables of romance or moral maxims, military exploits, hunting scenes, biblical stories – these last were much favoured at feasts following the consecration of a bishop – and all positively bristling with escutcheons. At bridal feasts a subtlety quite often foreshadowed the bride's happy future by depicting her in the last stage but one of conjugal felicity: that is, in urgent need of a midwife.

Meals, as distinct from feasts, were on a lavish scale for the nobility and rich merchants in those days. The poor were also relatively well fed, although on a much more meagre and probably healthier diet, provided the harvest did not fail, which it often did. At such times they existed on 'horse-food' – beans, oats, barley, lentils. In the year of Queen Elizabeth of York's coronation there were still many alive who could remember the terrible years from 1437 to 1439 when poor country folk had had to live on roots and herbs only, and thousands had died of want and of those diseases which attack and prove more fatal when hunger lowers resistance. Plague had followed these dearth years. In fact, as well as causing deficiency diseases, famine had always nourished plague.

We know a good deal more about what the rich ate and how much their food cost than we do about the food of the middling sort and the poor. In every nobleman's household accounts were kept of how much was spent and on what. But the poor and the not-so-poor could neither read, write nor cypher; they kept no accounts. Besides, those who lived and worked in the country, as most did, produced their own food and lived upon it and by barter. So for these we have to rely upon the accounts of contemporary historians who do note bad harvests and the control of prices, and also on what we can glean from various books written during or before the time.

'I haven't a penny,' says Piers Ploughman, 'so I can't buy you pullets, or geese, or pigs. All I've got is a couple of fresh cheeses, a little curds and cream, an oat-cake, and two loaves of beans and bran which I bake for my children . . . I haven't a scrap of bacon, and I haven't a cook to fry you steak and onions. But I've some parsley and shallots and plenty of cabbage, and a cow and a calf, and a mare to cart my dung till the drought is over. And with these few things we must live till Lammas time, when I hope to reap a harvest in my fields.'[4] This was written towards the close of the fourteenth century, but the book must have had relevance in all its aspects as it was reprinted no less than three times as late as 1550.

The diet of country folk can have changed little in the intervening century and a half, and Piers with his cow, his calf, his curds, cheese, parsley and cabbage, his mare to cart dung, was fairly representative of the agricultural folk of his own day as well as those of early Tudor times. Most villagers, however, unlike Piers, also seem to have had pigs and poultry, and some had oxen, or a sheep or two. Chaucer's poor widow who lived in a narrow cottage beside a grove standing in a dale, and who was only a 'manner deye' or farm servant, had three large sows, three cows, a sheep, a 'gentle cok' and seven hens. Nevertheless,

> No deyntee morsel passed thurgh hir throte;
> Hir dyete was accordant to her cote.
> Repleccioun ne made hir never syk:
> Attempree dyete was al hir phisyk.[5]

Chaucer's widow and Langland's Piers are contemporaneous and their temperate diets were enforced by circumstances. The widow, we know from her story, drank no wine, did not lack for brown bread, had a bit of broiled bacon, an egg or two upon occasion, but her meals were slender. The rich nobleman with his country estates fed lavishly, as did the rich and non-noble who could buy what they wished. Even so, the village labourer and the artisan class, although their diet was restricted, were far better fed than their counterparts in Europe.

When times were good, villagers fed upon coarse bread, cheese, eggs, milk, a bit of bacon and the occasional fowl, together with onions, leeks, parsnips, cabbage, peas, beans and, obviously, parsley. They had apples, plums, cherries and wild berries in season and this, though frugal, is undoubtedly healthy. They drank ale – the richer villagers brewed their own – and whey. The artisan in towns did even better: he had mutton, veal, lamb, pork, brawn, bacon, fowl, cheese, butter, eggs and fruit. He ate three meals a day and in good times ate as much meat as he could afford, which gave him a high animal-protein diet and must have been energizing. He breakfasted at six or seven on salted or pickled herring, cold meat, pottage, bread and ale. His midday meal, taken at about 11 a.m., he bought at a cook shop and took home or ate in a tavern – roast meat, pies, soup or stew, bread, cheese, ale or beer. At five or six o'clock he supped off cold meat with bread, cheese and ale. The only vegetable he seems to have had was onions, but the occasional cabbage was boiled to death in a soup or with the meat.

The food of the poorer classes does not seem to have changed to any great extent between the fourteenth and sixteenth centuries. Yet between Piers Ploughman's time and the Tudor era farming certainly did. Because of this change the diet of the poorer people became scantier. Before 1525 food was cheap. One penny bought two good-sized loaves of brown bread, or nearly one pound of beef. A chicken cost 2d.; so did a pound of butter, and a fine goose or capon could be had for 3d. or 4d. After this, a slow, steady rise in prices began, but there was practically no increase in agricultural wages – they barely changed at all in the one hundred years between 1541 and 1641. The poor landless labourers were thus badly affected. Artisans, on the other hand, were more fortunate; their wages did rise.

To understand this we need to refer briefly to the manorial system, even though this system, so common in medieval times, was all but finished. Open-field cultivation was still a characteristic of English farming, as it had been for centuries, and under the manorial system one or two great fields of the demesne were cultivated in strips by servants of the manor or by villeins. These last were serfs, free in relation to all but their lord and therefore not slaves. Villeins were, as often as not, villagers, and were bound to give the lord of the manor a certain number of days' work a year or, failing this, to pay him in money or in kind. This field service, even in medieval times in England, had occasionally been commuted for money rent and some villagers, or villeins, had been able to become tenant farmers.

This process of freeing the unfree tenant was speeded up by two catastrophes: first the Black Death (1348–9) and second, although on a very much smaller scale, the Wars of the Roses. The devastation caused by the Black Death was appalling; some historians hold that half the population was wiped out in the short period of eighteen months. This meant that many villages were left completely uninhabited, land values fell and labour was at a premium. Labour was in fact so scarce that labourers managed to get their wages raised for the first time in centuries. The rise was as much as 50 per cent. This meant that the lord of the manor could not cultivate his own demesne lands, and in every village strip holdings in the open fields reverted to him because the families who had once farmed them had died. As free labourers (those who held no land) were able to command higher wages, land-owners were now happy enough to let their land in farms, because an assured rent was better than having to worry about finding and paying labour to keep the land in cultivation. The same sort of thing happened to a much lesser extent during the Wars of the Roses – scarcity of labour, unrest, discontent and the freeing of land.

As by the mid fourteenth century a number of villeins had already been able to buy their freedom, the coming of plague and war helped many others to do so and, by the time of the Tudors, the yeoman had become independent. Independence brought him a new importance, while the old feudal lord was transformed into a commercial landlord.

But, if land tenure had changed, agricultural methods had not; they had remained virtually the same since Roman days and they stayed that way until well on into Elizabethan times. The simplest possible crop rotation was used and only a few crops, chiefly cereal and legumes, were grown. In the three-field system, the land was divided into parcels; crops were grown on two and the third lay fallow. Fortunately for agriculture and soil fertility, Virgil had said, 'See too that your arable lies fallow in due rotation/ And leave the idle field alone to recoup its strenth', and also 'Scruple not to enrich the dried up soil with dung,/ And scatter filthy ashes on fields that are exhausted.'[6] And Pliny had recommended that 'wheat should be sown in ground which has born a crop of lupins and vetch'.[7] Hence we rotated legumes with corn. Even so, yields were poor by modern standards and a three-fold return, that is, about seven and a half bushels an acre, was considered to be good.

When harvested, corn had to be taken to the manor mill to be ground – this was one of the few remaining manorial rights – and for this villagers and farmers had to pay, sometimes too heavily. As wheat and cereal crops provided the staple of everyone's diet, the price and the weight of bread for sale were controlled. Bread was of various qualities, white, brown or black, but none was in the least like our modern varieties. White, eaten by richer folk, was made from the best quality stone-ground wholemeal flour from which the coarse bran had been removed by bolting the flour through a fine linen or woollen cloth. The bread still contained the fine bran and a good deal of wheat germ and was rather yellowish in colour. Less fine white bread was produced by bolting flour through a coarser cloth; this, which produced a yellowish-white to a dirty-grey loaf, was called 'cheat'. It was cheaper than the first quality bread but 'raveled' was even less expensive, as it contained more bran. Brown bread was made from unbolted wholemeal flour, and if a little rye was added to it it was called 'meslin'. Bread made wholly from rye was black and cheap. Oatmeal was commonly used in the north and when times were really hard 'horse-food', that is, oats, rye and legumes, were ground together to make a flour from which the poor made their bread.

Country people of all classes made their own bread, but in cities and towns it was made and sold by bakers, who would also bake a customer's own home-made dough. Baking at home for the average person was still usually hearth-baking. Bread ovens were for large houses and were situated in a separate bake-house to avoid risk of fire. Not until fires moved from the central hearth to a side wall was it possible to build (into the thickness of the outside wall) a bread oven. Therefore for most of the Tudor period the average person who still lived in a thin-walled cottage or house would have to hearth-bake bread. Such loaves must have required a good deal of watching – as King Alfred had found to his cost centuries before.

The chaff of corn and the bins of beans were used as cattle-food, but livestock was also grazed on the stubble after harvest; this also helped keep the land in good heart. Only the healthiest stock could be over-wintered, so all weaker animals were slaughtered in the autumn and the meat powdered (salted) for winter use. Salt meat and fish and a consequent quenching of thirst were the chief features of a winter diet.

But a change did take place in farming in Tudor times – not in methods of agriculture, but in type of farming. This was due to an enormous increase in the wool trade. Profits from wool and its end product – manufactured cloth – were so rewarding that many land-owners, great and small, cast about for suitable grazing land and often turned their own arable into pasture. This caused a shortage of corn and a surplus of labour. Some great landlords raised rents so steeply that many tenants were forced out and the land, thus returned to the owner, became useful grazing land. In parts of the country, particularly the south-western counties, the common fields and land of the villages were forcibly enclosed. Although little arable land was taken in this way,[*] this was the real beginning of the enclosures and the subsequent enclosure acts which caused such misery in the eighteenth century.

[*] Enclosures in a very minor way began early in the thirteenth century. But in the Tudor era Henry VII passed two anti-enclosure acts in 1489, while in 1515 Cardinal Wolsey tried to enforce anti-enclosure legislation.

'Shepe in mine opinion is the mooste profytablest cattell any man can have,'[8] writes Master Fitzherbert in 1534. They were indeed profitable for those who had or could acquire enough land, but they spelled ruin for those who had not and could not. This change-over from mixed to sheep farming affected not only the national economy but also the 'look' of the countryside. Much arable land was no longer rich with corn and the changing colours of the seasons but was now pasture, clouded with sheep. As less wheat was grown there was a consequent rise in the price of bread. Sheep require less labour than does mixed farming, so unemployment rose. Villages could grow less of their own food, so villagers did without. By 1549 John Hales, in his *Discourses of the Common Weal*, was laying much of the blame for the economic troubles of the time on an over-emphasis on sheep-rearing. He believed that if one half of sheep ground, pasture and waste were turned into arable land there would be enough work for everyone and the price of food would come down. If, on the other hand, the 'insaciable ship pastures'[9] were allowed to continue encroaching on new ground we should never again have cheap food. He advocated, among other things, that for every eight sheep there should be one acre of tillage. Ahead of his time, he also wanted to see marshes drained and moors cleared.

In the *Decaye of England* (a decay which it was believed was due to over population of sheep) this problem is set out in a six-line 'proverb' which runs:

> The more shepe, the dearer is the woll,
> The more shepe, the dearer is the mutton,
> The more shepe, the dearer is the beefe,
> The more shepe, the dearer is the corne,
> The more shepe, the skanter is the white meat,
> The more shepe, the fewer egges for a peny.[10]

Eggs at that time, mid century, were four a penny.

Modern economists are not agreed that the great development of sheep farming was the primary cause of the inflation which set in around 1530, but inflation is inflation to the average person, no matter what its cause. It expresses itself in daily life by a rise in prices (which was not then offset by a rise in wages), and this results in a lowering of the standard of living – fewer clothes, less food, in some cases eviction and in all cases misery. That the rural poor saw enclosures and sheep farming as the sole cause of their plight was only natural, for to them land meant everything. In 1534 English farmers were forbidden to own more than 2,000 sheep, in an attempt to prevent further enclosures of common land and the loss of arable. To lose their own bit of grazing land meant the rural poor did not even have 'white meat' for their families.

'White meat' is what we now call dairy produce: milk, cream, butter, 'cruds' and whey. These had once been eaten by all classes but, as the sixteenth century grew older and so many people became rich, white meat began to be looked down upon as inferior food – chiefly, one thinks, because it was much eaten by 'inferior' people. By this piece of snobbery – and food snobberies and taboos die hard – the rich did themselves out of a good source of protein, calcium and Vitamin A. Harrison bears this out when he says 'white meats, milk, butter and cheese' which were 'wont to be accounted of as one of the chief stays throughout these islands, are now reputed as food appertinent only to the inferior sort, whilst such as are more wealthy do feed upon the flesh of all kinds of cattle accustomed to be eaten, all sorts of fish taken upon our coasts and in our fresh rivers, and such diversity of wild and tame fowls as are either bred in our island or brought over unto us from other countries of the main.'[11]

Cheese was of three kinds: hard, soft and green. Hard, made of skimmed milk, kept well, became even harder with keeping and was not eaten by the rich, although a staple in the diet of the poor. Soft cheese was made of whole milk or nearly whole milk and was matured for a short time before being eaten. This was a cream cheese and went to the noble or manor house if cheese was wanted (it was used in cooking). Green cheese was fresh curd cheese. It was not fully pressed out but shaped and stood upon straws or a bed of nettles to drain. Sometimes it was known as nettle cheese. Herbs were often added to a green cheese, and when this was done the cheese was called 'spermese'. Another curdled dish was junket, made of cream and rennet and set out to dry in small baskets made of rush – *jonquette* is the Old Norman French word for a rush basket. Frequently honey or sugar and rosewater were added, which made a delicious and very rich sweet.

The 'flesh of all kinds of cattle' included beef, veal, pork, lamb and mutton served in an astonishing variety of ways. There were far fewer haunches of venison and sides of beef than we like to think. The pot, rather than the spit, was the most used culinary implement in every household; every kitchen was equipped with pots great and small, choppers, pestles and mortars and mincing knives. Soups, broths, pottages, stews, hashes and ragoûts were all much favoured and eaten with a spoon. Guests brought their own spoons to a feast – apostle spoons were favoured by the rich – and people always travelled with their own spoons as a necessary part of their equipment. To go spoonless was, almost, to go hungry. Forks were scarcely known; nor were they needed, as many dishes using meat or poultry – rabbit for some reason counted as poultry – were pounded and, if that did not do the job, were passed through a coarse sieve. 'Blanch mange' was extremely popular, but it was not like ours. It was made of poultry pounded and boiled with rice and milk of almonds and sweetened with honey or sugar. A pinch of sandalwood turned it pink.

Food was often perfumed too, 'a custom borrowed from French cuisine, where it enjoyed a great vogue . . . It was never carried to the same lengths in England, nor was the range of scents employed so wide. The exotic musk and ambergris were added only occasionally to the foods of the well-to-do. But rosewater was ubiquitous, called for in sweet confections of every kind: cakes, puddings, creams and bakemeats.'[12]

'Mortrews' were greatly liked, and it will be remembered that Chaucer's cook who made 'blankmanger . . . with the beste'[13] could also roast, broil, fry and 'maken mortreaux, and wel bake a pye'.[14] Mortrews were made by pounding flesh, fowl or fish with other ingredients all together in a mortar, then mixing them with the yolk of eggs and 'poudre fort' (a mixture of hot spices). This

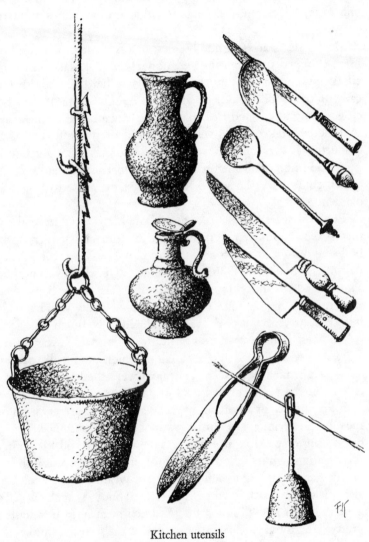

Kitchen utensils

was then boiled, presumably in a bag in a cauldron. The cauldron, a great lidded pot on three legs, was used to cook many things at one time, all carefully arranged within, rather like a modern pressure cooker.

'Bucknade' graced all good tables; it was made of any kind of meat chopped into thumb-sized gobbets with raisins, almonds, cinnamon and sugar – sugar was new, was hard and coarse and came in ten-pound loaves (it cost 8d. a pound in 1546) – onions, cloves, ginger, salt and rice, all pounded together and thickened with flour, then coloured yellow with saffron. Food had to be as colourful as everything else, and brilliant colours were given to it by the addition of alkanet, red sandal, mulberry juice and saffron, which could vary the yellow from palest primrose to brightest dandelion.

'Pumpes' were excellent fare – although we would call them meat-balls – and were usually made of lean and tender pork, boiled and minced fine together with cloves, mace and raisins of Corinth, and all rolled into small pellets. Over these was poured a sauce made of almond milk and rice flour, the whole being then strewn with sugar and mace. Pumpes could equally well be made with beef or veal, but pork was considered to be much superior.

'Allowes' were slices of beef or mutton upon which was spread a dressing or stuffing made of shredded onions, egg yolk, parsley and spices mixed with suet. The slices were then rolled up and either spit-roasted or grilled on a gridiron.

In the absence of any form of refrigeration, the preservation of meat both in winter and summer was of great importance. Heavy dry-salting or pickling in brine was the usual method for winter preservation, while light dry-salting or dipping the meat in brine or vinegar was thought sufficient for hot weather. In dry-salting, Bay salt with a touch of saltpetre was used, but too much saltpetre gave the meat an odd taste, though much meat must have tasted pretty odd anyway. Meat, after salting, was also often smoked in the kitchen or in the main room of a small house, where it could be hung from the rafters, which indicates how smoky such rooms must have been. When preserved meat was to be eaten it had to be 'seethed' for hours in water to which bran or hay had been added to help eliminate the salt. After this it could be fudged up, probably in a pottage of some sort.

Pottage was eaten everywhere and by all classes. Since it could be almost anything from a handful of tough old roots boiled in water to a superior meat stew thickened with oatmeal, bread-crumbs, eggs or rice – rice was imported from Italy along with spices and was only for the rich – it fitted the pocket, if not the stomach, of all kinds and conditions of people.

There was an enormous diversity about pottages. They were not all broth, gruel or thick stew; there is one which sounds very much like scrambled egg. This was called 'Hanoney' and was made by putting egg whites and yolks through a strainer, and shredding onions small and frying them in butter or grease. The eggs were then added and stirred in and the mixture allowed to fry for a short time. When ready it was served forth 'on a fayre disshe'.[15]

The less rich or the more economically minded often pieced out a meal with a nice dish of garbage – which sounds a trifle grue-some but isn't. Garbage was merely the name given to the giblets of fowl and the offal of animals. These were chopped and stewed, then thickened with bread and well spiced with mace and pepper. Meat seems always to have been eaten very highly spiced or sweetened, or both. The spicing was doubtless first used to disguise the taste of tainted meat – and meat was often tainted, particularly in summer, despite efforts to preserve it. Then prob-ably the taste of spices became the accustomed taste and meat, even when fresh, must have seemed flat and unpalatable if left unspiced. Sweetened meat sounds rather horrid, yet we still eat jellies and fruit sauces with certain meats, game and fowl.

Fowl, wild and domestic, was plentiful. There were pheasant, partridge – the last, perhaps, because 'it doth augment carnal lust'[16] – plover, pigeons, heron, bustard, tit-mice and wrens, larks and quail (we imported these from Flanders), crane and stork (where the stork came from I cannot say), bittern, shoveller, moorcock, moorhen and woodcock. In quantity were domestic birds – ducks, geese, capon, chickens, swan and peacock. Served whole, this last was a festal dish, but its wholeness was more apparent than real. The bird was first carefully skinned, feathers and all, the neck and head preserved intact, and the flesh was then cooked and minced fine or pounded, cooked and stuffed back into the skin. Neck, head and legs were then added in the right places and the bird looked magnificent, particularly with a bit of lighted camphor flaming in its gilded beak – sometimes the whole bird was gilded. This splendid piece was always carried in to a feast on a handsome charger.

The variety of fish of which Harrison speaks was abundantly eaten. Fast days and Lent saw to that. Sturgeon, whiting, roach, dab, thornback, cod and herring – these last two were chronic salt fish in winter – perch, gudgeon, turbot, pike and, sometimes, dolphin. Henry Machyn tells us in his diary that on 10 August 1552 three dolphin were taken in the Thames between Greenwich and Woolwich; one was sent to the king (Edward VI) and the other two to the market in Fish Street. Then there were smelt, trout, salmon – also to be found in the Thames – mackerel, bream, skate, flounder, hake, lamprey, and eels. Eels, it was believed, were so fond of music that they would swim bemused into the nets of singing fishermen. Shellfish, such as oysters, whelks, cockles, shrimps and crabs, were also eaten. So was porpoise when it could be had.

Porpoise was very special. It was now usually served whole – porpoise pudding had had its vogue in the previous century – and was 'entranched' by a special officer and eaten with mustard. In 1509, at a great feast given by Wolsey, a young porpoise (cost, 8s.) was served, and also strawberries and cream. Traditionally, Wolsey is credited with having made the combination of strawberries and cream fashionable. These were, of course, wild strawberries, and certainly by mid century they must have been grown in profusion, as they were sold in the London streets at a controlled price per pot. In fact in 1552 a man called Grege and an unnamed woman were 'on the pelere at Chepe-syde' because Grege, and probably his companion, had sold 'potts of straberries, the wyche pott was not alff fulle, but fylled with forne [fern]'.[17] Proclamations regulating the weight and price of food were fairly frequent and, later in the year which found Grege in the pillory, meat prices were fixed. Best beef, mutton and veal were pegged at 1¼d. the pound, necks and legs at ¾d. and best lamb at 8d. the quarter.

Oysters were cheap and plentiful – 4d. a bushel in 1491 – and were nearly always served cooked. There were many ways of doing this, some very complicated, some simple. A popular simple recipe, Oysters in Bastard Gravy, called for large oysters. The liquid was poured off them and mixed with ale and water; bread crumbs were then added and the mixture well seasoned with ginger, powdered pepper, salt, saffron and sugar. This witches' brew was well boiled and towards the end the oysters were added to it. The dish was then ready to be 'served forth'!

'Bastard' had no pejorative meaning then; on the contrary, it meant 'sweet and spiced'. Bastard was a sweet wine in its own right, but the name was also used for a wine of any sort sweetened with honey, sugar and spices. Wine was drunk in quantity. It was usually imported, although inferior wines were made at home. Good wines came from Guienne, Anjou and Poitou. Osney was a favourite sweet wine from Alsace. Compolet was another favourite; so was Romney from Hungary. Malmsey, much drunk, came from Napoli de Malvasia in the Morea. Verney was another sweet white wine and Mount Rose, a red wine from Gascony, was thought excellent. Algrave came from Crete, though whether it was a retsina I cannot discover. Antioch was made from grapes growing along the banks of the Orontes and Clare, or Clary, a favourite, was a kind of claret. Piment was a sour, thin wine sweetened with honey, and there was also a new drink, sack.

Sack began to be popular when, in the early years of the century, privileges were given to English merchants by the Duke of Medina Sidonia, allowing them to ship wines from Jerez. It is a melancholy thing to realize that in 1515 sack and claret each cost 8d. a gallon and that many bought these wines by the tun

(252 gallons) at a time. In 1556, when the Lady Anne of Cleves moved into a house in Blackfriars, among the wines bought to furnish her cellar were three hogsheads of 'Gascoyne' at £3 'the tonne'. There were also ten gallons of Malmsey at 20d. the gallon, eleven gallons of Muscadel at 2s. 2d. the gallon and 'Sacke, tenne gallons at xvid the gallon'.[18] By the end of the century sack had become a most popular drink, although in 1600 Dr William Vaughan warned in his *Directions for Health* that 'sacke doth make men fat and foggy'. Nevertheless, he also allows that it 'comforteth the spirits marvellously'. Hippocras, which usually ended a feast, was a red wine spiced with ginger, long pepper and grains of paradise. The Privy Purse accounts of Henry VII contain the following item for 10 November 1496: 'To Piers Barbour for spices for ypocras 6s. 8d.' The spices undoubtedly cost more than the wine.

Ale was drunk as freely as we drink water, which was just as well, as most water was polluted. It was the common breakfast drink of all classes and ages and came in various strengths. Here it should be noted that the court of Henry VIII was considered (by foreigners, of course) to be the most dissolute in Europe and that it had in particular a reputation for drunkenness – even among the Germans! But ale was the typically English drink, and a popular early drinking song of eight stanzas shows this. In it the singers state that they prefer ale to food, and each chorus ends with the refrain: 'And [or 'But'] bring us good Ale.' For example, they don't want brown bread, for that is 'mad of brane', which means only that it is made of bran. Eggs are unwanted because of too many shells. Butter contains, horrid thought, too many hairs. Bacon is too fat, and pig's flesh lets us in for some ham-fisted humour with 'for it will make us bores'.[19]

Beer was almost unknown until the beginning of the sixteenth century and very little was brewed in this country. The idea of adding bitter herbs, partly hops (though sweet herbs were used), to ale was regarded with great suspicion as being a form of sophistication, and thus charges of adulteration with hops were made. Henry VIII tried unsuccessfully to prevent the use of hops imported from the Low Countries* and forbade his own brewer to use either hops or brimstone. Beer, first brewed in London by Flemings and the Dutch, was a new and suspect drink and it took a good 150 years from the time of its introduction before it became popular with the masses. Beer made from barley ultimately replaced ale because it kept better, hops having a preservative action. Hop-less ale would not keep for more than a few days in hot weather unless brewed very strong. It was probably, therefore, much easier to get drunk on ale during the summer months than in the winter, and beer would have been considered poor stuff.

At a feast, dinner began with the guests washing their hands at a 'ewerie', a sideboard furnished with basins and ewers. The lord and master washed his in a separate basin brought him by a cup-bearer (the water had been previously tested to make sure it wasn't poisoned). The chief pantler then tasted the bread and salt. This tasting for poison always took place in royal households and began in the kitchen. Once a dish was ready to leave the royal kitchen it was tasted and immediately covered before being sent to the king's table. Even so, it was tasted again upon arrival in the room where the king was dining, just to be sure no one had lifted the cover and popped some poison in *en route*. Tasting was also the practice in the households of those great noblemen who were the sovereign's ministers of state. Lesser and non-office-holding nobility could dispense with this, although it may probably have been used on ritual or great occasions purely as a symbol.

In medieval and early Tudor times the pantler's chief duty was to cut and shape the trenchers of bread from which people ate. Trencher bread was made of wholemeal flour and the loaf, which was four days old, was cut into thick slices which sopped up the juice or gravy of the firmer meats – soupy ones were served in bowls. In rich houses these messy but nutritious slices were

---

* Hop cultivation was not understood in England then, but in 1549 hop-setters were brought over to teach English farmers how to grow them. By 1557 Tusser gives the farmer much information on this subject.

collected up after use and distributed to the poor. In lesser homes diners ate both food and trencher. Early in the sixteenth century wooden trenchers were slipped under the trencher bread, and these soon began to replace bread. Wood was subsequently ousted by pewter, and in rich homes by gold or silver.

When the dishes for the first course were placed upon dressers and sideboards the sewer (server), an early kind of *maître d'hôtel*, saw that these were tasted – not for flavour but for poison – before being served. If they were declared safe the carver began his operations on those dishes which needed his expert skill. Carvers may possibly have had to know all the carving terms, as set out in Wynken de Worde's *Boke of Kervynge*, although such terms as 'break that deer', 'lesche that brawn', 'rear that goose', 'sauce that capon', spoil that hen', 'unbrace that mallard', 'unlace that coney', 'disfigure that peacock', 'string that lamprey', 'chine that salmon' and 'side that haddock' may have been meant as instructions to the cook to suggest what he should do to meat, fowl or fish before or after cooking. Nevertheless, the carver certainly had to know all the 'fumosities' (inferior parts) of fish, flesh and fowl. These were the legs, heads, sinews and crops, which were never offered to the lord and his guests. Further, the carver always placed the meat on the king's trencher so that the sovereign did not have to fish it out of a dish with his fingers as other lesser mortals did. Men who wore daggers found them useful for spearing meat out of the dish and putting it upon their own trenchers or even, gallantly, first spearing a choice bit for a lady.

After each dish had been sent to the high table, it was sent down to the next-ranking table. Such dishes were known as 'the reward', as they were awarded from above. The remains of a feast were the perquisites of servants and, it is said, were called 'manners', which in this case can only mean 'custom' or 'usage'. There were good or bad manners according to the amount left, and it was apparently bad manners to clear one's trencher.★

★ This sounds like a Victorian invention. I can find no evidence for it earlier than that in J. C. Jeaffreson's *A Book About the Table* (1875), and he does not cite his authority.

When the wine came round, which it did very swiftly and frequently, the cup-bearer took the cup from the butler, poured a few drops into the cover, tasted it and gave it to his lord. Whenever the lord drank the cup-bearer had to hold the upturned cover under the cup to catch the drips. Slobbery drinkers must have caused a cup-bearer much trouble. Such offices as that of cup-bearer, carver and server were by no means menial, and members of the nobility held such positions in royal households. In 1526, for example, cup-bearers to King Henry were the Earl of Surrey, Lord William Howard and Sir Francis Bryan. Carvers were Lord Neville and Lord Clifton, and sewers Lord Thomas Gray, Sir Percival Hart and Sir Edward Warner. In addition to the server's usual tasks he, together with the master cook and the king's physician, had to determine the daily menus for the royal board.

The master cook of the sovereign was a man of considerable

Pewter jugs, cup, pricket-candlestick and earthenware charcoal burner

standing and possessions, whilst stewards and butlers were among the most trusted officers; eventually their offices became, like others, titular and honorary.

Yet as late as 1547, when the Marshal of France, Francis de Sceppeaux, Sire de Vieilleville, dined with the new young king Edward VI and the Duke of Somerset, he found the English custom whereby noblemen waited upon the king quite extraordinary. At this dinner they were served by knights of the Order of the Garter, headed by the Grand Master. All were bareheaded, all bore dishes, and upon reaching the king's table all fell to their knees. As they knelt, the Grand Master took the dishes from them to present to the king. Extraordinary as this custom seemed to the Marshal, he found English cooking even more so. He much preferred French, for by that date the French were already famous gastronomically. Good cooking had spread to France from Italy but stopped there, not daring to risk the Channel-crossing.

The office of sewer was, however, dying out in great houses by the beginning of the sixteenth century, and only at great feasts, such as that given by Edward VI, did noblemen undertake this duty. Yet the king, when he dined privately in his antechamber, was always served by bareheaded and kneeling retainers and strict ceremonial was observed. This custom seems to have been followed when dining privately by all the Tudor sovereigns throughout the whole century.

Dinner proper began with a salad, raw or cooked and dressed with oil, vinegar and salt. Although vegetables as such do not figure to any great extent or in any variety in meals of the time, far more herbs – and these included vegetables – were used in salads than we now use. Among these were the following: onions, leeks, garlic, turnip, winter cress, rocket, tarragon, succory, dandelion leaves, endive, 'lettuce of the garden' (as well as wild lettuce), beet-leaves and roots, spinach, orach, dock leaves, sorrel, purslane, rampion root, samphire ('dreadful trade'), water cress, water pimpernel, borage, bugloss leaves and hop buds. A good number of salad crops were also imported from the Low Countries.

After the salad came the first course which might run to as many as thirty dishes, including several sweet dishes at the end of it. This was followed by a second course of the same size or larger, but this course ended with rather grander sweets: tarts, custards, pies, cakes, jellies, in fantastic moulds, 'rapers' (made of figs and raisins boiled in wine) and various other things made from violets, primroses and roses, to say nothing of rich creams and fritters.

'Leche Lumbarde' seems to have been a long-standing favourite in the sweet line. One recipe for this calls for stoned dates – we imported dates, raisins, figs and prunes – first boiled in sweet wine, then brayed in a mortar and subsequently put through a strainer with a little white wine and sugar. This was then put into a pot and cooked until the moisture had all but evaporated. Next it was put on a board and ginger and cinnamon were added and kneaded into the dates. The final result was shaped by the hands into a square or oblong and cut into slices – 'leche' means 'slice' – and was served with a syrup made of sweetened red wine poured over it.

'Marchpane' was another old favourite, and an early recipe calls for two pounds of blanched almonds beaten fine in a stone mortar. To this was added two pounds of sugar, also beaten fine, and two or three spoonsful of rosewater. When the mixture became, after much pounding, a fine, pliable paste it was thinned down with a rolling pin and laid on a bottom of wafer paste (a fine, thin cake-mixture) slightly larger than the piece of marchpane; the edges of the underlying wafer were then turned up around the marchpane and the whole thing was baked. When ready it was iced with sugar and rosewater and then put back into the oven to dry off. When dry and cool it could be garnished with pretty conceits such as birds and beasts which had been made in moulds and then painted with (one hopes) vegetable colouring. Or the cake could be gilded and decorated with small biscuits, comfits and caraway seeds. Marchpane was often as decorative as it was delicious.

The dinner ended with an after-course or 'voider'. This consisted of wafers, fruit – fresh and dried – and cheese, and it was usual to serve cheese with fruit, nuts, raisins and Hippocras. After all this the diners were probably too inebriated or too surfeited to move.

Not surprisingly, we hear a good deal about the evils of surfeiting and 'Replecion' from Andrew Boorde, who gives a small dissertation upon the effects of over-eating and over-drinking. He tells his readers that when the stomach is stuffed with meat and drink the liver, which provides the fire under the pot, cannot cook the pot's contents, thus digestion is prevented. When digestion fails, horrid things can, and do, happen: the tongue can no longer speak, the wits or senses are 'obnebulated' [*sic*]; sloth, sluggishness and headache follow and sometimes 'the malt-worm plays the devil', so that all the world 'runs about on wheels'.[20]

At two feasts, at least, the world must have remained fairly stationary. One was a dinner for fifty members of the Worshipful Company of Salters given in London in 1506. The bill of fare shows that they had but one kilderkin (eighteen gallons) of ale at a cost of 2s. 3d., three and a half gallons of Gascony wine at 2s. 4d. and a single bottle of 'Muscadine', which cost 8d., among the lot. Leaving aside that miserable one bottle, this meant roughly three pints of ale and one half-pint of wine a head, which seems hardly calculated to breed the malt-worm.

As to surfeiting, who can say? The fifty Salters got through thirty-six chickens at a cost of 4s. 5d., or roughly 1½d. a bird. There were also: one swan and seven geese at 7s.; nine rabbits at 1s. 4d.; four breasts of veal at 1s. 5d.; two 'rumps of beef tails' at 2d.; six quail, which cost 1s. 6d., or 3d. each, a good deal more expensive than chicken and, considering their size, no cause of surfeit. Bread cost 1s., whilst two dishes of butter came to 4d. Bacon – we do not know the quantity – 6d. Then there were fifty eggs at 2½d., which is less than three farthings a dozen. A gallon of curds cost 4d. and a gallon of gooseberries 2d. Cherries and tart came to 8d. – the presence of gooseberries and cherries suggest that this feast was held in June or July – and perfume cost 2d. All this, together with other essentials such as herbs, saffron, spices, sugar, verjuice, vinegar, water (at 3d.), coal, faggots and the amount paid to the cook (3s. 4d.), totalled £1 13s. 2½d. No named vegetables appear on the bill of fare but they may have been included under the heading 'herbs'.

Neither do they appear, individually, on the menu of the second dinner. This was one chosen and given fifty-two years later by the Master and Wardens of the Stationers' Company, which had been incorporated in 1556, and it took place on 5 July 1558. We do not know how many people were present but we do know that they drank a stand of ale – probably thirty-two gallons – which cost 2s., so ale had gone down in price. They also had a barrel of beer (36 gallons) which cost 4s. 8d. and a pottle (half-gallon) of muscadel at 1s. 4d., plus twelve gallons of a nameless wine at 16s. They ate two dozen chickens at 9s. 4d., or roughly 4½d. each, so chickens had nearly trebled in price in the intervening half-century. Other items of food had risen accordingly. Twelve capons cost £1 6s., seven geese, 9s. 4d.; two rounds of sturgeon were 8s., and two breasts of veal 4s. 8d., that is, 2s. 4d. a breast, as opposed to the 4½d. paid by the Salters. A sirloin of beef came to 2s. 2d. and an unspecified number of eggs were 5d. Two necks of mutton cost 1s., four rabbits, 1s. 4d. – the Salters had paid 1s. 4d. for nine. Gooseberries cost 4d. and 'orynges' the same amount. Oranges by this date were fairly widely known but back in 1496 they cannot have been, for on 12 February of that year King Henry VII paid 'to a Portingale for oringes 6s. 8d.';[21] in the time of the first Tudor it seems that only the very rich could afford oranges.

It is perhaps interesting to note in passing that it was customary for the sovereign to receive all kinds of gifts from all degrees of people at all times of year, and that it was customary to 'reward', that is, tip, the servant or person who brought the gift. Thus the 6s. 8d. paid by Henry VII was probably a reward, not a price. The giving of food to the sovereign was a very popular custom and we find in the Privy Purse Expenses of Henry VIII that he was frequently given, among other things, cheese, sturgeon, cake – the Provost of Eton seems to have been peculiarly addicted to giving cake – medlars, lampreys, lamprey pie, pomegranates, apples, pears, grapes, dates, capon, chicken, deer, buck, doe, oranges, figs, to say nothing of 'Brawne and podings'[22] sent him by the Lady Wesyon, whose servant was 'rewarded' 4s. 4d.

To return, however, to our dinner, in addition to the major items there were some small items for which charges were made – marigolds, lavender, flowers and roses. The lavender may have been used for strewing, but the other flowers were probably not used for decoration but made into confections. Then there was the cost of coal, cherries, verjuice, vinegar, suet, spices, currants, prunes, flour and wafers, plus 5d. paid to the cook and his man for dressing the dinner, 4s. to the butler, who was obviously kept busy, and a further 14s. to a 'scrivener' – just why one does not know. The total cost of this dinner was £10 1s. There seems to have been less food in proportion to the amount of drink at this feast than at the one given by the Salters, so very possibly some of the guests may have found their wits and senses rather 'obnubilated'.

Much less grand and probably more fun in a simple way was the supper Henry Machyn ate with several friends at the home of Mistress Lentall, widow, at 'enley-a-pon-Temes'. When Henry and his friends had supped, in came a dozen masked men and women who sang and capered about while Mistress Lentall saw to it that 'a great tabull of bankett'[23] was prepared with dishes of fruit, spices, marmalade, gingerbread, jelly, comfits and many other sweets. Again, a year or so later, Henry notes with telling wit that 'Monser the Machyn de Henry'[24] and a number of friends ate half a bushel of oysters in the cellar of two of these friends, Masters Gytton and Smythe. They apparently used hogsheads for tables and accompanied the oysters with onions! They drank 'red ale', claret, muscadel, Malmsey – all at seven o'clock in the morning. Doubtless the world whirled on wheels after that.

To produce food, in no matter what quantity, takes space and cooking utensils. In great houses a mere kitchen and scullery were totally insufficient even for the needs of the family alone and its retainers. Kitchens, of course, varied in size, and in royal palaces as in very large houses there was sure to be more than one fire-place for cooking; there would be one for spit-roasting, another for boiling and stewing, and yet another for cake and pastry making. Spits of all sizes were used, from the very slender ones on which small birds were roasted to large heavy ones used for roasting a whole lamb or a side of beef. Each spit, when in use, had a long pan placed under it to catch the fat. Spits were turned by hand by a kitchen boy; in 1487 Lambert Simnel, the impostor, was given a job by Henry VII as a turnspit in the royal kitchens where, said Polydore Vergil writing in 1489, he 'is alive today'.*[25]

Dogs were also trained to turn spits; they were short-legged animals which were set within a 'dog-wheel' connected by an 'endless rope' to another wheel at the end of the spit. Hot coals were at first laid at the feet of the wretched animals to keep them running, so that they were soon conditioned to run within the wheel without the incentive of getting away from the coals. Whips were also used to keep them moving. Mastiff power was used to raise water from wells; the ass does not seem to have been allotted this task until the seventeenth century.

Pots of various shapes, sizes and kinds were numerous, from the large cauldron which stood on three legs to the hanging pot which swung from an adjustable chimney crane. Broilers or gridirons of different sizes were also used, as were kettles, skillets, ladles, and skimmers made of iron, brass or latten. In *The Names of All Kynd of Wares*, written about 1563 by Thomas Newberry, a travelling pedlar, crying his goods, chants that he has, among other things,

> . . . Ladels, Scummers, Anayrons and Spits
> Dryppynge pannes, pot hookes, ould Cats and Kits:
> And preaty fine dogs, without fleas or nits.
> What lacke you my friend? Come hither to me.[26]

He does not, however, mention those indispensable articles, pestles and mortars, some of which were made of stone, some of wood. There was also a wide variety of tubs, baskets and trays, to say nothing of choppers, mincers and dressing knives, as well as

* Simnel later became trainer of the king's hawks.

the 'pot-fork' or 'flesh-hook', that is, a long wooden handle to which a hook was fastened so that a piece of meat or a bag pudding could be fished out of the pot.

Kitchen and scullery were but two of the domestic offices; the other kitchen departments depended upon the size of the house. A brew-house and a bake-house, set apart from the main building, were essential in the country (though not in the city). For the rest, there was the pantry where, as the name suggests, bread was kept in large chests called arks, a ewery, a cellar, a buttery, to which wine was brought from the cellar and where the butler was the chief officer (all departments had separate heads), a spicery and a pitcher-house, where plate, cups and other silver vessels were kept. Often, if the house were vast, there would be a chaundry or candlery where the candles, tallow and wax were stored. The consumption of candles in great houses or in the sovereign's palace must have been enormous. In addition to these offices were the wafery, catering for delicacies such as sweets, and the saucery and napery.

The napery held tablecloths and napkins, and it is doubtful if either of these were very clean. Laundering, even if there was a laundry as part of the house, was a difficult and lengthy process and the age was not noted for an over-nicety in such things as clean linen for tables or bodies – or cleanliness in anything much else for that matter. Wooden trenchers were, as we have seen, now common, and they were kept clean between the various dishes served to the diners, who used a piece of bread as a mop. Drinking vessels were of wood, leather, horn, pewter and, for the rich, silver, silver gilt and gold. A very small amount of glass for drinking from was imported from Venice, but this too was in reach of only the very rich. Table-ware for ordinary folk was usually of wood and sold by the 'garnish', or set. A garnish comprised twelve platters, twelve dishes or trenchers and twelve saucers which, as the name implies, were used for sauces. Pewter vessels were sold by the pound, but were often hired out, probably to those who were giving a 'special occasion' dinner where the old wooden table-ware just would not do, or for which they hadn't

Pottery and pewter plate

enough of their own pewter to go round. Respectable families of the middling sort had both wooden and pewter-ware with, perhaps, a not too intricately designed silver standing-cup to be used by the head of the household on great occasions.

The rich and the royal – particularly the royal – seem to have had an incredible amount of silver plate, and Tudor monarchs, especially Henry VII and Henry VIII, appear to have had as great a predilection for silver as they had for jewels. 'The amount of extant plate made from the accession of Henry VIII through the short intervening reigns of Edward VI and Mary until the death of Elizabeth I (1603),' says Mr Gerald Taylor, 'exceeds by far that from the entire Middle Ages.'[27]

Silver was displayed and used in quantity in every noble household. A most important piece was the Nef, a silver ship completely rigged which held the royal – or the host's – napkin and cutlery. Standing cups and covers, elaborately wrought and jewelled; stemmed flat *tazze*; covered and uncovered mazers; magnificent salts and spice boxes; ewers, chargers, spoons by the dozen – apostle, seal or maiden-topped – these were all part of rich table-ware. Cardinal Wolsey's collection of silver, silver gilt and gold plate absolutely stunned foreigners and was said to exceed that owned by the king – a most dangerous exhibition of riches, as it turned out. New Year's gifts to the sovereign from relatives and nobles often took the form of silver – or money. On 1 January 1556/7 Queen Mary received from the Lord Cardinal (her cousin Reginald Pole) a salt with a silver-gilt cover set with a stone, presumably precious. It was also 'much enamyled',[28] with the edifying story of Job. The Dowager Countess of Oxford

Silver gilt salt and cup; drinking horn

presented a gilt salt with a pepper box, Sir Francis Englefields a silver spice box gilded and ornamented with a stone. Anne of Cleves, possibly more realistically, gave her step-daughter £20, but Lord Windsor presented two cruets of crystal garnished with silver and gilt.

One Henry Mills on this same day presented the queen with a most curious assortment of gifts: hose, waistcoats, perfumed gloves, a desk covered with crimson velvet, a 'cyttern', a glass of 'aqua compossata', a fire shovel, a box with a picture of Christ, two bolts of cambric, a little looking glass, 'two perfumers of silver with perfume in them',[29] a bottle of rosewater, a loaf of sugar, cinnamon and nutmeg 'in papers', pots of marmalade, a spiced cake, pots of green ginger and several partridges. But Henry, it seems, was a grocer – no doubt a member of the Grocers' Company – which means he was a wholesale dealer, trader or merchant. Perhaps his gifts were made on behalf of the Company or perhaps Henry enjoyed, or hoped to enjoy, the patronage of the queen.

All in all, gift-giving and great hospitality seem to have been characteristic of the Tudor period – particularly hospitality, although in many instances, especially if one lived in the country, hospitality was thrust upon one. Guests were frequent and they did not stay merely for dinner or supper, they often stayed for days on end. This was due to the small number of roads and their bad condition, the deficiency of transport, the scarcity of inns and, from the Dissolution onwards, the lack of monasteries, which in almost every locality had provided accommodation for travellers. So when any personage travelled throughout the country – and only the rich (apart from beggars) did – he had to plan his route so that he and his entourage could stay with friends or acquaintances on the way. Obviously some outstayed their welcome or were unwelcome in the first place, for we have an amusing medieval 'recipe' relating to dining which suggests how to get rid of the unwanted.

The host could induce his guest to wipe his hands and face with a wet napkin impregnated with powdered vitriol and gall – the guest then turned black. Or three hours before dinner he could be cheered with a cup of wine laced with belladonna which would, it seems, give him all the symptoms of lockjaw. Or at dinner his meat could be cunningly strewn with wake-robin which would 'bite his mouth' and 'skin his tongue' and make him 'gape like a fool'.[30] A fourth way was to smear his knife and napkin with colocynth which 'imparted a filthy and abominable taste to whatever he ate'.[31] Or the unwanted one's cup could be anointed with a mucilage made of syrup of figs and gum tragacanth which caused it to stick to his lips and was sure to get rid of him – which sounds very doubtful. If all these failed, however, as a last resort the host could speed his non-departing guest by making all the dishes at dinner look utterly repulsive by sprinkling them with a powder made of the dried blood of horses and small pieces of cat-gut, for 'if you cut harp strings small', says Baptista Porta, 'and strew them on hot flesh, the heat will twist them like worms.'[32]

Whether these simple and relatively harmless methods were still in use in guest-ridden Tudor households I do not know. They are all, however – bar the belladonna – of the practical joke variety, and we do know that our Tudor ancestors loved practical jokes.

CHAPTER FIVE

Of Physic

There was another enemy on the field of Bosworth that August day in 1485 when Henry of Richmond defeated King Richard III. This enemy, invisible, unfightable and hitherto unknown, swooped down upon the victorious army and decimated it. Some soldiers died within a few hours, some within a day. The attacker against the armed but helpless force was the Sweating Sickness, otherwise known as *Sudor Anglicus* or 'the English Sweat'; the emphasis is on the adjective, as this disease which has puzzled medical historians for centuries, no less than it puzzled the medical men of the time, was peculiar to England. It made its first appearance here[*] among Henry's soldiers after the battle which won him the kingdom, and spread so rapidly all over the country that it delayed his coronation. Holinshed notes, although he does not mention where the outbreak first occurred, that in this year 'a new kind of sickness invaded suddenlie the people of this land, passing through the same from the one end to the other ... being so sharpe and deadlie that the like was never heard of to anie mans remembrance before that time'.[1] Polydore Vergil says that it swept the city and was a 'baleful affliction and one which no previous age had experienced'; he adds that of all the affected 'scarcely one in a hundred escaped death',[2] which sounds improbable. He also claims it came over with Henry's troops, but gives no evidence of this. Vergil, writing well after the event,

---

[*] There is some evidence that it broke out shortly after the landing at Milford Haven, but Professor S. B. Chrimes says: 'the sweat, or something like it, was known in York at an earlier date.' See his *Henry VII*, ch. 1, p. 40, n. 1.

says that this fever was a sign that Henry should reign only by the sweat of his brow.

The onset of this new disease was sudden and the symptoms were a sense of agitation and apprehension, violent shivering, vertigo and headache, followed by a high fever, abdominal pain and profuse sweating, sometimes accompanied by a vesicular rash; then came prostration and collapse. People literally fell dead in the streets and, as usual, it was widely believed that this affliction was a visitation of God's wrath upon an impious people – although there were those who held that a politically minded Lord was angry with the Tudors, and it was thus considered to be an ill omen for that upstart line. How else explain that the sickness had first broken out amongst Henry of Richmond's troops?

How else indeed? It is a question which still vexes us. It might be thought that the disease had come with Henry's soldiers from the continent, but there is no record of its having been known there. Furthermore, there were four more epidemics. One, in 1507, was not severe. Another, in 1517, was very severe and was accompanied by epidemics of measles, putrid throat (diphtheria) and plague. There was yet another in 1528 and then the final one in 1551 which began in Shrewsbury, where 900 people died within a few days. These epidemics all began during the summer months and were usually preceded by a very heavy rainfall, which has led some authorities to conclude that climate was a contributing factor. With the exception of the epidemic of 1528, all were confined to England. The 1528 epidemic was the most severe of all, with an extremely high mortality rate, and by 1529 it had spread to northern Europe. From Hamburg it travelled to Germany, the Netherlands and Scandinavian countries, and then on to Vienna, which was being besieged by the Turks. The English Sweat devastated the city and the army besieging it and then travelled to Italy but this, as far as we know, was the only time it touched Europe. England was its home and the English were its prey. It existed for sixty-six years, covering only the reigns of the Tudor kings. Then it vanished.

Just what it was is still unknown. Many authorities believe it to have been a type of miliary fever allied in some way to rheumatic fever. Others think it may have been a form of typhus, while still others suggest it may have been a virulent influenza. Possibly all that can be said is that it was some form of what we would now call a virus infection. But this does not explain the most curious feature of the sickness. Why, with but one exception, was it known only in England? Also, why did it disappear in 1551, never to be seen in England again? A possible answer to this last is that bacteria can change in character and become non-lethal as, in our own era, the streptococcus has.

Dr John Caius (1510–73), who was working in Shrewsbury when the last epidemic began there, wrote the first clinical monograph in the English language* on the subject. Published in 1552, *A Boke or Counseill Against the Disease Commonly Called the Sweate or Sweating Sickness* described symptoms and suggested causes and treatment. Dr Caius, one of the most famous scholars and medical men of his era, thought that contributory factors might be eating too much meat, wearing too many clothes and drinking too much 'cyder' – just why cider should be a culprit is difficult to understand. He advocated as treatment diet, bed-rest and strict hygiene – not that hygiene was a strong point with anyone at that time. Once in bed the victim was not to be allowed to sleep, for fear it should be his last one. Dr Caius's book would doubtless have been more useful had there ever been another outbreak of the sweating sickness but there was not, which was something neither he nor anyone else could foresee.

Other physicians had had to cope with the previous four epidemics and one of them, Andrew Boorde (1490?–1549), also advises, in his *Brevyary of Helthe*, that the patient should be put to bed and covered entirely, bar the face, and that there should be a fire in the room. Whether this was a fire to fight the fire of fever or whether the fire was for the purpose of getting rid of 'impure air' we do not know but, once the patient was smothered in bed, no food was to be given for twenty-four hours, while plenty of

* Published also in Latin, as *De ephemera britannica*, at Louvain in 1556.

ale and warm drinks (but no wine) should be sucked up through a swan's or a goose's quill. Someone had to hold the vessel which contained the drink, because not even the patient's hands were to be uncovered, and whoever performed this office had to beware of falling ill himself as 'it is a kind of plague'.[3] (Just how to 'beware' or take precautions against contagion is not stated.) Further, the patient ought to drink a sapphire or, what seems a trifle simpler, hold it in his hand. A powder made of three ounces of myrtle and rose leaves sprinkled on the sheets was also useful – probably more for combating the characteristic stench of the sweat than for anything else. Yet the same powder was also of great assistance if taken in ale.

The Sweating Sickness and other epidemics such as the earlier Black Death, recurrent smallpox and the new one, syphilis, were so dramatic in their effects that knowledge of these has become a part of history, as has the fact that physicians of the time were virtually helpless against such diseases. But what might be called run-of-the-mill ailments, although to us they bear strange names, were commonplace and were suffered by everyone. The rich had doctors to attend them – often attached to their households; the rest of the people, as doctors were very scarce, made do with wise women, quacks and 'empericks', those skilled in herbal lore, sorcerers and witches.

Medicine in England in early Tudor times was still much as it had been in the later Middle Ages, and much as it had been in Italy before the Renaissance. With the coming of the Renaissance, the initial impact on medicine of the new learning stimulated the discovery or re-discovery of original Greek writings on the subject, just as it had stimulated the re-discovery of Greek architectural proportions, so that the Gothic was succeeded in both medicine and architecture by the new classical (which did rather better by architecture). As the golden age of Greece was held to be the high point of civilization, when all was known, work on original medical texts was concerned chiefly with making pure translations, and thus became more of a literary exercise than a medical or scientific inquiry. For example, the re-translation of

Aristotle's *Metaphysics*★ merely brought about a revived interest in astrology, alchemy and the occult sciences. Physicians had to have a knowledge of astrology, or work closely with an astrologer, so astrology and medicine ranked equally as sciences.

Here one must go back rather a long way, for the knowledge of medicine in Europe came originally from the writings of Hippocrates (fifth century B.C.), Aristotle, and later Graeco-Roman physicians such as Dioscorides (*c.* A.D. 50), Celsus (first century A.D.) and Galen (130–200). Dioscorides, a physician in Nero's army, wrote a *Materia Medica* which was the leading textbook on pharmacology for sixteen centuries. Celsus, largely ignored in his own time, wrote *De medica* which during the Renaissance became the most influential of textbooks and was first printed in 1478. Galen, whose medical system, based on the Hippocratic collection, was theoretical, became most influential of all, but those Greek writers who came after him were 'imitators and abstractors and they mainly imitated and abstracted Galen at his worst'.⁴ Yet these men and their disciples were considered to be the source of all medical wisdom, and so it is hardly surprising that the practice of medicine had made little progress for more than a thousand years.

With the fall of the Roman Empire, Greek and Roman learning passed to the Arab world and to the Arab Empire and was preserved, but often in a debased form. There were, however, great Arab physicians too: Avicenna (980–1037) and Rhazes (865–923 or 932). Rhazes (Abu-Bakr Mohammed ibn Zakariya Ar-Razi) was the greatest physician of the Islamic world and also a philosopher, as many Arab physicians were. He wrote a treatise on smallpox and measles in which he carefully distinguishes between them. It became famous in Latin and various modern-language versions. His philosophical works have been neglected until the present century. Avicenna and Rhazes made original contributions to medical knowledge, and when the Arabs conquered southern Europe in the twelfth century all the

★ This is a composite treatise of different 'layers' of thought put together by later editors.

old Greek and Roman works were re-introduced, but mainly in faulty translations or transliterations. Arabic works had also been translated into Latin and thus, up to the Renaissance, medicine was based upon corrupt texts preserved by the Arabs, as well as upon Arab medicine.

Independent schools of medicine did spring up in Spain during this time (Córdoba in the twelfth century was the great seat of Arab learning) and several famous figures arose. Isaac Judaeus (845–940), who wrote a treatise on fevers which was available in the Middle Ages, and Averroës (1126–98), who wrote a complete handbook on medicine as well as works on astrology, were two such men, and their works on medical matters remained in use until the eighteenth century. Albucasis the Moor (eleventh century) left a textbook on surgery which became an important element in the revival of the subject in Italy and France. There was also in Italy the famous School of Salerno, which began in the eleventh century, but this was not independent as it came under the aegis of the Church – though not altogether, as some of the early Salernitan doctors were laymen and some, even, were women.

The influence of the Church on medicine stemmed from the fact that for six or seven centuries after the fall of the Roman Empire it was the sole arbiter of all intellectual activities, and pre-Reformation Tudor physicians, no less than their European confrères, were chiefly in the service of the Church. Disease was considered to be a natural result of defects in the constitution or environment or a direct result of sin and hence – possibly in both cases – a sign of God's wrath. God's mercy was capricious but no one doubted at that time that he proved his omnipotence with cruelty, which often took the form of wholesale visitations of epidemics or by the singling out of individuals to be stricken with something dire.

Those best capable of dealing with God's wrath, when expressed by disease, were priest-physicians (or sometimes a witch). But as papal authority had decreed during the twelfth century that no priest should shed blood, the priest-physician was in an awkward position, since he could not undertake surgery. This was therefore left to his servant, a lay brother who was usually also the barber who shaved the priest's tonsure. This lay brother – who was at least familiar with a razor – bled the patient, drew teeth and, doubtless, sawed off a leg when necessary. Often it was not even a lay brother who did the bloody work; sometimes apothecaries, barbers and even smiths carried it out. Thus surgery sank to a very low level, while doctors, deprived of this side of their profession, took to a more learned field and emerged as scholastics. By the fifteenth century the split between medicine and surgery was total. The humble surgeon with little book-learning was scorned by the well-educated and often incompetent physician.

Surgery was first rescued not by those who practised it, but by artists such as Michaelangelo, Raphael, Dürer and, above all, Leonardo da Vinci (1452–1519). These men needed to know the anatomy of the human body in detail for their own work and, despite prohibitions against dissection, did manage to dissect and learn. Da Vinci was interested not only as an artist but as a scientist, and wrote a book on physiology which he did not publish, but for which many of his meticulous drawings and notes survive. One of the things he did was to question Galen's anatomical findings – these dealt with animals, chiefly monkeys, which was hardly helpful – and in so questioning and experimenting found these much-revered findings to be wrong. His views, although not published, were well known to his contemporaries.

The work of writing an anatomical textbook fell to Andreas Vesalius (1514–64) of Brussels, who studied medicine first at the University of Louvain and later at Paris, where anatomical teaching was still well stuck with Galen and the Middle Ages. Vesalius then went to Padua, a noted university where more modern instruction was available. At the age of twenty-three he became a professor there and it was he who founded the still well-known scientific tradition at that university. Students from all over Europe, including England, flocked to hear his lectures and watch his demonstrations. In 1538 he published a brief guide to physiology and anatomy which was not very useful as it was based on Galen and Aristotle, both of whose views he soon discarded. Four years later he wrote his major work, *De humani corporis fabrica* (1543), which he further revised in 1555. As Vesalius and Titian were great friends, he was able to get Titian's favourite pupil, John of Calcar, to provide the illustrations. This wonderful book so advanced the knowledge of the human body that it is probably safe to say that descriptive anatomy today is just a correction and enlargement of Vesalius's work. More important at that time was the fact that the book stimulated many new investigators, and the new knowledge of anatomy had an immediate effect in that it improved surgery.

Surgery and the barber surgeons were not well thought of in early Tudor times. Surgery was not, in England, a profession for gentlemen – nor did it become one for several centuries. But, as early as the fourteenth century, barbers and surgeons had joined in a fraternity and were organized into 'gilds'. John of Arderne (fl.1370) was a famous surgeon and probably under the patronage of the Black Prince. Thomas Morstede (d.1450) was surgeon to the army at the battle of Agincourt, 25 October 1415. He was paid 12d. a day plus 100 marks a quarter for supervising the surgical care of the whole army. Both men were members of the London guild. Every important town had its guild and there were probably twenty or thirty such associations, but we know very little about them or their members. It is not until we come to Thomas Vicary (1495–1561), who became sergeant-surgeon to Henry VIII, that we really begin to know something about the barber surgeons.

The barbers had been incorporated in 1462 by a charter granted by Edward IV, and this allowed them to let blood, engage in minor surgery, pull teeth, cut hair and shave. Specifically, the charter was granted to 'free men of the Mystery of Barbers of our city of London exercising the Mystery or Art of Surgery'.[5] Amongst other privileges the barbers were exempted from jury service. Surgeons proper also secured the same privileges and in 1491 were even let off keeping watch and bearing arms, but this exemption was so far forgotten that in 1513 the wretched surgeons had to appeal to Parliament for the privileges already granted them. On the other hand, the surgeons were considered to be socially and professionally a cut above the barbers and could be distinguished from them by their long robes – appropriately enough, the barbers' were short.

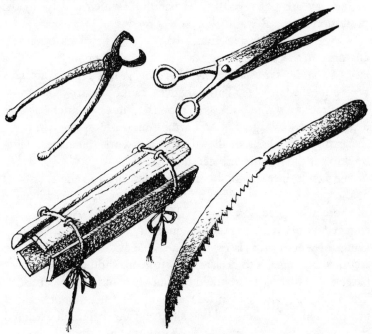

Barber surgeon's tools

In 1530 an Act which lumped bakers, brewers, surgeons and scriveners together, under certain prohibitions, made even more clear the great distinction between physicians and surgeons. Further, by this time the physicians had their own college. The 1530 Act, however, had one good result. Bakers, brewers and scriveners were hardly the right company for surgeons, so the surgeons grew closer to the barbers, for the barbers had gone from strength to strength, which the surgeons had not. This stronger bond was finally statutorily effected by an Act of Parliament of

12 July 1540 which incorporated the two into the Barber-Surgeons Company; Thomas Vicary became first Master of this united company.

Holbein commemorated this great event by one of his most famous paintings, which shows the king presenting the charter to a kneeling Vicary. Many famous barber surgeons and physicians of the day are portrayed in the painting, which is now in the possession of the Royal College of Surgeons.

Vicary, a remarkable man, wrote the first textbook on anatomy in the English language, entitled *A Treasure for Englishmen Concerning the Anatomie of Man's Body*. It is reputed to have been published in 1548. This, however, cannot be proved because it is untraceable. The book was 'reprinted' in 1577, after Vicary's death, by his colleagues at St Bartholomew's Hospital. Although the anatomy is of the medieval type, the work remained a textbook until the seventeenth century.

The newly incorporated company, desiring to raise the status of the profession, organized a course of systematic teaching for all those who practised surgery. Well-educated physicians were engaged to teach and lecture on anatomy, and of these Dr John Caius (of whom more later) was one. One of the things which the Act of 1540 did was to declare that surgeons should no longer be barbers and that barbers should confine their surgery to dentistry. The company also had power to impose fines on unlicensed practitioners in London and was allowed two corpses of executed criminals a year to enable anatomy to be studied at first hand.

Internal medicine, despite the prestige of physicians, was less fortunate. The discoveries and reforms of Vesalius were not accompanied by any similar advance in this field. Hence physicians generally remained bogged down in the Middle Ages with, among other things, the four humours and astrology to aid them. They were, in fact, still very like the physicians of whom Chaucer writes:

> With us there was a DOCTOUR OF PHISYK,
> In al this world ne was ther noon him lyk

> To speak of phisick and of surgerye;
> For he was grounded in astronomye . . .
>
> He knew the cause of everich maladye,
> Were it of hoot or cold, or moiste, or drye,
> And where engendered and of what humour;
> He was a verrey parfit practisour . . .
>
> Wel knew he th' olde Esculapius,
> And Deiscorides, and eek Rufus,
> Old Ypocras, Haly, and Galien;
> Serapion, Razis, and Avicen;
> Averrois, Demascien and Constantyn;[6]

This physician 'grounded in astronomye' was obviously an expert in astronomy's sister science, astrology. Astrology, like alchemy, had come to Europe with the Arabs and was then a branch of scientific astronomy, that is, the kind of knowledge useful for steering ships – what sailor could do without the Pole Star? (The astrolabe* is probably the oldest scientific instrument in the world.) Astronomy's half-sister, astrology, was held to be just as important and as scientific as astronomy. Soon astrology itself became a very lucrative profession.

The Tudor belief in astrology was very nearly universal and quite understandable. There were changes in the solar system, all of which could be foretold. The moon had her cycle; so did women. The stars moved in a fixed course, so it was more than probable that God had fixed the tides, fortunes, patterns and courses of men's lives just as He had fixed the universe, with the earth and man, around which everything else revolved, as its centre. Thus, what was to happen could be foretold. Even Aristotle had pointed out that man was a microcosm reflecting the macrocosm, so it was held that the knowledge of the movements

---

* Chaucer's unfinished treatise on the astrolabe, written for 'Litel Lowis my son', is still fascinating reading.

and conjunctions of the planets enabled the skilled astrologer to foretell the future and also, when necessary, give the prognosis of any disease. It was also believed that epidemics, when not due to a sudden and direct explosion of God's wrath, were under stellar control, and many held that plague returned regularly in a twenty-year cycle. No competent physician, then, could study man apart from the much greater universal environment in which he lived, and few, if any, Tudor doctors would have doubted the value of astrology. Like medicine, it was a 'science', but unfortunately there were as many if not more 'quack' astrologers as there were 'quack' doctors, for true astrology was a most difficult and complicated subject with its own language and disciplines. So important was astrology that in Paris and at some other universities the chair of astrology was combined with that of medicine.

There were two main branches of astrology; both affected man: first, the Natural or Horary, which combined astronomy with predictions on the fate of mankind in general; second, the Judicial, which dealt with individual and personal matters. A Judicial astrologer was much engaged in casting horoscopes and dealing with separate individuals on personal matters. Such things as the nature of a disease and of its cause came within his knowledge and scope and it was upon the Judicial astrologer that the physician – if not one himself – relied.

Astrology was much used in forecasting the fate and character of a new-born child. Procreation was not thought to be possible without divine help and, as the spark of life came into the heart of the foetus from the sun, it was perfectly clear that the child would derive his individuality from the time of his birth in relation to the position of the sun and from the particular planet from which the 'cosmic' ray came.

Two things in particular were regulated by consulting the astrologer; the best method and time for getting rid of harmful humours, and when to bleed and purge. It was Jupiter which largely influenced this, and doctors still use its symbol, Rx, prefixed to their prescriptions. The actual site where the patient

Zodiacal man

was to be bled was found by reference to the signs of the Zodiac, since every part of the body came under a Zodiacal sign. So anatomical charts showing Zodiac Man were included in many medical textbooks. Various medicines were also more effective when given under the correct Zodiacal sign. Purges were more efficient when the moon was in Scorpio or Pisces. Emetics, shaving and medical baths – a somewhat odd collection – did better when the moon was in conjunction with Cancer, and so on.

It is hardly surprising, then, that this was a perfectly splendid era for quacks. Belief in magic – white and black – and the supernatural, which had persisted for centuries and was to continue to persist, saw to that. So there sprang up a type of 'doctor' who, possessing 'knowledge' denied to ordinary mortals, was able to effect cures by getting in touch with the unseen. Incantations in Latin, holy relics and holy wells were all part of the stock-in-trade of such men, some of whom may have started out as monks before the Dissolution of the Monasteries. Far lower in the scale were those who sold charms, amulets and potions – the last, of course, prepared under favourite planetary influences. There were also witches and sorcerers, usually herbalists who gathered plants, brewed their concoctions at various phases of the moon and sold them in a suitably darkened room, whilst chanting an unintelligible incantation. Naturally, every respectable witch or sorcerer had a skull as a part of his equipment. Country folk fared rather better; they usually had a local wise woman who knew from experience and from handed-down wisdom how to deal with simple complaints and prescribe simple herbal remedies. These may have done no good but undoubtedly did far less harm than quacks and 'empericks'.

Here it is only fair to say that not all dealers in herbs were quacks: apothecaries grew herbs too and were a very different order of men. By the mid-Tudor period three branches of the medical profession could be clearly differentiated: first, the physician, famous for book-learning and knowledge of Greek and Latin, and master of at least one of the occult arts – usually astrology; second, the surgeon, who was a species of barber and noted for his skill in bleeding, bone-setting and bandaging; and, third, the apothecary, who was familiar with worts and drugs and who provided doctoring for the population in general.

Although many physicians preferred to make up their own prescriptions, the good apothecary was what we should now call a pharmacist. He specialized. Most apothecaries grew their own herbs and simples in their own physic gardens – as did most great households – and this protected their clients from the adulterated or bad herbs whose unscrupulous sellers flourished in the cities. It was, however, believed by many apothecaries that herbs growing wild were better, and more potent, than those domesticated in physic gardens, and so they went out, or sent their assistants, into the woods and fields to collect them.

Apothecaries increased in number after the Dissolution of the Monasteries, as many lay brothers and members of the minor clergy took to growing herbs – an art they had learned in the monasteries – and set up in business. Of course apothecaries also had very complex and exotic remedies such as Theriac and Mithridatum, each of which contained a minimum of fifty ingredients which all had to be added to the brew at the right time. The right time, in this case, was one which was astrologically propitious. Early apothecaries were affiliated to the Spicers' and Pepperers' guilds, but by Tudor times the genuine apothecary was a member of the Grocers' Company, which had a monopoly on all imported drugs. Although they gained in status they were reminded by Dr William Bullein (d.1576) in *A Booke of Compoundes and the Apothecaries Rule* (1558) that they were 'the Physician's Cook'. There could be far worse things to be.

But medicine was still based on the humours. The humoral theory of man's complexion – we should call it temperament – was as old as Hippocrates and Galen, but had been much added to during the intervening centuries. It was held that the four elements, fire, air, earth and water, with their attributes, heat, cold, dryness and moisture, fixed the 'complexion' of every human being. Although all four were present in every individual, two were normally predominant; but these were not necessarily fixed, so that other humours at different times enlarged or grew, the natural complexion or temperament was affected and the body became ill. Keeping the natural complexion in, or restoring it to, proper balance was the first object of every physician, and for this he had to know the natural temperament of his patient. There were four of these: Sanguine, where fire and water were the two natural humours; Choleric, where fire and earth combined; Phlegmatic, in which air and water predominated; and Melancholic, where the two elements were air and earth.

Chaucer's Physician, like all good physicians, knew well the basis of 'everich maladie', were it hot, cold, moist or dry, for Zodiacal man was also humoral man and the four humours, together with Animal, Natural and Vital spirits, were what made man what he was.

The body was alive because of the 'life soul' which inhabited it. It was not just an inn but a residence where the life soul could show its power. This life soul was unseeable, untouchable and had various ways in which it could control or direct the body. This was done by certain 'spirits', and each spirit controlled an individual body process. Spirits, or *pneumata*, were circulated in the blood – this theory went back to Galen and beyond – and the 'Natural Spirit', the lowest of the lot, controlled growth and nutrition. When further refined by the heart it was the 'Vital Spirit' which endowed the various organs with their special functions. When the blood which carried this Spirit reached the brain it was further refined and became the 'Animal Spirit', the breath of the soul. This spirit could direct or mis-direct judgement, memory and imagination. These three, when properly directed, produced that immaterial product, 'reason'. Thus, the faculties of the life soul were useful to physicians in that they could account for or be used to explain any physiologically unknown quantity. This sounds like a very early attempt at psychosomatic medicine.

But heat, cold, moisture and dryness were fundamental and were of decisive importance, not only to man but to every living thing. All living matter was considered to be made up of humours, and medicines and remedies were compounded with this in mind.

According to the famous dicta of the School of Salerno,★ Sanguine man was 'gamesome', loved wine, women, pleasant tales, news, dice and good company. He was cheerful-looking, given to laughter, loved mirth and music. He was neither 'ireful' nor apt to take offence easily, but he took little thought for the future and if not careful ran to fat. Too much of the Sanguine humour was indicated by a swollen face, red cheeks, staring eyes, protruding veins, constipation, headache, restless sleep and dreams which would make one 'blush to tell'.[7] Much of this sounds as if Sanguine man was given to high blood pressure, and surely this description of him fits, at least in part, Henry VIII?

Choler was 'a humour most pernetious' and Choleric man was violent, fierce, full of fire, quick, ambitious, out to make a fortune, proud, bountiful, but also malicious. He was as bold a speaker as he was a liar, angered easily, ate a lot but remained thin – which sounds as if he were hyper-thyroid – grew quickly when young and produced quantities of hair on his face and breast when old. Too much Choler produced a ringing in the ears, wakefulness, a rough tongue, vomiting, great thirst, slimy excrement, squeamish stomach, loss of appetite, a fast heart, sour spittle and dreams of fireworks – perhaps such symptoms indicate diabetes.

Phlegmatic man was quite different. He was inclined to be short, square-built and fat, and was much given to ease, rest and sloth. Quite happy in knowing very little and quite unable to take any pains over anything, his spirits were as dull as his senses and he was given to day-dreams. An excess of Phlegm caused a bad taste in the mouth, too much saliva, a sore chest right down to the waist, a distaste for food, slow digestion, head and shoulder

---

★ The first European medical school of continued fame. The poem *Regimen Sanitatis Salernitatum* encapsulated its teaching in easily remembered Latin verse. It was added to and emended by various hands during the intervening centuries and first translated by Thomas Payne in 1530, who translated commentaries only. Other editions appeared 1541, 1557, 1597. I have used the edition of 1607 throughout.

pains and dreams of rivers and seas – was Phlegmatic man bronchitic?

As for Melancholy man, he came off worst of the lot. Unlike the others he refused sport, ease and company, was studious and 'ever solitary', inclined to pensiveness and musing. Worse, he often secretly hated others, but he had the virtue of being constant in his choice, though 'long a choosing'. He was also extreme in love, but not lustful, though he was also suspicious and mistrustful. He possessed a wary wit and sparing hand and was unenterprising in spirit and heavy in looks. Too much of the Melancholy humour was very dangerous as it sometimes made one mad. This humour was distinguished by a hard pulse, a dark, bad colour, false grounds for joy or else 'perpetual sadness' – which sounds a bit on the manic-depressive side. The Melancholic victim was often frightened by dream-like visions (visual hallucinations?) and was much troubled by bitter belches and a humming in the left ear.

Then there was the doctrine of 'contraries' – 'allopathy', as it was later called. This taught that heat would drive out cold, moisture would drive out dryness, and the other way round. All that needed to be done was to discover the quantity of each element in any drug and the quantity of the excessive humour to be purged in the patient. Thus any imbalance would be equalized. The humble prune, so cold and moist, was most effective in driving out hot, dry Choler, while pennyroyal purged cold, dry Melancholy and also comforted the stomach and spirits. To get rid of corrupt humoral fluids, however, bleeding, cupping, leeching and drastic purges were necessary and were tried in turn or in combination. For a patient already weakened by a severe illness, these methods of drawing off corrupt humours might well have drawn off life itself.

A large leech of the English variety could suck three drachms of blood, while another three subsequently oozed from the wound. But to remove the usual twenty ounces, twenty-four leeches were required. Galen had advised snipping the tail off the leech so that more blood ran through, but although the patient may have survived this the leech did not, and leeches were not all that easy to come by. They were caught and collected by apothecaries who lent or hired them out, but the best physicians had their own and applied them themselves. Leeching in most cases was considered to be as good as phlebotomy or cupping, but was more used by the lower classes and a few cowardly uppers who were frightened of the lancet. Leeching was also used on those too weak to stand other methods of blood-letting or who were in a coma or delirious. In delirium leeches were applied to the head.

Clysters were used for weak stomachs, fever, debility, constipation, headache and colic. The bag was made of the dried bladder of a pig with a tube fixed to it and the enema was given in the usual way. The favourite mixture used was a weak saline solution infused with herbs and honey. About one pint was given and the patient directed to retain it for one or two hours. In cases of great debility, nutrition was supplied *per rectum* and various mixtures of honey were used. This is very modern in thought and anticipates

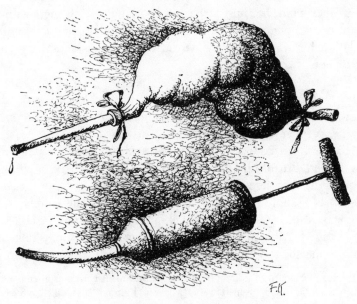

Animal bladder and piston enemas

the Murphy* drip (which was in turn supplanted by the glucose drip) by about four hundred years. There was, however, another and positively terrifying gadget which had made its appearance towards the end of the fifteenth century. This was a piston syringe made of metal and, if used with any force, it must have been agonizing. Physicians were far too grand to give clysters, so this job was left to apothecaries and surgeons.

Humours could also be kept in balance by the right diet. Andrew Boorde is very keen on diet and in his *Dyetary of Helthe* gives pointers on the correct food for each of the four temperaments. Of Sanguine man, hot and moist, he says that the purer the complexion the more easily it is corrupted; therefore he should eat no fruit and herbs, no garlic or onions and, above all, no 'muddy fish'.[8] His sleep and diet should always be moderate, else he will become fat and gross. Hot, dry Choleric man should not get hotter and drier – which seems a thought obvious – and must avoid hot spices, wine and choleric meats, such as venison, even though he can eat 'grosser' meat than any other complexion. On the other hand, he must never fast too long, which suggests his choleric temper might be due to low blood sugar. To purge Choler, fumitory, centaury, wormwood, violets and whey are excellent.

Phlegmatic man should never indulge in viscous or white meat, fish or fruit, and should keep away from marshy ground. Hot, dry meats, if taken in moderation, are good, as are onions, garlic, pepper and ginger, which dissolved phlegm. As for Melancholy man, that cold, dry creature later made so famous by Robert Burton, he should never eat fried meats or anything 'sour or hard of digestion'[9] such as hare – a sure breeder of melancholy. Nor should he drink 'hot', that is, red, wine (surely bad advice). Milk is good, and egg yolks, but the eggs must be boiled, not roasted. All easily digested foods are to be favoured. Pills to purge melancholy were made of quick beans, senna, hart's

---

*John Benjamin Murphy (1857–1916), eminent American surgeon and teacher, also invented the anastomosis (Murphy) button (1892), which reduced danger in intestinal operations.

tongue, maiden hair, borage, organum, sugar and white wine. It sounds as if Melancholy man was given to dyspepsia, which doubtless caused the insomnia he was well known to suffer. Hours of sleep were regulated for other complexions – seven for the Sanguine and the Choleric, nine for the Phlegmatic – but the Melancholy were allowed to sleep where and when they could, for they, Boorde says, a trifle nastily, one feels, were 'the receptacle and dregs of all humours'.[10]

As we saw in the previous chapter, a royal physician had to assist in preparing the menus for the sovereign. Diet, although what was eaten sounds extraordinary to us, was sensibly considered to be a part of medicine. 'A good cook is half physician,' Boorde says, and adds: 'For the chief physic (the counsil of a physician excepted) doth come from the kitchen; wherefor the physician and the cook for the sick man must consult together for the preparation of meat . . . For if the physician without the cook, prepare any meat except he be very expert, he will make a worse dish of meat, that which the sick cannot take.'[11] Whether most physicians added cookery to their other required accomplishments is not easy to say, but either the physician or the cook – or both – must have been well up on what foods were right for each complexion, and also on which foods would help overcome any imbalance of the humours.

Boorde, here, is reiterating what the Salernitan School had advocated for centuries:

> Good diet is a perfect way of curing,
> And worthy much regard and health assuring.
> A King that cannot rule himself in his dyet,
> Will hardly rule his Realme in peace and quyet.[12]

Added to this is the advice not to eat until one is hungry, because adding food to food breeds repletion. Also, it is wise to be sure to vent wind when necessary or cramps, dropsy and colic will ensue, to say nothing of 'Mazed Brains for want of vent behind'.[13] Then, too, diet should be suited to the season. Food should not be taken in excess during the spring and very little should be eaten during summer, while too much fruit should not be eaten in autumn; but during the winter a certain amount of gorging is permitted. This is very sound advice, bar, perhaps, eschewing fruit in autumn – at least in England, for the book was written with the Italian seasons in mind. Even so, it should be remembered that it is an old country belief that the devil spits on blackberries in October.

Still another piece of good advice comes in another verse of the same poem:

> They that in Physicke will prescribe your food,
> Six things must note, we here in order touch,
> First, *what it is*; and then *for what 'tis good*.
> And *when*; and *where*; *how often*; and *how much*.

As for remedies in general, Pliny the Elder (23–79 A.D.) had taught in his *Natural History* that every plant had a therapeutic value and, although most of his information seems to have come from earlier authors, he nevertheless added various observations of his own. Few educated Tudor gentlemen were unacquainted with Pliny and, as home doctoring was of great importance, doubtless Pliny's advice was followed where possible. It is equally possible that doctors of the time were well aware of Pliny's theories of the therapeutic qualities of plants and minerals, although their knowledge was more likely to have come from later sources. Boorde was, as we know, a doctor, and some of his prescriptions use the same plants for the same diseases as those recommended by Pliny.

Boorde, an ex-Carthusian priest – physician and one-time suffragan bishop of Chichester – an office which he does not seem to have taken up – applied in 1528 to be released from his vows, travelled abroad and settled for a time at Montpellier, then the greatest medical centre of the known world. Here he took his M.D., which he later 'incorporated' at Oxford, since only Oxford and Cambridge graduates had the right to practise freely.* At

---

* Most ethical doctors studied abroad and took a foreign degree which they incorporated at either of the two universities upon returning to England.

both universities medicine was almost a dead art or science; it was scholastic, that is to say, erudite, codified and purely academic. It consisted of book-learning only. Boorde accepted the humoral teachings of Hippocrates and Galen, but not all of them, and he believed that if doctors always followed books alone more harm than good would come of it. He also believed that mirth was one of the best medicines and for this was jeeringly called 'Merry Andrew'. Nonetheless, he was physician to Thomas Cromwell, Sir Robert Dudley (d.1536) and the Duke of Norfolk. He died in the Fleet, where he had been imprisoned either for debt or for keeping three whores at Winchester. In 1542 he wrote his *Dyetary of Helthe*, following it in 1547 with the *Brevyary of Helthe*. They were the first medical books to be printed in the English language.

The second of these was fully entitled, *The Brevyary of Helthe, for all manner of sycknesses and diseases the which may be in man, or woman doth follow. Expressing the obscure termes of Greke, Araby, Latyn and Barbary into English concerning Phisicke and Chieurgury completed by Andrew Boorde of Phisicke Doctour an Englishman.* It was addressed not only to fellow practitioners but also to the general reader. It was a medical home-help for those who could not afford to keep a physician-in-residence and had to cope with illness at home and compound their own remedies. Boorde warns against quacks and adds that, in addition to his regular studies, a physician 'must surely have his Astronomy to know how, when and at what time every medicine should be administered',[14] and also that if a physician lacks the 'science' of 'Logic' by which he distinguishes truth from falsehood, grammar – which seems curious – and natural philosophy or the knowledge of natural things 'he shal kyll many more than he shal save'.[15]

To the general reader he speaks in a different voice.' Gentyl reader,' he says, 'I have taken some pains in makynge this boke, to do syke men pleasure and whole men profit, that sicke men may recuperate their helthe and whole men may preserve them selfe from sickeness (with goddes help).' The book is, in fact, a brief encyclopedia of illnesses and their cures, plus many suggestions on diet. It is arranged in alphabetical order and covers nearly everything then known from 'abhorring of the stomach' and 'abortion' to 'Worms in the ears' and 'Wrinkles'. Simple things such as dandruff, warts, superfluous hair, sunburn, belching, gurgustation, or 'croaking in ones belly', freckles, bad breath, 'gaping' (yawning) and nose-bleed are dealt with among the more serious complaints such as Apoplexy – a cold humour which stops the brain and arises possibly, he thinks, in the 'hinder' part of the head. This condition was characterized by 'a sudden striking down and taking away of a mans wit, reason and moving'[16] and the cure, among other things, was to purge the head, then use a sternutation (sneeze) made of white hellebore, pepper and castery blown into the nostrils. Pliny had said that white hellebore made the best sneeze and recommended it also for epilepsy (thought by Boorde to rise in the 'hindest' part of the head), melancholy, insanity, giddiness, tetanus, dropsy and white leprosy.

White leprosy might have been the white morphew with which the Tudor era (and earlier times) was sadly afflicted. Boorde describes it as a kind of leprosy – many skin conditions were confused with or called 'leprosy' – which he states might be caused by poor nutrition or by 'usinge too much Venus actes in youth'.[17] To effect a cure, the finely powdered root of gentian mixed with gentian juice and white vinegar or a decoction of powdered madder root stamped with sugar and vinegar was applied to the affected area. Or, more curiously, the site could be rubbed with a scarlet cloth and then with mandragora leaves. Was the doctrine of contraries in operation here? Or was it that red cloth, held to be of great use when draped around a room and over the windows of a smallpox victim, had in itself a specific therapeutic – or magic – value?

Cancer, in English, as defined by Boorde, is not carcinoma but a canker or corroding ulcer that eats sinews and bone and comes from a Melancholic or Choleric humour or – and this is more likely – from a neglected wound. If the bone turned black there was no remedy for it other than to amputate the arm or leg if either were involved. (This was as likely to kill one as the infected wound.) If, on the other hand, the canker had not 'putrified' the site should be scoured for three or four days with white wine – at least this contained some alcohol which would be mildly disinfectant – and then the wound should be anointed with burnt lead* mixed with oil of roses. Or a salve could be made of one ounce of white poppy, one dram of opium or henbane, half an ounce of gum arabic and four ounces of oil of roses. One hopes the opium helped to deaden the pain.

Then there was diabetes, called in English 'immoderate pyssynge'.[18] It was probably *diabetes mellitus*, with its consequent polyuria, or it may have been the much rarer *diabetes insipidus*, which is even more immoderate in its effect. For this a purge of manna and cassia and forcing the patient to drink cold water until he vomits are highly recommended. Taking clary in which a cockerel had been stewed or eating, every morning, four eggs prepared with powdered red nettle and sugar was also of great use.

As for Pestilence – a vague term – when not a direct punishment from God it comes from corrupt and contagious airs and, says Boorde, one infected man can infect another. Pestilence also arises from the stink of dirty streets, open, unclean channels (sewers), standing puddles, stinking water, shedding of man's blood, corpses not deeply buried and of 'great company in too small a room', as well as from 'common pyssynge places'.[19] The chief remedy? To submit oneself to God, amend one's ways and, sensibly, flee from infected places. A good diet should be followed, rooms and houses should be perfumed, one should not go out in the night air nor rise early and the sun 'should have dominion over the ground to waste and consume all contagious mites and airs'.[20] The use of the word 'mites' is interesting because, although it was commonly held that evil odours bred diseases, it suggests a nascent theory of germ-born disease.

Megryme is well defined as a sickness 'keeping to the middle of

---

* It is impossible to know now what this means. It may have been white basic lead carbonate or red lead (Pb_3O_4), both of which were in use at this time. It may just possibly have been molten lead, which was used on severe wounds.

the skull and descending to the temple' and making a half circle 'like a rainbow'.[21] Its cause is given as a rheum or wind in the head which becomes trapped and unable to escape, and must therefore be purged with gargles and sneezes – and what could be more painful than being forced to sneeze when suffering with a migraine? Various pills are prescribed, and salves for anointing; so is a mustard plaster. Garlic, onions and related vegetables are to be avoided; so is strong beer and constipation. No pottage, ale or new bread should be taken. From this we can see that Boorde knew as little about the causes and cure of migraine as we do. One small point, however, is the advice to avoid onions. Today some authorities hold that onions, chocolate, cheese and whisky can precipitate migraine. The Tudors had neither chocolate nor whisky.

When it comes to Wind, which sounds so simple, apparently it could be trapped in various parts of the body and, astonishingly enough, 'especially and most commonly . . . under the skin'.[22] A wind-inflated skin sounds highly unpleasant. For this complaint phlebotomy, purgatives, scarification and boxing (cupping) were necessary to let the wind out. Just what wind under the skin can have been defeats the imagination, although it conjures up in the brain some rather startling images.

Boorde also deals with urine and uroscopy in fourteen pages, for uroscopy was the great diagnostic feature of medicine at the time. It was not useful in the smallest degree, as there were no scientific means of testing urine. But uroscopy, or water-casting, was used until the seventeenth century as a means of recognizing any disfunction of the humours. It was also used as a test for pregnancy. 'The urine of pregnancy was believed to have special features, particularly if it were stored in a glass container for a few days. One characteristic was the pearly film . . . reported to form on the surface . . . It appears that the surface layer is the result of the stimulation of bacterial growth by the hormones of pregnancy . . . Avicenna, Hippocrates and Savonarola . . . were aware of these changes'[23] – but it cannot be said they understood or interpreted them correctly.

Nevertheless, the urine flask was as much the symbol of the Tudor physician as was his long, fur-sleeved gown and circular, biretta-shaped or close-fitting black velvet cap. The flask, made in the shape of a bladder, had a wide mouth and was divided into three zones, superior, middle and inferior. The first related to the head and brain. The second showed the state of the heart, lungs and stomach, while the third indicated ailments related to other parts of the body below the belt. Urine was thought to be excess blood filtered of its red colour, but blood in the urine was considered to be a bad sign. An even worse sign was passing less liquid than had been drunk – which is true enough and indicates that physicians must have measured fluid intake and output in their patients but, again, they can have known too little to make use of this.

Boorde also has a delightful small note on music, one of the seven liberal arts, which, he says, is a comfort to man in sickness and in health and, like medicine, is divided into theory or speculation and practice.

Other diseases have very strange names such as 'Poose', caused by too much rheum and apparently little more than a cold, and 'Egestion or Seege', which was costiveness and required clysters and purging with mercury. Strangest of all are Boorde's remarks on *Ambustio meretricis*, which he calls 'burnynge of an harlot or of a hoore'. This is a perfectly good translation, but the cause of the condition seems rather peculiar. It is 'when a harlot doth hold her breth & clap her handes hard together & toes in lyke maner. And some harlotte dothe stand over a chafynge dyshe of coales into which she doth put brymstone and there she doth perfume her selfe.'[24] If a man has intercourse with such a woman and 'do medle with another woman within a day, he shal burne the woman that he doth medle withal'.[25] Should a man be so burnt he should 'wash his secrets' two or three times with white wine or sack and consult a surgeon, 'or els the gutts will burne and fall out of the belly'.[26]

Altogether, this is an unpleasant prospect which may, on the harlot's part at any rate, have involved black magic – one

Harlot fumigating herself

wonders a little about that brimstone. 'Hell' was certainly a cant term for the female pudenda. What is of some interest here is Boorde's statement that a man so burned can affect another woman and transmit the burning to her. It sounds as if the disease were gonorrhoea, and it took some time before it was realized that syphilis too was a venereal disease and infection was spread only by intercourse.

The confusion as to just what Boorde can have meant by *Ambustio meretricis* is that he deals with gonorrhoea and the 'French Pox' separately, and, though he says the latter can be caught by sitting in a draft where a 'pocky' person has sat, he also says it is especially taken when 'one pocky person do sin in lechery with another'. We cannot tell whether 'another' refers to one similarly infected, but certainly it sounds as if 'sin' and 'lechery' were the key words here. The cure was boar's grease, powdered brimstone, verdigris, the inside bark of the vine and five ounces of quicksilver 'mortified by fasting spit', all beaten together and used to anoint the sores, or plantain water with sublimated mercury – only the mercury could have been helpful, and it had long been used for abrasions of the skin of any kind. Boorde also mentions 'Gonorrhea' by name but defines it as *'profluvio somnis'*, and also as 'sodomy'. There is no remedy for this last other than great repentance – or marriage.

Syphilis was possibly brought to Europe by Columbus's sailors after his voyage of 1492, although there is no indisputable evidence for this. It spread with the utmost rapidity, often assuming epidemic form, and it was named after each country it had left as it reached the next one. Until 1530 when Frascatorius* wrote his poem *Syphilis*, which fixed its name permanently, *Morbus Gallicus* was the most common term used to describe the disease. Syphilis probably reached England around 1487, and by 1529 its venereal nature was known, but it was first thought to be airborne, entering the body through an abrasion in the skin – like rabies. As mercury had been used in the treatment of skin diseases for years, it was used externally for syphilis and also given orally, sometimes in doses large enough to kill. In passing, it should be noted that the mercury treatment for syphilis was not superseded until 1909.

Four hundred years before this, in 1506, and again in 1546, when syphilis reached epidemic proportions here, the Bishop of Winchester had to close, temporarily, his highly profitable stews in Southwark. By the last date there was an additional cure, lignum vitae. It had been introduced into Europe some thirty years before from the West Indies and Central America, and it was given the name 'lignum vitae' because it was reputed to be the West Indian cure for venereal disease. The wood itself was

---

* Hieronymus Frascatorius (1483–1553) of Verona came of a noble family. He studied mathematics, geology and astronomy and practised medicine. He also pursued music and poetry. At Padua with his friend, Copernicus, he concentrated on medicine. In verses modelled on Virgil, his *Syphilis sive morbus Gallicus* tells of a mythical shepherd, Syphilis, who by some impiety offended the gods and was smitten by a loathsome and contagious disease.

turned into sawdust mixed with water and fed to the afflicted in the form of porridge. It cannot have been easy to make sawdust of lignum vitae, as it is very hard, and so heavy* that it sinks in water.

There is a theory, long current, that Henry VIII suffered from syphilis and a number of medical men have put forward their reasons for believing this to be so. Others with equal vehemence have denied the theory. This is not the place to go into a matter on which both contentions are upheld with great skill and knowledge. Believers hold that Mary Tudor had syphilitic stigmata – bossed forehead, deep voice, patchy hair, poor sight. Edward VI and Queen Elizabeth escaped because the disease in their father had reached the tertiary stage by the time they were conceived, and therefore their mothers were not infected.

Those changes in the king's character noted by his contemporaries may have been due not to syphilis but to cerebral damage caused while jousting in 1536 (he was then forty-four years of age), when he received such a severe head injury that he was unconscious for two hours. Certainly the king, who was enormously robust, had illnesses during his life. At twenty-two he contracted smallpox, at twenty-nine, malaria – the benign tertiary kind, which recurred until he was fifty. In 1524 he had also received a head injury in a tournament, and in 1527-8 an ulcer broke out on his leg. This was cured temporarily by his surgeon, Thomas Vicary, and is thought to have been a varicose ulcer. After the head injury of 1536 he suffered from severe headaches, and shortly afterwards ulcers broke out on both legs. In 1538 he was very ill with, possibly, a pulmonary embolus. But he did not suffer from consumption which, it is generally thought, killed his father, his elder brother, his illegitimate son (the Duke of Richmond), and his heir, young King Edward VI.

There were two very important things connected with medicine which Henry VIII did: one bad, one good. The bad was, in a sense, inadvertent and came about by the suppression of the monasteries. By 1539, when 655 monasteries, 90 colleges and, later, 2,374 chantries and free chapels had been put down, many hospitals

* Density about 88lbs per cubic foot.

went down with them. This was a terrible blow, particularly in the provinces, where twenty-three of the principal cities and towns were left with no hospitals at all and there was no one to look after the sick and the poor. London fared rather better, thanks to Sir Richard Gresham,* Lord Mayor, who in 1538 wrote to the king that the remaining hospitals there, St Mary's Spital, St Bartholomew's and St Thomas's as well as the Abbey on Tower Hill, should be placed, with their revenues, within the disposal of the Lord Mayor and aldermen, as there were so many poor, sick, blind, aged and impotent people lying about the streets 'offending every clean person passing by with their filthy and nasty savour'.[27]

Despite this horrifying picture of ill and wretched human beings lying about in the filthy, crowded streets, nothing was done. But the matter continued to be pressed by the court of aldermen and finally, in 1544, the king, who needed money from the city, refounded 'Bart's' (he subsequently took possession of it again). It was not until he was on his death-bed that he made an agreement with the city concerning the maintenance of hospitals. This grudging act of a dying king earned him the totally un-merited title of founder of Royal Hospitals.

St Bartholomew's, however, was not re-opened until the reign of Edward VI, and in 1552 Christ's Hospital for poor children and Bethlehem for the insane were opened. In this year the young king also added St Thomas's to the list which, in the end, totalled five Royal Hospitals. The sick were tended at St Bartholomew's, the permanently infirm at St Thomas's. Bridewell was also given by King Edward as a prison–workhouse–hospital, but Queen Mary was reluctant to part with it and it did not come into the city's fold until 1556.

The medical good done by Henry VIII was less immediately apparent than the bad. But he did found the College of Physicians in 1518. Until this time no real distinction had been made between

---

* His second son, Sir Thomas Gresham (1519?–1579) founded the Royal Exchange (1566–8) and Gresham College. He was financial adviser to Edward VI and Queen Elizabeth.

bona fide physicians and quacks and, as we know, quacks were the more plentiful. It has been estimated that there was only one qualified physician to every 25,000 head of population. In addition there were the empericists who, either from ignorance or contempt for medicine, set themselves up as healers and dealt chiefly with epidemic diseases, mumps, whooping cough and the like. They made extravagant claims, and here the recently invented printing press aided them, for they printed and distributed handbills in which they claimed to cure everything – gout, ague, cancer, the pox and every other ailment to which the flesh ought not to be heir. Curiously enough, one of these frauds, a certain Master Gernais, was lodged at St Thomas's! Mountebanks and charlatans also came to this country from abroad, principally from Germany and Italy, and brought with them all sorts of panaceas, elixirs and secret remedies compounded of rare ingredients. These were capable of curing every disease known to man and some that obviously were not, such as Moon-fall and Rockogrogle. There were quacks among apothecaries too, as we know, and such a one was Heywood's 'Potecary', who purveyed remedies such as the following:

> . . . diosfialios,
> Diagalanga, and sticados,
> Blanka manna, diospoliticon[28]

Dentistry was almost, but not quite, entirely in the hands of quacks, and here two instruments of torture were known and used, the 'Pelican' and the 'Davier'. In November 1537 Nicholas Sympson, who was not an empiric, was sent by Henry VIII to draw a tooth from the mouth of the Princess Mary. He must have used the Pelican; for this and for the pain she must have endured Nicholas was paid '6 angels'.[29]

Toothache, it was believed, was caused either by a humour descending from the head or by worms which corroded or ate into the teeth. Purges and gargles were good if the ache were due to a descending humour, so was chewing horehound root. Getting rid of worms in the teeth took a good deal more trouble. A wax candle impregnated with henbane seeds had to be made; then the patient sat gaping over a basin of cold water while the candle was held close enough to his open mouth to permit the 'perfume' to enter the affected tooth or teeth. This was guaranteed to stupefy the worms so that they fell into the basin of water, where the sufferer could catch them and 'kill them on your nail'.[30] Why the stupefied worms were not allowed to drown is not stated, but Boorde warns to beware of pulling out a tooth. 'Pull one and pull out more,' he says, and recommends that the teeth be washed every day with cold water and rock alum. The alum would have tightened, temporarily, spongy gums.

But to return to medicine proper. It was because of that very great man, Thomas Linacre, that in 1518 letters patent were obtained from the king to set up a regular body of physicians which in 1551, under Edward VI, became the Royal College of Physicians of London. This association of qualified physicians had the power to decide who should practise in or within a seven-mile radius of London and, more important, it was allowed to license and examine practitioners throughout the whole country. The college was also granted the authority to examine drugs and prescriptions in apothecaries' shops and was empowered to fine or even to imprison those who broke the law. At last the Tudor mess and muddle of medicine was being cleaned up and some sort of order imposed.

Thomas Linacre, the man responsible, was one of a band of young scholars who had studied at Padua and brought home that 'new learning' which was ultimately to replace medievalism. Educated at Oxford and a fellow of All Souls, Linacre went to Italy in 1485–6 and became an M.D. of Padua. Returning to England in the same year in which Columbus set out upon his surprising voyage, he translated many Greek manuscripts and, using the original texts, freed them of much of their later accretions which were as useless as they were confusing. Hippocrates, Galen and Dioscorides emerged in Linacre's translation looking a good deal cleaner and saner; the doctor really showed Greek thought to have been precise and scientific, not muddled and medieval. This was to become the basis of the precise thinking which, in the next century, produced Harvey and his great discovery.

In 1501, Linacre had become domestic physician of Henry VII and tutor to Prince Arthur. He was intimate with all the great scholars of Europe. Sir Thomas More was his pupil and Erasmus his patient. He became one of Henry VIII's physicians, lectured at Oxford in 1510 and received many ecclesiastical preferments. Linacre seems unique because he appears to have been the only person to have realized that the standard of contemporary medicine must be improved. At the age of 58 he gave medicine a 'corporate existence' through the charter of 1518 and the consequent founding of the College, of which he was first president. He lodged the college in his own house in Knightrider Street in the City, paid all its costs and founded a medical library. Added at a later date were an anatomy theatre and a physic garden of which John Gerard (1545–1612), the great herbalist, was at one time curator. The Church, incidentally, now anxious about its waning influence, was delighted to have this most distinguished priest–physician within its ranks.

When Linacre founded the college, he had a number of his co-physicians with him. Among them was John Chambre (1470–1549), physician to King Henry VIII and the first of the six mentioned in the original charter, and Edward Wotton (1492–1555), also physician to the king, who wrote the first book on Natural History in English, *De Differentiis Animalium*. Published in 1553 and dedicated to King Edward VI, this work achieved a European reputation because Wotton was the first to realize the importance of anatomy as taught in European universities. There were also John Clement (d.1572), tutor to Sir Thomas More's family and later his son-in-law,★ who became president of the College in 1554, and Richard Bartlot (1471–1557), who was president in 1527–8 and again in 1531 and 1546. The latter was a most distinguished physician, and his obituary was written by no less a person than Dr John Caius.

★ He married More's adopted daughter and cousin, Margaret Gigs.

Caius, who is said to have modelled himself on Linacre, was an outstanding scholar and linguist and, as we have already seen, wrote the classical account of the 1551 epidemic of the sweating sickness. This was the prototype of all clinical description but, like all other physicians of the time, Caius believed in the humoral hypothesis. Born in Norfolk and destined for the Church, he went first to Cambridge and then to Padua, where he lodged with Vesalius of whom, unfortunately, he makes no mention in his writings. He took his M.D. in 1541 and then toured Europe visiting private and public libraries, trying to find uncorrupted texts of Hippocrates and Galen. He succeeded in finding two originals, which he translated, and it must be said that at this time his interest was really much more philological than medical.

When Caius returned to England he caught the attention of Henry VIII – who collected scholars – and, at the royal request, in 1546 started a series of lectures at the Barber-Surgeons' Hall. These lectures were attended by all the leading surgeons of the day. Caius continued to lecture there for twenty years and, further, introduced the subject of anatomy into the medical curricula at both universities, as well as into the College of Physicians. He became physician to Edward VI and, later, to Queen Mary and King Philip, and was then converted to Roman Catholicism. For this reason, when Queen Elizabeth succeeded her half-sister he ceased to be chief physician, but the Royal College, less encumbered with prejudice, still considered him to be the most learned physician of the time.

Learned he was, and he was also a most successful general practitioner; he remained a bachelor, made a fortune – the two are not necessarily linked – and devoted his fortune to the advancement of learning and science. In 1558 he was granted a charter by Queen Mary and King Philip to reform and endow his old college at Cambridge, Gonvil Hall. 'He bestowed good land *on*, erected fair buildings *in*, bequeathed thrifty statues *to*, produced a proper coat of arms *for*, and imposed a new name *on* this foundation. Gonvil and Caius College.'[31]

Medicine, although still far from being a science, became

under such men a centre point for scientific thought and most scientists (although we should hardly call them that) were physicians.

Linacre, whom Fuller calls 'the first restorer of learning in our Nation',[32] referring to him and to John Caius as 'the two phoenixes of their profession',[33] was the prototype of the great scholar–physician and was, as we know, for a time tutor to Prince Arthur. The prince died at the age of fifteen, at Ludlow in April 1502, of the consumption which may have killed his father or, as some hold, of the sweating sickness, which in that year seems to have been prevalent in that particular pocket of rural England. It is said that his bride, Catherine of Aragon, contracted the sweat too, but recovered. Perhaps later events made her wish that she had not.

On 18 June 1502 a laconic entry was made in the Privy Purse Accounts of King Henry VII. It reads: 'Payd to the Under-Treasurer the rest of his boke made for the buriall of my Lorde Prince £556 16s.' On the same date Morgan Knightly was paid £3 1s. 2d. for 'burying of Owen Tudder'.

CHAPTER SIX

Of Pleasures and Pastimes

The high season for revelry was then, as now, the twelve days of Christmas, and in the fourth year of his reign King Henry VIII kept 'a solempne Christmas at Grenewiche':[1]

On the twelfe daie at night came into the Hall a Mount called the riche Mount. The Mount was set full of riche flowers of silke, and especially full of Brome slippes full of coddes, the Braunches were grene Satin and the flowers flat Gold of Damaske, which signified Plantagenet. On the top stode a goodly Bekon giving light, round aboute the Bekon sat the king and five other, al in cotes and cappes of right Crimosin velvet, enbroudered with flatt gold of Dammaske, their coates set full of spangelles of gold, and foure woodhouses drewe the Mount till it came before the quene, and then the king and his compaignie discended and daunced: then sodainly the Mount opened, and out came sixe ladies all in Crimosin satin and plunket, [a woollen cloth of grey or light blue] embroudered with Golde and perle, with French hoodes on their heddes, and thei daunced alone. Then the lordes of the Mount toke the ladies and daunced together: and the ladies reentered and the Mount closed, and so was conveighed out of the hall. Then the king shifted him and came to the Quene, and sat at the banquet which was very sumpteous.[2]

As we are explicitly told that the Broom signified Plantagenet, it can be surmised accurately enough that the 'riche Mount' signified Richmond. Since the Plantagenet line had once split into the two houses of Lancaster and York, and these two warring factions had been brought together by Henry VII and Elizabeth of York, the mount was a symbol of their reconciliation (by marriage), of which Henry VIII, seated on top, was the living testimony. Obviously, this grand and final entertainment of the season at court – and there were other and more elaborate ones throughout the whole period – carried with it a graceful and easily read message. The Tudors were much given to making use of symbolism in their entertainments, but much of this must be lost to us today.

It is also clear that for such an elaborate 'set-piece' no expense was spared, and that those responsible for it knew a good deal about what we would call stage machinery. Although the Mount was drawn in and 'conveighed' away by four men dressed as wild men – wild men were great favourites – it apparently opened by means of some mechanical device. Mechanical devices were much used in the miracle plays of the time.

Christmas at court, although it represented the apex in entertainment, was merely a more expensive and spectacular reflection of the usual festivities indulged in all over the country at that time of year. The Lord of Misrule, sometimes known as the Abbot of Misrule, reigned not only at the king's court but also in noblemen's houses and in towns and cities as well. At the feast of Christmas, we are told, 'there was in the king's house wherever he was lodged a lord of misrule or master of merry disports and the like had ye in the house of every nobleman of honour or good worship, were he spiritual or temporal.'[3] This also applied to various cities, towns and parishes, as 'the mayor of London, and either of the sheriffs had their several lords of misrule, ever contending, without quarrel or offence, who should make the rarest pastimes to delight the beholders'.[4] In London and elsewhere houses and parish churches were 'decked with holm, ivy, bays, and whatsoever the season afforded to be green'[5] and in London, at any rate, 'the conduits and standards in the street were likewise garnished'.[6]

A good deal of mumming and disguising went on too, not

only at court, where disguising was a particular indulgence of Henry VIII, who loved to dress up and show off, but also in private houses of all sizes as well as in the streets and taverns. In town and country masked mummers paraded the streets in groups and entered houses to dance or play at dice and were rewarded with cakes and spiced wine. Those masked and singing men and women who burst in upon Mistress Lentall in December 1554, when Henry Machyn was supping with her, were given, as we have seen, even better fare than this.

Mumming, a very old form of entertainment, was engaged in not only at Christmastide but also at other holiday seasons, such as May Day. In May 1554 there was 'a goodly May-game at sant Martins in the fields with gyants and hobbehorses, with drumes and gonnes and mores dance and with other mynstrelles',[7] Henry Machyn tells us, while at Westminster were also great doings with giants, morris dancers, drums, bagpipes, viols and many 'disguised'. The hobby horse seems to have been a part of the mummers' stock-in-trade.

Mummers had once been silent and were sometimes costumed to represent the virtues, goodness, plenty and so on, but by the fifteenth and sixteenth centuries mumming had expanded and little plays were often a part of it. These simple plays may have arisen from the old games or song dances, such as *London Bridge is Broken Down* or its earlier equivalent, where dramatic action accompanies the words of the song or game, But, whatever their origins, these unsophisticated playlets at Christmastide usually contained a 'death and resurrection' theme of some sort. A favourite Christmas mumming play was of St George and the Dragon, with the Dragon becoming, in time, a comic character. These playlets later contained stock characters – at Christmas, the doctor who cured all wounds, a pretty girl to carry mistletoe and a boy with a wassail bowl made their inevitable appearance. In May-day mumming the Lord and Lady of the May, Robin Hood and Maid Marian, were to be seen all over the country – as of course were the maypole and the morris dancers.

Gambling has always been a part of the Englishness of the

English and gambling and wagering were almost a national pastime, but, since both contributed to idleness and vice, prohibitions against servants and apprentices dicing and playing cards were introduced in 1495 and remained in force for many years, save at certain seasons. Stow says that in London to play cards was permitted only from 'Alhallon eve' until 'the morrow after the Feast of the Purification', and that during this time cards were played 'for counters, nails and points more for pastime than for gain'.[8] This obviously applied only to the lower orders, since the Privy Purse Accounts of various Tudor monarchs show they lost money at cards and dice at times other than those specified. On 6 October 1532 Henry VIII paid £5 13s. 4d. for losses at primero. During May 1537 the Princess Mary had a run of bad luck and lost a number of small amounts at cards. Even earlier, in the Privy Purse Accounts of her grandfather, £7 15s. was paid to Hugh Denes 'for the Kinges pley at dice upon Friday last passed'.[9] This was, however, within the permitted time, but the king often played at dice and cards throughout the year and seems to have been fairly unlucky.

Perhaps the king's dice were 'a paire of silver dice'[10] like those sent by Alice, wife of Arden of Feversham,★ to regain the favour of that 'blacke, swart, man'[11] the tailor Mosbie. Or they may have been 'a paire of dees of gold'[12] like those sent in scorn to Demetrius by the King of Parthia. Gold and silver dice were expensive, but there were also ivory dice, wooden dice and bone dice. These last two must have been in common use. Cheating with dice was far from new; as Beatrice says of her heart: 'once before he won it of me with false dice.'[13] False dice were those which were loaded so that they were heavier on one side, or they could be 'high cut', which means they lacked the four. Certain games such as 'tables' (backgammon) required the use of dice and we know that

★ The squalid history of this lamentable affair, which took place in 1550–51, is given five pages in Holinshed. It was not written as a play until some time between 1585–92 and is by an unknown author. It is the first 'domestic' tragedy, as opposed to high tragedy, in the English language.

Catherine of Aragon played 'tables, tick-tache, or gleek, with cardes and dyce'.[14]

Probably the most popular, chancy and addictive dice game was Hazard, which had been known for centuries and continues to be known. Its rules were variable; in fact, 'Hasard is verrey moder of lesinges [lies],'[15] is the way Chaucer's Pardoner defines the game. References to hazard appear frequently in *The Canterbury Tales*: 'Your bagges been nat filled with *ambes as* but with *sis cink* that renneth for your chaunce.'[16] Here *ambes as* means double aces; *sis cink* is six and five and may refer to two dice. Later 'ambes as' became 'aumsace' or 'ambsace' and it is possible, though not very probable, that 'ambes as' could refer to cards. In *Thinterlude of Youth*, Ryot tells Youth:

> Syr I can teache you to play at the dice
> At the quenes game, and at the Iryshe,
> The treygobet and the hasarde also[17]

All these games were played with dice. Iryshe was rather like backgammon, 'treygobet' meant that the player had to throw better than a three and the 'quenes' game must have been played with two dice, for the same number had to turn up at a single throw.

Card games were also popular. Ryot again tempts Youth in the same play by offering to teach him

> ... many other games mo.
> Also at the cardes I can teche you to play,
> At the triump and one and thyrtye,
> Post, pinion and also aumsace,
> And at an other they call dewsace.

A great many games seem to have been known and played and card games were as good a way of losing money and passing time as any.

Playing-cards were relatively new – compared with dice – and we do not know exactly when they were first introduced into this country; it may have been at the end of the fourteenth century, but possibly not until the fifteenth. Two things suggest – but it is only a suggestion – the later date. First, in the third year of the reign of Edward IV, a statute prohibiting the importation into England of a variety of dissimilar things was enacted. Among the proscribed imports were tennis balls, dripping pans, wood knives, daggers, razors, bodkins and 'Cardes a Juer'. This was obviously protectionist in intent and meant that such things were made here and no foreign competition was wanted. So it is arguable that playing-cards were first made in this country by, say, the mid fifteenth century and that hitherto they had been imported. The second piece of evidence is a bit more flimsy. It would seem that playing-cards are not mentioned by any fourteenth century English writer. Langland does not mention them in *Piers Ploughman* among his exhaustive list of vices and, unless 'ambes as' refers to cards and not to dice, neither does Chaucer.

Both Langland and Chaucer died in 1400 and the lack of reference to card-playing by either – and certainly Chaucer's pilgrims reflected the fashions and foibles of the time – would seem to indicate that it was unknown in England before that date. Admittedly, this is negative evidence which may be put entirely out of court by the fact that in the Chester miracle play, *The Harrowing of Hell*, which is probably late fourteenth-century, the very last verse refers to the ale-wife 'using cards, dice and cups small'. However, it is generally accepted that this episode concerning the ale-wife (Scene III) is a later addition and it certainly reads very differently from the previous two scenes.

But, whenever introduced, the use of playing-cards must have spread fairly rapidly and seems to have been known to all classes, with the possible exception of those living in remote rural areas. Just what the cards looked like is difficult to say, since we have no extant examples earlier than about 1675. It is both possible and probable that English playing-card-makers copied the French, and the late Sir Gurney Benham, in that excellent book *Playing Cards*, gives abundant evidence that cards made at Rouen were the prototype of English cards. All court cards were then – and remained for centuries – full length, but the faces of the kings, queens and knaves of the Rouen cards all wear a sly or slightly sinister look.

Card games of the day bear odd-sounding names and many games cannot now be defined. Primero, one of the oldest of these, was very popular. In it every card seems to have had treble its value, while the knave of hearts was the 'quinona', which counted as any card of any suit the holder desired. 'Come you from the king, my lord?' Sir Thomas Lovell asks Bishop Gardiner at one o'clock in the morning; to this the bishop replies, 'I did Sir Thomas; and left him at primero, with the Duke of Suffolk.'[18] The king lost this time to Charlie. And Falstaff admits to Dr Caius, 'I never prospered since I for-swore myself at Primero.'[19] Hence, Primero must have been fairly universally played. Prime was another game and seems to have been related to Primero.

Gresco was an old game about which I know nothing. Gleek, sometimes called 'Cleke', was a game for three players in which forty-four cards were dealt, twelve to each player, and the eight remaining formed a common pool. Lodam, probably a corruption of Loadum, may have come from the Italian game *Carica l'asino*. Losing Lodam seemed popular, as he who won lost; that is to say, the lowest score was the winning score. Noddy was hardly a game to be played in a semi-somnolent state, as it was much used for gambling; it may have slightly resembled Cribbage, which was not invented until the seventeenth century. Noddy was also the name given to the knave in other card games. New Cut was also played, and about this little is known. Put or Putt resembled our Nap. All Fours was the Tudor version of Seven Up. In Post, or Post and Pair, each player received three cards and bet on them; it was also known as 'bone ace' and the chances of winning were so slight that it had a third name, 'the fool's game'. Pinion was certainly a card game but has winged its way into total oblivion. Then there was Ruff, which was similar to Triumph or Trump.

Trump, too, was an old game and popular with all classes. Dame Chat in *Gammer Gurton's Needle*, which was written no one knows quite when, but probably some time between the reign of King Henry VII and the early years of Queen Elizabeth I, is 'fast set at trump' when the mischievous beggar Diccon enters. She invites him to play. He refuses, and she turns to her maid Doll and says:

> Come hither, Doll! Doll, sit down and play this game,
> And as thou sawst me do, see thou do even the same –
> There is five trumps beside the queen, the hindmost thou
>   shalt find her.
> Take heed of Sim Glover's wife, she hath an eye behind
>   her![20]

The last remark may have been a slander upon Sim Glover's wife, but certainly the unknown author indicates that the game of Trump was known and played by ordinary village 'gossips', although the play was of 'academic origin'.[21]

These were indoor games played at home or in taverns and inns, but there were as many, if not more, outdoor pastimes. A very old game was Prisoners' Bars or Prisoners' Base, which had been known since the days of Edward III (1327–77) at least. The game probably came from, or was picked up in, France, where it was known as *les barres* or *Jeu aux barres*, and it was played by boys and men. Royalty was not above playing this game and the young Edward VI notes in his journal that at this particular sport 'the King wanne'.[22] This game, with time-altered rules, survives today.

Unlike Prisoners' Base, which could be played by any team anywhere, tennis, sometimes called 'paume' or 'palme', was a game for the rich and noble. Henry Howard, Earl of Surrey, the courtier–poet, speaks of this as being one of the delights of the court of Henry VIII at Windsor:

> ... The palme playe, where, dispoyled for the game,
> With dased eyes oft we by gleames of love,
> Have mist the ball ...[23]

Henry VII, who played chess, backgammon, cards and dice, shot at the butts, watched bull-baiting and 'throwing at Cocks' (a Shrovetide custom), and seems to have participated reasonably

Late fifteenth-century inn

thoroughly in all the sports and pastimes of his age, also played tennis. On 14 July 1493, Sir Charles Somerset and Sir Robert Curson 'with the balls'[24] won £1 7s. 6d. at tennis with the king. The king seems to have been no more lucky at tennis than at cards, for frequent losses at 'tenes' are listed.

Tennis was played on a covered court – lawn tennis is a nineteenth-century game – and covered courts had to be specially built; also the game itself was complicated. Henry VIII, who was a very keen and a very good tennis player, had new covered courts built at Whitehall and Hampton Court and he played the game abroad as well as at home. In 1532 at Calais, playing against 'Cardynall De larenero and Mouns. le guyse',[25] he lost £45 13s. 4d., a large sum, but not nearly so much as he often lost. And we know from Hall that in 1511, when the king was nineteen, he was 'much entysed to playe at tennys and at dice' by crafty persons who imported Frenchmen and Lombards to play against him, 'and so he lost much money'. Hall does not say how much his hero lost – but he does tell of another game which the king played in 1522 with the Emperor Charles V. 'They playd at tennice,' he says, '... agaynst the prince of Orenge and the Marques of Brandenborrow ... they departed even handes on both sydes after xi games fully played.'

Other ball games far less exclusive and far more generally played were Hand Ball and Balloon Ball. This last was played by batting an inflated bladder about with the hand. Bandy Ball was played with a small leather ball stuffed with feathers which was struck with a crooked or bent – hence bandy – bat. Ring Ball was much the same, but here the object was to drive the ball through a ring set in the ground.

Football was known and was a very rough game indeed. Appropriately enough, one of the customs of the shoemakers of Chester was to play the game every Shrove Tuesday. Starting from a field outside the city they played through the city streets to the Common Hall. This caused such inconvenience and such bashing about of players and of citizens going about their lawful business that it was prohibited in 1540.

Sir Thomas Elyot (1490?–1546) is positively choleric about football, 'wherein,' he says, 'is nothing but beastly fury and extreme violence; wherefore proceedeth hurt and consequently rancour and malice do remain with those that be wounded; whereof it is to be put into perpetual silence.'[26]

Still, a good deal of blood could be drawn by other sports, such as cudgel-play, in which, armed with heavy sticks, opponents tried to see which one could lay open the other's scalp first. A variant of this was played with shorter sticks weighted at each end with lead – rather like a primitive dumb-bell – which when brandished about 'opened the chest',[27] but whether of the bran-disher or of some unfortunate opponent is not clear, since the phrase 'opened the chest' can have two meanings. Wrestling, too, was great sport and apparently differed in different parts of the country. The fashion in the adjacent countries of Cornwall and Devon differed only in that although all holds were legal above the waist or on any part of the jacket or smock, and each wrestler wore loose canvas shoes, Devon wrestlers had theirs very thick-soled so they could kick each other's shins with great gusto and vigour.

Sword-play was now more used to exhibit skill than to do damage. Running at the quintain and tilting were great favourites, splendidly done and with much pageantry at court and simply done in the country. Tilting at the quintain began as a military exercise before becoming a sport. At first the quintain had been merely a post to be struck by the rider with his lance as he galloped past. Then the post became a carved wooden figure on a pivot; the figure held a sword and, if not struck in the right place, swivelled round and hit the rider on the back with it.

A much more simple quintain, and one more commonly used, consisted of a cross-bar on a pivot. On one end of the bar hung a bag of sand or flour; on the other a broad piece of wood was fixed. If the tilter were not swift enough in getting away after hitting the piece of wood, then the cross-bar swivelled and he himself was hit by the bag which, were it a sand-bag and not a flour-bag, could inflict some injury. This unpretentious quintain and the sport of running at it were popular throughout the country – in towns as well as in rural areas. The 'youthful citizens' of London practised running at the quintain at Christmastide and also during the summer. Stow recollects that he has seen the quintain in Cornhill and says: 'he that hit not the broad end ... was of all men laughed to scorn and he that hit it full if he rid not faster, had a sound blow on his neck with a bag of sand hung on the other end.'[28] Then there was a form of water quintain where the rowers in wherries faced the bow instead of the stern and the participants tilted against each other with sticks – 'and for the most part one or both [were] overthrown and well ducked.'[29]

The overthrown probably came to no harm, as swimming seems to have been an accomplishment and a sport more practised by all classes then than now. There is mention of swimming in Book XII of *Piers Ploughman*, while Sir Thomas Elyot refers to it as 'an exercise which is right profitable in extreme danger of wars'.[30] When the water froze in rivers, lakes and ponds, sliding and skating were favourite pastimes. Skating, we know from William Fitzherbert's *Description of London*,★ was popular in the twelfth century. Skates then were made by binding the shin-bone of an animal to each shoe by means of a leather thong threaded through holes made at the front end and back end of the bone. The skater propelled himself along with an iron-shod pole. Sometimes two skaters would skate towards each other and engage in combat with their poles as weapons; 'either one or both of them fall,' Fitzherbert says, 'not without some bodily hurt ... and whatever part of their heads comes in contact with the ice is laid bare to the very skull.' Broken arms and legs were quite usual, and we have no reason to believe that this sport did not persist into Tudor times and later, although wooden skates shod with iron or steel may have been introduced from the Low Countries.

There were, too, a number of throwing games, among them

★ Fitzherbert (d. 1190?) wrote a biography of Thomas à Becket, *Vita Sancti Thomae*, in which the Description appears. Stow printed it with his *Survey of London*.

quoits: the quoit was a flat disc of metal or stone which, when thrown, cut into the ground or, if off the mark, did the same office for an unwary spectator. Tossing the weight required more brute strength than quoits and was a favourite in country districts. The weight was a beam or bar and this sport was much favoured by Henry VIII in his youth. In fact, when a young king, he exercised himself daily in 'shotyng, singing, dauncing, wrastling [and] casting of the barre'.[31]

Shooting was, of course, with bow and arrow and this again was a necessary military art as well as a sport. In the reign of Henry VII, although in 1492 the king lost 13s. 4d. 'at the Buttes shooting with his cross Bow'[32] against Sir Edward Borough, he forbade the use of the crossbow, and this prohibition was reinforced but later withdrawn by his son.

Henry VIII, who in his youth was good at all sports, was, as might be expected, a magnificent archer and could 'draw the bow with greater strength than any man in England'.[33] He further promoted the practice of shooting with the longbow by an act which compelled every male subject to keep a bow and arrow continually in the house. Exceptions were made for those over sixty, the physically handicapped, ecclesiastics, justices of the two benches and of the assizes and barons of the exchequer. Further, fathers or male guardians of boys had to teach them the use of the bow and had to provide the child with a bow of his own at the age of seven. Masters had to supply bows to apprentices and compel them to go shooting with them at the butts on holidays. The short-lived Prince Arthur was such a good shot that, it is said, expert archers were often called 'Arthur'. The prince, we know, had been provided with a bow which cost 6s. 8d. when he was about six years old. It may or may not have been his first bow but he must have practised regularly to have become so expert at such an early age. The young Edward VI was an excellent archer, too, and also indulged in hunting and tennis. In fact, it was becoming overheated at tennis and then over-drinking which caused the king's fatal illness, according to that nonentity poet, William Baldurn (fl.1547), in his *Funerelles of King Edward the Sixt*.

When shooting for practice and for sport (apart from live game) archers shot at butts – tall mounds surmounted by a target, usually at each end of the field – at pricks or rovers. A prick is the bull's-eye of a target and a rover is a mark selected at random and not at any fixed distance from the archer. 'At rover or pricks,' Elyot says, 'it is at his pleasure that shooteth how fast or softly he listeth to go. And yet it is the praise of the shooter neither more nor less, for as far or nigh is the mark of his arrow when he goeth softly as when he runneth.'[34] Elyot was, of course, writing about sports suitable for young men of the nobility and gentry who were destined to become 'governors' – a classless society was unthinkable in the sixteenth century – who were those gentlemen who helped the king to rule. These fledgeling officials were urged to shoot with the longbow, as this 'excelleth all other excercises and games incomparably'.[35]

That brilliant educator, Roger Ascham, who was, it is said, addicted to cock-fighting, wrote the first book in English on archery. Entitled *Toxophilus or the Schole of shooting* (1545), it stressed the importance of physical training in education and gave much information on equipment. Bows, he says, are best made of yew – elm and ash are also good – and should taper from the middle to each end. Bow-strings should be of good hemp, flax or silk, while the wood of the 'wand', or stick, of the arrow should be according to the different purposes of shooting: ash for military arrows, oak for pastime or sport, followed by hard beam or birch. Feathers from the wing of a grey goose were best for fletching, although there was argument over whether the second feather or the pinion were the better. Feathers of other birds were also used, and it was necessary for every archer to have several arrows differently fletched to allow for varying wind direction. Arrows had broad or forked heads, but Ascham thought round, pointed heads, similar to a bodkin, were best. The notch could be varied according to the occasion or the wish of the archer.

Shooting was used in the sport of kings, hunting, when the quarry was not brought down by dogs or driven into the 'toils' (nets). And there were heavy penalties for those who destroyed game in the royal forest. Although the severity of the forest laws had been modified since the time of King John and, fortunately, death or the loss of an arm or leg were no longer penalties, an offender could be massively fined, and in default of payment be put in gaol for a year and a day and subsequently have to find surety for his good behaviour.

There were a few exceptions: an archbishop, bishop, earl or baron, when travelling at the king's command through a royal forest – and there were many such forests – was permitted to kill one or two deer in the sight of the forester, provided he happened to be near. Were he not, a horn had to be sounded to show that the archbishop, or whoever the travelling dignitary was, did not intend to steal the deer.

Henry VIII, a tireless and constant horseman, could stay in the saddle for hours and often tired out eight or ten horses a day. Although deer, roe, buck and hart were the 'big game', our Tudor forebears hunted everything that could flee and beasts of the chase then included hare, fox, wolf, wild boar, marten, bear, cat, weasel, otter and even the squirrel, as well as beasts of 'stinking flight' – otherwise known as polecat and stoat. Both men and women hunted, and women too used the bow.

They hunted with hounds, harriers, greyhounds, bull-dogs, spaniels and mastiffs. They went at the fox and wolf from Christmas to the Annunciation, roebuck from Easter to Michaelmas, roe from Michaelmas to Candlemas, hare from Michaelmas to Midsummer and boar from Christmas to the Purification of Our Lady.

Hawking too was a sport for both sexes. Despite the fact that Elyot can find 'no notable remembrance that it was used of ancient time among noble princes' (adding, 'I call ancient times before a thousand years passed, since which time virtue and nobleness hath rather decayed'),[36] noble princes and princesses had been hawking in England since Anglo-Saxon times – and in China for some two thousand years. All the Tudor sovereigns and some of their consorts hawked, and the king's falconer was an important official. Other noble and gentle households also had falconers.

There was plenty of game to be had, and great open spaces where the goshawk, or goose-hawk, could pursue grouse, woodcock, duck and even seagull. The hawk was also used for rabbit, hare and magpie, but most splendid was when the hawk's prey was a heron. For partridge and snipe the 'tiercel' was used, whilst the merlin – one of the smallest but one of the boldest birds of prey – was used for small birds, particularly larks. The male, or jack-merlin, was noted for its beautiful plumage.

Training hawks was a long and sometimes difficult process. When the trained bird finally flew from the left wrist of the gauntleted hand of its master or mistress and pursued, stooped and brought down her prey, that prey was located by the jingling of bells tied to the hawk's legs. Hawks were not just hawks, as we have seen; there was a nomenclature for them – for example, a 'haggard' was a wild female caught when adult. A 'tiercel', 'tercel' or 'tassel' was any male hawk, but the name was applied more particularly to the peregrine falcon. 'Hist, Romeo, hist – O, for a falconer's voice/To lure this tassel-gentle back again,'[37] says Juliet from the balcony when trying to call Romeo back, thus indicating that she was well-versed in the art of falconry, for the falconer had a special call or whistle he used with the hawks.

A falcon required much training and was thought to be better when bred from the nest and not caught wild. Every bird required special paraphernalia: a hood of leather to blind her when not pursuing game, jesses – short straps of leather, silk or other material for each leg – to tie her to the wrist before loosing, and at the free end of the jess a varvel, to which the leash of thong or string was attached. During training, a creance or cord was fastened to the leash to keep the bird from flying away and a lure was used – a bunch of feathers to which the meat constituting the trainee's food was tied. When falcons were moulting they were kept in mews – not until much later did the word become connected with horses. And, rather unexpectedly, hawks could become very affectionately disposed towards their master. Sir

Thomas Wyatt (1503–42) expresses the faithfulness of the falcon in one of his short *Songes*. It begins, 'Luckes, my faire falcon and your fellowes all/Ye not forsake me that faire might ye befall,' and he swears by their bells, 'Ye be my fryndes, and so be but few elles.'[38]

Fortunately for friendship's sake – as well as that of sport – a falcon will keep for twenty years if properly looked after and will remain a sporting bird the whole time.

In his *Dyetary of Helthe*, Andrew Boorde, who gives exhaustive advice on how a gentleman's house and grounds should be constructed, insists that a pair of butts and bowling alley should be included to provide interest and amusement. Bowling was a popular pastime, not only in gentlemen's private grounds but on village greens all over the country. Allied to bowling was Kayles, rather like ninepins, only the pins were set in a single row and a club or baton thrown at them. Closh or Clash was similar to Kayles, but a bowl was used instead of a stick. Loggats was another variation of Kayles or Clash, and Hamlet has a grim little reference to this in the grave-diggers' scene: 'Did these bones cost no more the breeding but to play at loggats with 'em?'[39] he asks Horatio. This may imply that bones were used either as pins or as the throwing-piece in this rustic game.

Various games and ceremonies were associated with seasonal events other than Christmas and May Day. On Shrove Tuesday pancakes may or may not have been tossed but, traditionally, stones were tossed at a cock on this day. At other times and everywhere cock-fighting was a sport much favoured, and Henry VIII had a new cock-pit built at Whitehall. On May Day, apart from mumming, everyone went out into the fields or woods to gather flowers and green branches and to bring back the flower-bedecked maypole around which there was dancing. Sometimes little bowers were set up and used for feasting. 'Maids and men' going into the woods together on May-day eve often had the usual, delayed, result.

There were also games at Whitsun, and probably much leaping and vaulting, for both were popular throughout the century. On

Midsummer's Eve, the Vigil of St John the Baptist, bonfires were lit, dangerously in the towns and more safely in the country, and around these young people, garlanded and carrying bunches of flowers – violets for preference – gathered to dance. The young men showed off by leaping over the fire, which was kept alight until midnight and sometimes until cock-crow. It was believed that if the dancer looked at the fire through the flowers no pain would be felt in the eyes. The flowers were cast into the fire at midnight and then the dancers began their devotions, asking God to protect them, particularly from the ague.

Then there were annual feasts at Sheep-shearing in the spring and Harvest Home. These were country affairs and at Harvest Home the last load of corn brought in was decked with flowers. A 'kern baby' or corn dolly was also made and brought home, and around this the villagers sang and danced to pipe and drum; then followed a feast. There were also Church Ales, usually at Easter and Whitsun. These were essentially fund-raising affairs and, rather naughtily, the church-wardens and other parish officers brewed a very strong ale for the occasion. The parishioners paid for the ale and became rather more generous with their contributions as a result of the strength of the brew. So the church gained both in ale-money and contributions. In extenuation it should be said that this eased the parish rates a bit.

Courtly, as opposed to country, amusements included jousts and tournaments, the last romantic relic of the age of chivalry. With these Henry VIII was obsessed; he held them and participated in them upon every possible and impossible occasion. He was a notable jouster. 'The kyng being lusty young and couragious greatly delited in feates of chivalrie,' says Hall, adding that 'justs and tourneys' were a particular 'delite'. Even so, the court was afraid the king might come to some harm. At one joust in 1511, when the king and his men dressed in green silk and the Earl of Essex and his cohorts in blue, there was good running and many a broken spear, 'but for al the sport every man feared, lest some yll chaunce might happen to the king, and fayne would have had him a looker on, rather than a doer, and spake thereof

Henry VIII's armour: youth to old age

as much as thei durst, but his courage was so noble that he would ever be at one end.'⁴⁰ The king was temperamentally no looker-on at anything. He was a doer and fancied himself as such. It sometimes seems as if he must have thought of war as being merely a bigger and better form of tournament in which he, of course, was the principal jouster. He broke his head once in a tournament, as we have seen, and he broke the country by his wars.

Tournaments may have been a form of palpable nostalgia for the old chivalric days but the same can hardly be said for bull- and bear-baiting, both of which had been popular with all classes for centuries and were to continue to be popular for centuries more. Most towns and villages, especially market towns, had a bull-ring where chained bulls and bears were baited by dogs. There were bear gardens on Bankside 'whereon', says Stow, 'there be prepared scaffolds for beholders to stand upon',[41] and they were 'much frequented'. At one bear-baiting at Bankside, however, the scaffold offered no protection to one spectator, for 'the grett blynd bere broke losse, and in a ronnynge he chalkt [caught] a servyng man by the calff of the lege and bytt a gret pesse away'.[42] Doubtless this caused the spectators almost as much pleasure as the baiting of a blind bear, for it was an age when people were just as cruel to each other as they were to animals.

It was, of course, an adolescent age as well, and when all else failed or the weather was poor, which was not unusual, there was nothing like a merry jest or a riddle to enliven whatever proceedings there were or to while away a dull evening. Riddling was a splendid form of amusement; often the riddles are either coarse or childishly simple. 'What is it,' asks one, 'that freezes never?' and the answer is, 'That is hot water.' This is hardly a side-splitter, but men rolled on the floor or slapped each other in an ecstasy of delight with the embarrassment of the ladies of the company at such riddles as the following – and in verse too!

> A vessel I have
> That is round like a pear,
> Moist in the middle,
> Surrounded with hair,
> And often it happens
> That water flows there.[43]

The answer is – Oh, ha, ha – 'An Eye'.

Equally schoolboy is a French riddle (many riddles were French) which is hardly noted for its Gallic wit: 'Qu'est-ce que plus on quiert et moins on le trouve?' The reply – 'C'est le fond d'un con.' Farting too was a subject much dwelt upon in riddles and jests, as was excrement. As to the old one still known to us: 'What came first the hen or the egg?', they had the irrefutable answer straight from Genesis: 'The hen when God made her.'[44]

Although there was no theatre as such in those days – the first playhouse was not built in London until 1576, at Shoreditch* – there were plays of well-defined types which had both a public and a limited appeal. These can be rather loosely termed Mysteries, Miracles, Moralities and Interludes. Mystery and Miracle plays really cannot be differentiated and, since the term 'Mystery' does not appear in this particular connection until 1744, 'Miracle' is the older and better word to use in describing this type of play, which has its roots in early medieval times.

The progenitors of the Miracle play were 'tropes', or chanted Latin dialogues, which were added to the mass at Easter and at Christmas. An integral part of Divine Service, they were performed by the clergy, and out of these more or less static additions to the service the Miracle play evolved. Its subject matter – of which more later – came originally from stories in the New Testament, and later on from the Old Testament; later still, the lives of the saints were added to the repertoire. The saint plays do not survive in this country; they were destroyed at the Reformation.

The Morality was different and of later origin. It was intended to edify the onlookers as, indeed, was the Miracle. But the Morality edified by personifying vices and virtues fighting for the possession of the human soul. Probably the most famous Morality play, or the best known to us, is *Everyman*, written in the late fifteenth century and very probably of Flemish origin. Its theme, however, was based on the then very universal emotion, Everyman's fear of death, and his spiritual victory over this fear. An unquestionably English play, although written by an

* The first building of wood was erected by James Burbage (d. 1597), a joiner by trade, one of the Earl of Leicester's players and father of Richard Burbage (1567?–1619) the celebrated actor.

unknown author in 1553* or a bit later, is *Respublica*. It too is a Morality play, although often classed as an Interlude.

The Interlude, as the name seems to suggest, was possibly set between two main items of a larger entertainment.† It was a short play performed more often than not by strolling players or Interluders on festive occasions in the hall of a great house, at the Inns of Court, in colleges and certainly at Court. 'To two players in the Hall £1 6s. 8d.'⁴⁵ is one of the payments made on behalf of Henry VII during the Christmas festivities of 1495, and on 2 January 1503 another item reads, 'To the pleyers of Essex in rewarde £1', which suggests they were strolling players.

Unlike the Morality, the Interlude did not always aim at uplifting the character and morals of the audience; it was often a serious enough piece but it was also often comic and combined 'mirth with modesty'.⁴⁶ It could be serio-comic and sometimes had all the qualities of a farce. It was also occasionally used for propaganda purposes. For example, the Bishop of Ossory, John Bale (1495–1563), who wrote the first English historical play, *King John*, also wrote a number of excessively bad plays attacking the Roman Catholic Church, and to one of these, *The Whore of Babylon* (1546), Edward VI was either persuaded to lend, or willingly lent, his name. The one really savage riposte to this kind of attack was *Respublica* where, understandably enough, the new queen, Mary Tudor, is represented as Nemesis, whilst a clutch of Protestants represent Avarice, Indolence, Oppression and Adulation, all of which cheat and delude Respublica, a widow of the 'poore Commontie'. The theme of the play, although like other Miracles, Moralities and Interludes it has comic touches, is retribution, the usual method then of restoring the fallen fortunes of the virtuous.

A still readable and amusing Interlude is *The Playe called the*

---

* Earlier than this is *Ane Pleasant Satyre of the Thrie Estastis* by the Scottish poet, Sir David Lindsay (1490–1553). It was produced before James V in 1540.

† Sir E. K. Chambers in *The Medieval Stage* (1903) holds that the word, deriving as it does from *Interludium*, was a *ludus* carried on between two or more performers.

Foure PP by John Heywood (1497?–1580), first published around 1544. Heywood wrote a number of Interludes, but 'The Four Ps' harks back and shows us three typical medieval figures, the Palmer, the Pardoner and the Pothecary, who hold a contest to show off their skills in telling lies. A further stock character, the Pedlar, is the judge. The lies told are preposterous, amusing and coarse; at one point the Pardoner displays a relic with these words:

> . . . behold, here may ye see
> The great-toe of the Trinity.
> Who to this toe any money vow'th,
> And once may roll it in his mouth,
> All his life after, I undertake,
> He shall be rid of the tooth-ache.[47]

The winning liar is the Palmer, but the Interlude ends on a serious note when the winner beseeches the Lord 'to prosper you all/In the faith of the Church Universal!' As Heywood, a Catholic, was much in favour with Queen Mary and had to withdraw to the continent upon her death, by 'the Church Universal' he doubtless meant the Roman Catholic Church. This brings us back again to the Miracle plays.

Tropes, it seems, developed within the 'Church Universal' into what might be called tableaux, which grew in context and size and finally became the Miracle play. They also moved from the chancel to the nave, where they could be set up in a series of incidents to be seen, in sequence, by the spectators moving through the body of the church. Finally, as they were further elaborated, the church became too small to hold them and they moved outside to be performed in any space beside the church or on some other piece of open ground. When this again grew too small for the press of people, the scenes were mounted upon pageants and drawn through the streets – the word 'pageant' means a movable stage, that is, one on wheels, as well as what is produced upon that stage.

Pageants of the wheeled variety may have looked rather like

a large Punch-and-Judy stand, with a stage for the actors on top, covered perhaps by a painted canvas roof and, below the stage and concealed by painted cloth, a dressing-room, a place for props and a space into which Lucifer fell, as he always ultimately did, or from which a dragon could emerge to be slain, as he always finally was. These pageants, upon which the story was depicted serially, were hauled through the streets and stopped, in turn, at certain specified points or open spaces where the spectators waited to see each scene as it appeared or, if lucky, saw it in serial form from a window along the route.

It was in the mid thirteenth century that Miracle plays received the real impetus which was to turn them into great cycles of religious dramas★ and when they also became as much connected with the laity as with the clergy. This was because in 1246 Pope Urban IV proclaimed the hitherto local feast of Corpus Christi an annual festival to be celebrated throughout the Roman Catholic world.† The Latin liturgical playlets continued within the church as part of the celebration of different liturgical seasons but the Miracle plays, by now in the vernacular, were not, as we know, so restricted as to either language or form, and in England they became a part of the festivities usual at Whitsun and, more particularly, at Corpus Christi – probably because in our climate the weather is more favourable then for outdoor performances than, say, at Christmas or Easter.

Thus our great Corpus Christi dramas, which embody the whole scheme of Christian salvation, began to grow. A very much wider interpretation was given to the stories presented and they became enormously popular with the people. A recalcitrant and angry Mrs Noah – an English interpretation – having to be

---

★ Our four great cycles, York, Chester, Coventry and Wakefield (Towneley) are called after the towns where they were, or are traditionally thought to have been, performed and have come down to us almost intact. Many others have not survived, while others still, such as the Cornish cycle (in Cymric) and the Beverley cycle are very fragmentary. There were independent plays as well, a favourite theme of these being *The Conversion of St Paul*.

† This Bill was confirmed by the General Council of Vienne in 1311.

persuaded to leave her gossips and enter the Ark and then giving poor Noah a sound box on the ear must have convulsed spectators, because it is both realistic and funny. The Second Shepherd's Play has its comic side in Mak the sheep-stealer, yet this is allied to the seriousness of the nativity scenes.

By the fourteenth century the Corpus Christi dramas had become the special province of the trade guilds, and the Thursday after Trinity Sunday had become a high festival for everyone. The Host was carried in procession through the streets and exhibited at various pre-arranged places. The procession was secular as well as religious, for the municipal authorities and the trade guilds formed a most important part of it, and thus, in a sense, the Miracles moved into the market place.

The guilds, which were the firm foundation of the middle and upper working classes, were active in community affairs and took an enormous interest in the Miracles, which soon became the special object of their care and attention. This ultimately led to the fostering of the great dramatic cycles of York, Chester,* Coventry and Wakefield. Each guild, wherever the Miracles were performed, would contribute to the series of episodes according to its own particular skill. The guilds also paid for, and produced, the episodes. Thus, *The Marriage at Cana* (now lost) was the concern of the Vintners, *Noah's Flood* appropriately fell to the Shipwrights, *The Adoration of the Magi*, with all its emphasis on splendid apparel and gifts, was presented by the Goldsmiths – only they could supply the right props – whilst *The Last Supper*, which must have required an extra-long pageant to hold the table, was the province of the Bakers.

Nor was there any nonsense about not representing God on stage. He was a part of daily life and He appeared when necessary and spoke or, more probably, intoned His lines as occasion demanded. God, like nearly all actors, must have been a local person (members of the guild were often the actors too), so

---

* At Chester the cycle of twenty-four plays was performed on Corpus Christi and moved to different stations. The whole twenty-four were played at each.

when the time came to reckon the cost it would be common knowledge in the town and surrounding district how much the skins of white leather for His gloves had cost and how much the gold leaf which made His countenance shine had come to, as well as how much the actor himself had been paid. Indeed, in a performance of the Noah pageant at Hull on Plough Monday, 1483, one Robert Brown received 6d. for his role as God.

Some ordinary man must have had to assume the role of Christ in various pageants but the man chosen for such a part, we may reasonably assume, must have had a deep religious conviction, since through him Christian salvation was expressed. The Passion plays formed a large part of the cycles, but the *Crucifixion* of the York cycle is so merciless that it makes almost unbearable reading even today.

Some, if not all, of these plays contained singing and music and it is not too far-fetched to see in them, as well as in some of the Moralities, the germ of the oratorio which, in its present sense, originated around 1600.

Reading was also a pastime, but a limited one: only a very small percentage of the population was literate and there were very few books available. Or, rather, there had been very few books until the late fifteenth century when William Caxton (1422–91), a successful English merchant, took to printing because he, like William Morris later, wanted to publish books to suit his own taste. Caxton, who had lived much abroad and had had a printing press at Bruges, returned home in 1476 and set up the first English printing press in the precincts of Westminster Abbey at the sign of the Red Pale. He enjoyed the patronage and custom of the Yorkist kings, Edward IV and Richard III. His first English author was in fact the brother-in-law of Edward IV, Anthony Woodville, second Earl Rivers, whose translation from the French, *Dictes or Sayeings of the Philosophres*, was the first book ever published here. It came out in 1477 and in the same year, or possibly the next, Caxton brought out Chaucer's *Canterbury Tales;* a second edition followed in 1484, and between 1492 and 1498 his *Parlement of Foules, Hous of Fame, Boece* and

Troilus and Cryseide were published. So printing with the new movable type came to this country only eight years before the first Tudor won the throne and the earlier Tudor period saw its rapid and lusty growth.

In a very short space of time, printing became the chief vehicle for conveying ideas, and it remained so until the present century. Whether this new form of rapid communication created a greater demand for subject matter we cannot say, but it seems probable, on the analogy that wireless and television, both voracious media, have done so in our own time. But there was also a backlog of centuries of manuscripts to be transformed into books in the new 'artificial script', as it was first called, and 'of early printed books hardly any are by contemporaries'.[48]

A lively interest in past history was one of the main features of this early period, probably because countries which have just emerged from protracted wars do not, as a rule, face the future with great self-confidence and are apt to look back upon the past as containing a 'golden age'. This 'golden age' tends to vary according to the century which does the looking back. Dryden, for example, thought of the Elizabethans as a Giant Race before the Flood, while we used to think of the eighteenth century as a golden era. Thus, in the time of Henry VII people looked back to the days of Edward III, Chaucer and Lydgate. One of the most popular of early publications was John de Trevisa's translation of Ranulph Higden's *Polychronicon* (1495). As Higden had died in 1364 and Trevisa (1326–1412) had made his translation from the Latin in 1387, this universal history can hardly have brought the reader up to date, but it was vigorous reading, as was Sir John Mandeville's *Travels* (1496). Who Sir John was is still a matter of speculation, but his *Travels*, written in French around 1370, were a wonderful compilation of adventures in the Middle East, complete with details of fantastic monsters and even more fantastic human (or sub-human) beings. This remarkable literary forgery engendered wonder, amazement and belief in its readers. Quite different was *The New Chronicles of England and France* (1516) by Robert Fabyan (d. 1513). This was printed by

Richard Pynson and reprinted with enlargements three times between 1516 and 1560. It was the first of the Tudor histories and it is doubtful if anyone who enjoyed reading failed to read it, while dramatists found it excellent for source material.

Caxton and his successors* published translations, the classics and original works by English authors, and it is with a few of these we are briefly concerned. English authors at this period were, on the whole, relatively dull. It is not until we get to the Elizabethans that we emerge from what C. S. Lewis terms the 'Drab Age' in literature. (By 'drab' he means artificial and heavy prose, with verse lacking in richness of sound and imagery.)

Of course, contemporary work may not have seemed drab to those who lived then, and it must have been a fresh excitement and interest to buy newly printed books on all subjects and to build a special library to accommodate these new volumes, rather than sticking to the shelves and chests which held manuscript works. We do not know how many books constituted an edition, so it is difficult to estimate readership, but 'the average edition of a book printed in the fifteenth century was probably not more than about 200 – which, however, it must be kept in mind, was a 200-fold increase upon the scribe's work'.[49]

Yet the next century saw what must have been an explosion in printing. The new medium made rapid progress and gained in popularity; presses were set up all over Europe and the 'best seller' arrived. As a matter of interest, this was *De Imitatione Christi* by Thomas à Kempis, and its first appearance in English was in 1503. This was a translation from the French of the first book and it was made by the Lady Margaret Beaufort. In the same year, or a year later, William Atkinson translated the first three books, and Richard Whytford made a complete translation in 1556, towards the close of Mary's reign. Indeed, the greatest publishing successes of that time were theological, liturgical and legal books, which suggests a large readership amongst students and the serious-minded.

* They were, in the period under review, Wynkyn de Worde, William Fawkes, Richard Pynson, Richard Grafton and Edward Whitechurch (d. 1562).

One book, published abroad in 1526 but banned in this country, had nevertheless a wide circulation here. This was the New Testament in an English translation. The translator, William Tyndale (1494?–1536), also translated the Pentateuch, other parts of the Old Testament and various controversial works; for these sins he was strangled and burned at the stake near Brussels as a heretic. His most vigorous opponent in England was Sir Thomas More, but More himself was made a martyr by his friend Henry VIII when the king turned from the persecutor to the patron of translators.

In 1534 Miles Coverdale (1488–1568), sometime Bishop of Exeter, translated the complete Bible. It was published abroad, bore an unauthorized dedication to the king and was brought into England in 1535. Then in 1537 appeared the so-called 'Matthew Bible'. It purported to be the translation of one Thomas Matthew, whom no one has been able to trace, but it was 'edited' by John Rogers (1500–55), the first victim of the Marian persecutions. This Bible was published by the king's special licence so, in a sense, it is the first 'authorized' version in our history. In 1539 the 'Great Bible' appeared, revised by Coverdale and printed in Paris, as English presses were not good enough for the work. The second edition, known as 'Cranmer's Bible', came out in 1540 and bears a statement on its title page: 'This is the Bible appointed to the use of churches.' Although it was a large and bulky book, there were many reprints – it was very popular.

By 1543, however, the king felt that 'unrestricted reading of the Bible was a dangerous thing',[50] and that 'free disputation by unlearned men was improper',[51] so an act was passed which condemned heretical books as well as 'all craftye, false and untrue'[52] translations of the Bible, including that of Tyndale. Even the reading of the approved version was severely curtailed. None save those appointed by the king could read it in churches. Noblemen and gentlemen were permitted to read it to their families. Merchants, if well-established, and gentlemen could read it to themselves, but no one else was allowed to read it at all.

There, must, however, have been secret readings by those prohibited to do so.

The next edition was the Geneva Bible, smaller and more manageable. The New Testament was published at Geneva in 1557 and was proscribed by Queen Mary. The entire Geneva Bible, also known as the 'Breeches Bible' and dedicated to Queen Elizabeth, did not appear until 1560. Like Tyndale's version, it has extremely tendentious marginal comments.

There were also, as we know, two Edwardian prayer-books. In the revised edition of 1552, Archbishop Cranmer fixed the liturgical order of the English Church in most beautiful prose. The book must have been within the reach of many, as it cost 2s. 2d. unbound and 3s. 8d. bound. In 1550 John Merbecke (d. 1585), musician and theologian, who in 1543 had narrowly escaped being burnt for heresy, compiled and put together *The Booke of Common Praier Noted*, and this provided the first printed musical setting of the English liturgy. Thus the Bible in English and the Book of Common Prayer first became a part of our English literature.

There were other translations too; those of French romances were common, and there is at least one English prose work which was probably of much interest to the Tudor monarchy, particularly to Henry VII.* This is the *Morte d'Arthur*, by Sir Thomas Malory (fl. 1470), which was published in 1485 in time to welcome the first Tudor to the throne. Although, strictly speaking, the work is not originally English, for it is a translation from the French with additions from other sources, Malory gathered together the chief body of Arthurian legends and so produced a seminal book which has been read, used, worked over and drawn upon from that day to this.

As for 'all-English' works, they were less interesting and had less merit. There was *A Treatyse of Fysshynge with an Angle* (1495), which may have appealed some thirty years later to Henry VIII,

---

* Miss Agnes Strickland says that while he was a virtual prisoner in Brittany Henry of Richmond had no other amusement than the stories of Arthur and that 'much of the royal brain was occupied in ballads of the "Mort d'Artur" '.[53]

as we know that on 13 August 1530 he rewarded John Tylson for 'Two Angelyng Roddes' which were brought to him at Hampton Court. The treatise, or teach-yourself type of book, seems – apart from the translations – to have held the publishing field and this does make English literature appear rather drab. Among the treatises published during the period was Anthony? Fitzherbert's *Boke of Husbandrie* (1523), the first practical manual on agriculture. The first Latin–English dictionary came out in 1532 and another by Sir Thomas Elyot followed in 1538. Robert Recorde (1510?–88), the mathematician who either invented or was the first to use the equal (=) sign, wrote in 1537 *Introduction to lerne to recken with the Pen*, followed in 1540 by *The Ground of Artes*. Then came Ascham's *Toxophilis* (1545), which uses dialogue, later to become a fashionable technique. In 1551 came another two books by the indefatigable Recorde: *The Pathway to Knowledge*, on geometry, and *The Castle of Knowledge*, which deals with astronomy. He rounded off his career with *The Whetstone of Witte* (1557), which discourses on algebra and can hardly be called light reading. Thomas Tusser's *A hundreth good poyntes of husbandry* also appeared in this year and was undoubtedly more enjoyable to many readers than sharpening their brains by learning algebra. In any event, Tusser's book is still interesting and instructive.

Mention should be made here of Sir Thomas More's *History of Richard the Thirde*, notable for its narrative prose style, but as it is based on information supplied by Cardinal Morton (some critics think he wrote it) the picture of Richard is too vindictive and not to be trusted. The *History* was printed in Richard Grafton's *Chronicle* (1543) eight years after More's execution, and was rather imperfectly done. More's principal literary work, *Utopia*, written in Latin and printed in Louvain in 1516, was not translated and published in this country until 1551.

Poetry of this period had its own difficulties. A change in language from what we call Middle English to Modern English had taken place during the century after the death of Chaucer. Pronunciation had altered and was altering, the old metre had virtually collapsed and the patterns used and established by Chaucer had become impossible. Poets had to struggle with shifts of emphasis and stress because of these changes.

John Skelton is what might be called a transitional poet, in that he looks back to fifteenth-century poetry and forward to the Renaissance, and he was given the purely academic distinction of being made Poet Laureate by both Oxford and Cambridge. His verse is generally satirical: *The Bowge of Court*, in traditional rhyme-royal stanzas, is a satire on the court life of Henry VII, while his *Speke, Parrot* and *Why come ye nat to courte?* attacked Cardinal Wolsey so bitterly that Skelton had to seek sanctuary in Westminster, where he died; *The Boke of Phylyp Sparowe* contains a parody of certain parts of the Latin liturgy of the Church, including the Office for the Dead. *A Garlande of Laurell* is full of self-praise, whilst *Colyn Cloute* had some influence on Spenser. His very vigorous *The Tunning of Eleynor Rumming* deals humorously with contemporary low life, and he also wrote a Morality, *Magnyfycence*.

Skelton's verse is lively, rough, very personal, outspoken and, as he himself said of it in *Colyn Cloute*, '. . . ragged/Tattered and iaggéd'. But 'a new company of courtly makers'[54] – 'maker' means poet – came into being at this time. Its two chief exponents were Sir Thomas Wyatt,* said to have been a lover of Anne Boleyn before her marriage, and Henry Howard, by courtesy Earl of Surrey, who was executed at the age of thirty on a frivolous charge of treason. Both men had travelled in Italy and learned much of Italian and French poetry and they returned home to polish the metre and style of English poetry. Wyatt did much translating of foreign verse and experimented with a number of metres and stanza-forms. While in Italy he had come under the spell of the great fourteenth-century Italian poet, Francesco Petrarcha, the master of the sonnet of love (idealized), and he translated some of Petrarch's sonnets into English. He often follows Petrarchan forms in his own verse, albeit rather awk-

* Father of the Sir Thomas Wyatt who led the rebellion of 1554 against Queen Mary's Spanish marriage.

wardly, but he did re-establish – or establish – a new metrical discipline and style in English poetry. Wyatt's lyrics are far from awkward; they are charming, often poignant, and many are obviously meant to be sung. His 'Blame not my lute' is, perhaps, best known to us today.

Although Surrey is neither so subtle nor so strong as Wyatt, he undoubtedly enlarged the range of the English poetic voice. He is smoother, more assured and more graceful than his older contemporary and master, Wyatt, and his nature imagery is wider in scope. He too experimented with the Italian sonnet and seems finally to have settled for what is now known as the Shakespearian form. He also experimented with 'Poulter's Measure', a sort of dot-and-carry-one metre with lines of twelve and fourteen syllables alternating – a form which was to become very popular later in the century. But Surrey owes as much to Latin as to Italian poets and his translation of Books II and IV of Virgil's *Aeneid* (published by Tottel in 1557) introduced the use of blank verse into English poetry.

Some of Skelton's verse was printed during his lifetime (though dates are difficult to ascertain accurately) but, generally speaking, new poets were not printed. They circulated their poems in manuscript amongst their friends. But in 1557 Richard Tottel (d.1594) published *Songes and Sonnetts*, otherwise known as *Tottel's Miscellany*, which included poems by Surrey, Wyatt and Nicholas Grimald (1519–62), as well as other poems by 'Uncertain Authors'.* Grimald, who helped with the publication, has little to say and says it chiefly in Poulter's Measure.

Songes and Sonnetts, the forerunner of future compilations, went on being popular throughout the remainder of the century. There is an obvious reference to it in *The Merry Wives of Windsor* (1599?) when Slender, who wishes to woo Anne Page, says 'I had rather than forty shillings I had my book of Songs and Sonnets here',[55] and in the next breath asks his servant, Simple, if he has

---

* One of these is now identified as Thomas, Lord Vaux. Amongst the others may have been Sir John Cheke, John Heywood, Sir Anthony St Leger and Thomas Norton.

'The book of Riddles' with him. Clearly, Slender was the type who softened up his women with merry jests and song.

Singing, and all music for that matter, was not only a pleasure and a pastime; it was, as it had been for centuries, very much a part of daily life. Right from the beginning of the Tudor dynasty, music played an important role in all great and small events. In January 1486, for the marriage of the first Tudor to Elizabeth of York, there was much music. Thomas Ashwell (d. 1518?), a young composer who subsequently became master of the choristers of Lincoln Cathedral, wrote a five-part anthem, 'God Save King Harry', for the occasion, while Gilbert Banestre (d. 1487?), master of the Children of the Chapel Royal, wrote another, 'O Maria et Elizabeth', especially for the queen. The greatest amount of music – at least of that which survives – was church music (although there were no hymns★ as we know them) and Erasmus, for one, thought there was too much of it and that the monks, who should be lamenting their sins, attended to nothing but music, as though God were to be pleased by this gurgling. But then, great as he was, Erasmus was perhaps not musical. The English, great and small, were.

Music was, and had been for a very long time, a part of the education of gentlemen and an accomplishment they had to acquire, while for ordinary folk it was a joyful recreation. The court and many a noble household kept their own bands of musicians – minstrel galleries are a common feature of great houses – and in villages groups of villagers provided music in parish churches and for singing and dancing on festive occasions.

The Tudor sovereigns were all musical – perhaps their Welsh blood came out most strongly here – and Henry VIII, who had received musical training as a part of his ecclesiastical education,

---

★ An undated version of nineteen psalms to the metre of *Chevy Chase* was made by Thomas Sternhold (d. 1549) and dedicated to Edward VI. Sternhold and John Hopkins (d. 1570) were jointly responsible for metrical versions of all the psalms. In 1549 the Psalter of David in four-part harmony was set by Robert Cowley. These were probably the precursors of the Anglican hymn, which did not become common until the late seventeenth century.

was an excellent musician, had a fine voice, played several instruments and was also – like King Henry VI – a composer. His son, Prince Edward, certainly played the lute, and we know that when king he at one time (1552) employed sixty-five secular musicians at court. The Princesses Mary and Elizabeth also inherited this love of music. The Princess Mary played the virginals uncommonly well and had done so since the age of five. She also played the lute and supported court musicians throughout her reign, as did her half-sister when she became queen.

Sir Thomas Elyot, although commending music as a necessary part of education, is not so sure that an indulgence – or overindulgence – in the art might not have very ill effects: '... I would not be thought to allure noblemen to have so much delectation therein that in playing and singing only they should put their whole study and felicity; as did the Emperor Nero.'[56] He felt it would be better that a nobleman should not be taught music than to take an 'inordinate delight' in it 'and by that be elected toward wantonness, abandoning gravity and the necessary cure [care] and office in the public weal to him committed'.[57]

What with musical-headed fling-brain officials helping to govern and the thought of Henry VIII, metaphorically speaking, playing the lute while London burns, Sir Thomas seems to treat our musical propensities with suspicion and alarm. This in itself suggests that as a nation we were indeed musical.

Further, very early on we had university degrees in music, something which countries of the continent did not have. The earliest Cambridge doctorate goes back to 1463 at least. Oxford lagged behind and it was not until 1511 that Robert Fayrfax (1464–1521), who had taken his degree at Cambridge, became Oxford's first Doctor of Music. Fayrfax was considered in his day to be the leading English composer.* He was organist and choirmaster of St Albans Cathedral and, when Queen Elizabeth of York visited St Albans in 1502, wrote a five-part motet for her, 'Aeterne laudis lilium'. In 1509 he sang at the funeral of Henry VII

---

* His music, published in 1960 by the American Institute of Musicology, shows that his work was most certainly worthy of the praise it received.

and at the coronation of Henry VIII. The latter granted him an annuity of £9 2s. 6d., which was less than a royal gardener received. But there were compensations. Fayrfax, a Gentleman of the Chapel Royal, was also made a 'poor knight' of Windsor in 1514, with a pension attached. Also, from 1514 to 1519 on each New Year's Day he was handsomely paid for copying and composing books and anthems. Perhaps the high point in his career came not long before his death, when the king took the Chapel Royal with him to the Field of the Cloth of Gold (he had also taken them to France in 1513). Here Fayrfax and the choir, combined with that of the Chapelle de Musique du Roi, sang before the French and English kings. Henry, as a musician, thought, or pretended to think, that music would link the two countries together and provide a bulwark against diplomatic quarrels. All, as we know, did not turn out to be as harmonious as expected.

Another famous musician–composer who attended this notable event was William Cornyshe (*c.* 1468–*c.* 1523). He was at the courts of both Henry VII and Henry VIII. He must have been a man of many and varied talents, for he was also an actor and singer, as were all Gentlemen of the Chapel Royal, and a producer of Interludes and pageants. In 1509 he became Master of the Children of the Chapel Royal. He wrote secular music for court banquets and masques and a few secular songs – some satirical – for instruments and voices, among them a setting for Skelton's 'Jolly Rutterkin'. His works also include motets, madrigals, magnificats and, in at least one instance, a prophecy! In 1493 he was paid 13s. 4d. by Henry VII for a prophecy, about what we do not know, but this was considerably less than the king paid to 'An astronomyer for a prognosticacon'[58] in 1500. This lucky fellow got £3 6s. 8d. Yet it is encouraging to see that in 1493 the king paid £30 for 'a par of organnes',[59] and in the previous January William Newark (*c.* 1450–1509), also a noted composer, Gentleman of the Chapel Royal and, later, Master of the Children, was paid £1 for 'making a song'.[60] The accounts of Henry VII are full of payments to poets and musicians, professional and amateur, and payments for songs or for instruments – and from one item we learn that it cost 13s. 4d. to 'sett the Kinges' clavy-cordes'.[61] We know too that, wherever the king went, music went with him.

Today the best-known musicians and composers of the early Tudor period are the three 'Ts', Taverner, Tye and Tallis. John Taverner (*c.* 1495–1545), organist and composer, became in 1526 Master of the Choristers at Wolsey's new Cardinal College (now Christ Church), for which he received £10 a year for living and commons. In 1528 he was convicted of heresy but apparently was not imprisoned, and he left or was dismissed from the college in 1530, whereupon he became a well-paid agent of Thomas Cromwell. These two professions must have been incompatible, for Taverner gave up music! Most of his work prior to giving up was, of course, church music, but some time in 1530 he contributed songs to Wynken de Worde's *Song Book* (printed musical notation had recently arrived): 'The bella', for four voices, and 'My Harte, My Minde' and 'Love wyll I', for three voices. In 1538 he helped to suppress with great violence four friaries in Boston, Lincolnshire, which sounds almost incredible but is not when we learn that he was later presented with two of them. Cromwell's agent, a rabid Protestant, seems to have fared better than Wolsey's slightly heretical musician. One of Taverner's best-known Masses, 'The Western Wind', is so called because it is based on a folk song of that name which does not survive.

Christopher Tye (*c.* 1500–73) was a composer and a poet, and around 1541 was choirmaster at Ely. In 1545 he took his musical doctorate at Cambridge and it is possible that he was music master to Edward VI. Certainly his *Actes of the Apostles*, in an English metrical version and set for four voices, is dedicated to the young king. This work, with lute accompaniment, was primarily intended for domestic education. Tye was chiefly noted for church and choral music but, as a poet, he probably set some of his own work.

Thomas Tallis (*c.* 1515–85), the youngest and last of the

three 'Ts', is called the father of English cathedral music. He served in the Chapel Royal under four Tudor monarchs, Henry VIII, Edward VI, Mary I and Elizabeth I, and was in fact the master of the great Elizabethan composer, William Byrd (1538?– 1623). His works include two Masses, two Latin Magnificats, Lamentations for five voices and more than fifty Latin motets, as well as psalms, litanies, thirty anthems and various secular songs. Tallis lifted the English school of music to heights never before reached, and it remained at that level until the death of its last representative, Orlando Gibbons, in 1625.

Church music was heard by all, as all went to church. Splendid music was composed and played by musicians and sung by trained choirs in cathedrals and private chapels. Much more simple melodies were produced in parish churches by the local inhabitants with their few instruments, and there must have been many an amateur composer, like Chaucer's Squire who 'coude songes make and well endyte',[62] whose music was never written down. There were also 'folk-songs . . . which are the common creative possession of many minds',[63] and, of course, rounds.

As for non-church music, there are records extant of vocal music but we have little to tell us what instrumental music was like, although we know what instruments were in use. However, the practice of 'playing vocal music on instruments indicates that it must, as a rule, have closely resembled sung music until the fashion of playing to audiences and with it the varieties of virtuosity arose.'[64]

This practice of playing sung music persisted until Elizabethan times: a song for any number of voices could be transferred to an equal number of instruments, a consort of instruments in fact. It must not be forgotten that we loved to sing and had many choirs and groups of singers, great and small. In churches, great houses, cottages, inns and taverns voices were raised in praise, relaxation and pleasure.

Ballads were popular, as they had always been, and so were carols, which include song–dances and joyful songs as well as the more specific 'nowells' and Easter carols. But ballads, traditional and new, often recounted not only tales of the past but also events of the day, tragic, heroic, marvellous, and they were often fashioned of new words to suit the topical event, although sung to old music. Formerly, bards had moved from place to place to sing ballads – famous bards visited castles, humble ones went to village fairs and markets, but now, with the coming of printing, this minstrelsy disappeared slowly and the broadsheet hawked by a chapman took its place.

The ballad, as the name implies, was once a song to be danced to, and dancing was also one of the great pleasures of the age. In villages, dancing to the accompaniment of voices, a stringed instrument, a bagpipe or a pipe and tabor was a common form of entertainment, and villagers capered about the green whenever weather or opportunity permitted. The traditional dances of country folk, and of gentlefolk too, were the circular or round dances for any number of people, the double file, also for any number, which was either in processional form or danced in 'sets', and 'sets' themselves, which were for two, three or four couples. There were also other gambols of a rustic type and, just as there were folk songs, there was folk-dancing, for the two cannot be separated.

Higher in the social scale dancing was even more popular and far more elaborate, and at court 'it is possible that more musicians were regularly occupied in providing dance-music than for any other purpose'.[65] Among the dances was *la volta*, much favoured by the young. It was a lively dance full of turns and bounds in which the dancers, facing each other in pairs, had to revolve like teetotums and at one point the lady was seized and lifted off her feet by her partner. Many an oldster doubted the propriety of this and *la volta* only became really respectable when Queen Elizabeth herself danced it at court.

There was the coranto, a quiet running dance probably in triple time. The gay galliard, a zestful dance, was a great favourite and, as it usually had five steps, *cinque pas*, in our English fashion it became known as the Sink-a-pace, which sounds far from zes.ful. There were also the new pavan, slow, stately and in simple duple time, and for which the dancers dressed elaborately, and something known as the 'bace' or basse-dance, also slow and stately, for which there is music still extant.

As usual when comparing modern activities with ancient ones, Sir Thomas Elyot seems to have little use for contemporary dancing: 'we now have base dances, bargenettes, pavions, turgions and rounds,'[66] he complains. These were nothing like the dances so commended by the ancient philosophers, particularly Socrates. A bargenette, or bargaret, was probably a rustic song–dance, whilst a turgion, or turdion, was a lively measure rather like a galliard.

Dancing at court was a chief amusement throughout the era, more particularly during the reign of Henry VIII. It was at this time that a different type of court entertainment, which had dancing as its basis, was introduced. This was the masque which, under Queen Elizabeth and the earlier Stuarts, was carried to great heights in which dancing, acting and vocal and instrumental music were all combined around some central theme. The very first mention of a masque in England comes in Hall's *Chronicle*, with Henry VIII – who else? – as its chief exponent. This took place on the night of Epiphany, 1512, when 'the kyng with xi other wer disguised after the maner of Italie, called a mask a thing not seen afore in England, thei wer appareled in garments long and brode, wrought all with gold, with visirs and cappes of gold, and after the banket doen, these Maskers came in with six gentlemen disguised in silke bearyng staffe torches, and desired the ladies to daunce, some were content, and some that knew the fashion of it refused, because it was not a thing commonly seen.'[67] This refusal on the part of those who 'knew the fashion of it' is a trifle equivocal. Did they think it vulgar, were they unenterprising, or did they think tripping this particular light fantastic too light morally or physically?

Most dances, like instrumental compositions, were brief, and from the sixteenth century on were in suite form. Thus, the music was also in that form. A suite at that time contained four obligatory dances, an allemande, or Alman haye, which is of

German origin, a quick courante, a slow sarabande and a lively gigue – to give them their French names. They were almost always in the same key, as they were probably written for the lute, which would otherwise have had to be tuned anew for each different key. Other dances could be, and subsequently were, added, so that in later centuries we find the gavotte, minuet, bourrée, rigaudon, and so on, forming part of the suite, which by the time of Purcell, Bach and Handel had become a highly complicated form of instrumental music using dance-rhythms. The suite, born in the sixteenth century, was also the forerunner of the sonata.

Lutes were the most popular instruments of the day. Although 'no English lute music (noted) can be dated earlier than 1540',[68] no household of any pretensions was without several lutes, and even inns and taverns had them available for customers to use. The lover and his lute is a commonplace in poems and literature of the time; Dobinet Doughty says this of his master who fancies himself in love with every woman:

> Then up to our lute at midnight, twangledom twang;
> Then twang with our sonnets, and twang with our dumps,
> And heigho from our heart, as heavy as lead lumps;[69]

Dobinet is being sarcastic, but this half-pear-shaped instrument of Arabic origin (*al' lud*) is beautiful: it can be marvellously ornate or quite simple in decoration. Lutes usually had six pairs of gut strings – that is, six courses – two to each note, and, as strings were expensive, to give a person a set of lute strings was considered to be a correct, charming and unostentatious gift.

Another stringed instrument was the cittern; there are many variations on its name. It is not unlike a lute in shape, but has wire strings and is the ancestor of the guitar. Its strings, in double courses, were rarely if ever tuned below the treble clef. There were also virginals, with the strings running parallel to the keyboard or keyboards; these oblong instruments were placed on tables to be played, but were sometimes supplied with legs. Virginals (a member of the harpsichord family) also often had

Harpsichord

exquisitely ornamented and painted cases. The same applies to the clavichord, whose tone is produced not by plucking but by a kind of pressure stroke from below, delivered by a small metal 'tangent'.

There was an endless variety of flutes, all descended from the recorder – they had no reeds – and some, the fipple-flutes, were end-blown. The recorder itself was the head of the fipple-flute family and came in different sizes, bass (four feet long and played through a side pipe), treble, descant and sopranino, making a complete range of four octaves.

Among other instruments to blow were the sackbut, parent of the trombone, the indispensable trumpet and the shawm or shalm, a very primitive ancestor of the oboe family. It had a double-reed mouthpiece and a wide bell. The largest had bent tubes to the mouthpiece and resembled a bassoon. Very large shawms were often called bombards, which gives some idea of their blasting qualities.

Blasts could come from organs, and some great organs worked

by eight or more bellows created such a noise that the sound has been likened to cracks of thunder. But the small positive organ or 'regal' of five or six octaves was now in use, as was the small portative organ. These could be carried about; some were so small they were fitted into a leather case and looked like a large book. Among the musical instruments found at Westminster at the time of Henry VIII's death were five pair of double regals, all beautifully decorated, some with pipes covered with purple velvet and embroidered with gold and pearls, and eight pair of single regals, equally beautifully made. There were upwards of a dozen virginals, there were clavichords and viols, 'great and small', gitterons (citterns), lutes, flutes aplenty, crumhorns, recorders, shawms, tabors and one bagpipe.

There was also an instrument described as one 'that goeth with a wheel without playing upon'. It was of wood, varnished yellow and painted blue with six round plates of silver 'pounced with antique' and 'garnished with an edge of copper gilt'.[70] This must have been a mechanical instrument of some sort, perhaps worked on the barrel-and-pin principle, that is, having a revolving barrel with pins in it which released some striking mechanism when the barrel was turned. We know, too, that as early as Henry VIII's time there was such a thing as the mechanical virginal, which this instrument clearly is not.

But, at a guess – and the description is too inadequate to do more than that – I think it might have been some kind of hurdy-gurdy. This instrument, which originated in the Middle Ages and was used for training choirs, was also 'favoured with periods of courtly use'.[71] The hurdy-gurdy* is gut-stringed and the sound is produced by turning a wheel at one end. The strings are usually double and are stopped by wooden blades set on transverse wooden keys as in a clavichord; these are pressed down by the player's left hand as he turns the handle of the resined wheel with his right. The blades are hidden inside a key-box with a hinged lid. Other strings which the instrument may have are drone strings or 'bourdons'.

* A descendant of the tenth-century *organistrum*, which required two players.

A hurdy-gurdy, especially one for 'courtly use', was often most beautifully painted and ornamented. The six silver plates 'pounced with antique', that is, embossed or engraved with classical heads, and the edge of 'copper gilt' may have been rich embellishments and not part of the mechanism. However, I hold no brief for this; it is merely a theory.

The king wrote a number of songs, instrumental pieces and at least two masses which were performed. We are not sure if these were all his own work or if he had assistance from court musicians, but there seems no reason to believe he could not or did not write the songs attributed to him. One, 'If Love now reigned', is a rather heavy, elaborate melody, but 'Whereto should I express' is simple, expressive and slightly melancholy, while 'Pastime with good company' is still sung today.

Some time not long before the king's death in 1547, John Redford (who also died in the same year), a well-known musician–poet, friend of John Heywood and Master of the Choristers of St Paul's from 1531 to 1534, wrote an Interlude possibly intended to be performed by the boys at court. This Interlude, *Wit and Science*, is amusing and contains a fair amount of music, as Interludes did; even the galliard is danced as part of it. It incorporates in its stage directions the titles of songs together with their accompanying instruments.

Most appropriately, *Wit and Science* ends with the following direction:

> Here cumth in fowre with violes, and sing
> 'Remembreance', and, at the last, quere [choir] all make
> a cur[t]sye, and so goe forth syngyng.[72]

CHAPTER SEVEN

Of Gardens and How They Grew

It may as well be admitted at once that about gardens and gardening in Tudor times, excepting the Elizabethan era, we know very little. Unlike buildings, furniture, jewellery and other domestic artefacts which remain to speak of themselves and of their own day, gardens by their very nature do not survive unchanged, while gardening itself is a continuous process and, as it develops, leaves little trace behind of what has gone before. Gardening, although it is probably the most popular and most practised art in England today, does not seem to have begun, as such, much before the end of the fifteenth or the beginning of the sixteenth century.

Before then, gardens were largely utilitarian. They produced flowers and fruit, it is true, but essentially they appear to have been used for growing medicinal, pot and strewing herbs and certain flowers, chiefly because they, too, had medicinal properties. This was the primary purpose of gardens.

About medieval monastic gardens we know a little. A few accounts remain, showing, for example, how much gardening boots and mending an orchard gate cost the monks, and what they paid for vegetables when, by some mischance, their own crops failed. For instance, in 1451, Mr Miles Hadfield tells us, there is 'a suggestive item' in the Gardener's Account Rolls at Norwich, where Brother Robert Brettenham was in charge of the gardens. It reads: 'To the cellerer, when herbs failed, 3s. 4d.'[1]

But the monks were the skilled horticulturalists, and had been for centuries. As they lived quietly, relatively undisturbed by wars, they could cultivate their gardens. They must have grown flowers as well as food, for flowers were used on many special feast days of the Church; and priests, particularly at Corpus Christi, were garlanded with roses – a charming custom which was banned at the Reformation. Flowers were also used at weddings and funerals.

There were more than 700 religious houses in England at the time of the Dissolution, but not all can have had gardens, for some were located in towns and cities, while certain religious orders did not go in for agriculture. On the other hand, we know that the Benedictines and Cistercians were large land-owners, farmed their own land and were adept at horticulture. That abbeys such as Glastonbury – where we know vines were grown – Netley, Jervaulx and Fountains had large gardens we can, I think, take for granted. All country priories and abbeys also had fish ponds (as did many private houses), kept for utilitarian purposes, and doubtless when monastic buildings and land were granted to, or bought by, Henry VIII's men they still remained utilitarian, although it is possible that in time some became ornamental ponds as well.

The monks also paid great attention to grafting; grafts were inserted into stock, clay laid round the scion and then moss bound round to keep the graft moist and in place – very similar methods are still in use. Orchards seem to have been Tudor favourites and we know that the poet–soldier–courtier, Henry Howard, Earl of Surrey, had a large garden made around his new house, Mount Surrey, which he built on the site of St Leonard's Priory, Nor-wich. Not a trace of the house remains and one of the few things we know about the gardens is that a dozen years after the earl's execution the apple trees in his 'appleyard' were destroyed by the followers of Robert Kett. The destroyed trees were apparently used to make huts for the rebels, so the orchard must have been fairly large.

Unfortunately for us, no pictures of English gardens before the Tudor era exist as they do on the continent, where they occur chiefly as illustrations in French or Flemish manuscripts and devotional books. We have no wall paintings, carvings or illuminated manuscripts to give us the smallest clue as to what gardens were like. It may be that such things were destroyed at the Reformation, we cannot tell, but there seems to be nothing pictorial left from which we might attempt to re-create a medieval English garden and so lead from that, even if only imaginatively, into the Tudor.

It is reasonable to assume, however, that the peaceful conditions which followed the accession of the first Tudor brought with them many changes in gardens. We have already noted the changes which took place in domestic architecture – castles and fortified manors giving way to unfortified family houses. Gardens, hitherto bounded by strong, battlemented walls and more practical than beautiful, must also have altered, as there was now no necessity to confine them exclusively within such fortifications. Nevertheless, about the gardens of great houses we can only hazard a guess – but a reasonable enough guess – that in early Tudor times they escaped from confinement and began to become places of pleasure and beauty as well as of utility; and we can reinforce this piece of guesswork with the knowledge that all great country houses were self-sufficient. Such gardens, and the much smaller and simpler gardens of country folk, produced flowers, fruit and herbs – which included vegetables – for culinary and medicinal purposes. We know that later, in great Elizabethan gardens, separate plots were used for the growing of flowers for beauty and flowers for physic. We know, too, that vegetables were kept separate and that the flower garden proper was formally arranged. It was cruciform in shape, with four beds formed by two walks, a 'straight forward' which ran from the garden front of the house to the far wall, and another which ran from one side of the garden to the other and intersected the 'straight forward' in the middle and at right angles to it, making four equal plots for planting, usually with knots. It was all very formal, regular and 'tight'; we would think it stiff and unnatural. This pattern must at least have had some faint beginning in earlier Tudor times.

During the first years of the sixteenth century, in 1511, to be exact, the ill-fated Edward Stafford, Third Duke of Buckingham (1478–1521), began to build himself a great new house, Thornbury Castle, in Gloucestershire. Curiously enough it was built in the old, castellated style, and it is said to have been based on Henry VII's palace at Sheen. Stafford was a royal favourite, but so arrogant, so rich, so noted for his lavish hospitality to powerful nobles, as well as for the fact that he had royal blood in his veins – via King Edward III – that at last Henry VIII became both jealous and suspicious. The inevitable result was that the Duke was tried and executed for treason – a flexible term – in 1521. But he had already completed a good deal of the garden of his new home before going to the block.

In a survey of Stafford's lands made in May 1521 we are told something about the gardens:

> On the south side of the inner ward is a proper garden, and about the same a goodly gallery conveying above and beneath from the principal lodgings, both to the chapel and the parish church. The utter [outer] part of the said gallery being of stone, embattled, and the inner part of timber covered with slate. On the east side of the said castle or manor, is a goodly garden to walk in, closed with high walls embattled. The conveyance thither is by the gallery above and beneath and by other privy ways. Beside the same privy garden is a large and goodly orchard, full of young graffs [grafts] well loaden with fruit,* many roses and other pleasures. And in the said orchard are many goodly alleys to walk in openly. And round about the same orchard ... [are] other goodly alleys with roosting places covered thoroughly with white thorn and hasel.²

Beyond this orchard, from which there were a number of exits, lay a newly made park. It was not particularly woody but 'it had many hedgerows of thorn and great elms'.³

The mention of galleries may be confusing to us because the word 'gallery' suggests indoors. But garden galleries, a distinct

* Fruit in May? Perhaps the promise of fruit, blossom, is meant.

feature of sixteenth-century gardens, usually ran around the inner side of the outer walls of a garden. Wooden posts, often arched, formed the other side and overhead was a covering of vines, creepers or wood to give better protection. In the case of Thornbury the walls were crenellated and the solid stone or brick wall formed one side of the gallery. It seems to have had its inner side covered with slates, which sounds most unattractive. Galleries sometimes ran around three sides of an enclosed square or rectangular garden, but often a gallery led from the house to the mount.

Mounts, a feature of Tudor gardens, were developments from those mounds of earth which, back in the thirteenth century, were raised against monastery walls so that the inmates could climb up and have a good look outside, gazebo-fashion. It was just as well to know who had arrived at the front gate. Such simple mounds were later used in lay gardens, but in Tudor times the mound was transformed into a fashionable feature and was termed a 'mount'. Made of earth, not necessarily against a wall, mounts were planted with fruit or other trees and were frequently sited in orchards. The top was reached by a special stair or by a cork-screw path bordered with sweet-smelling herbs, shrubs or flowers. On top was usually an arbour made, perhaps, of trellis-work and covered with climbing plants. Or the building might be of a more substantial kind and used as a banqueting house.

The mount at Hampton Court was vast and splendid. It was built at the end of 'The King's New Garden', which Henry VIII had made in 1533. Raised on a brick foundation, it was planted with quick-set and three pear trees and further ornamented by the king's beasts, as were other parts of the garden. These animals were made of wood, gaily painted, and there seem to have been sixteen of them climbing the mount, which had a wonderful banqueting-house or arbour surmounting one side. This must have been a relatively permanent structure, as it rose two storeys and had glazed windows and a gallery made of wooden trellis-work which connected it with another arbour, possibly an open one, on the west side.

We have some information about what the Hampton Court garden – or gardens – looked like, but not enough to enable us to picture the general plan and layout. Both Cardinal Wolsey and, later, Henry VIII made extensive alterations to the garden but, unfortunately, no plans are extant of the work set in hand by either cardinal or king. Both men had roughly 2,000 acres to play with, a good deal of which was park-land, and Wolsey certainly extended the court around the original manor house. Here he laid out orchards and gardens separated by brick walls. Part of the old manor-house garden he apparently kept as it was, so this must have been late medieval. John Chapman was his head gardener, and he remained head gardener at a salary of £12 a year when, in 1529, Henry VIII took over the palace and greatly altered it.

As we already know, in 1533 the king was much engaged with extensive alterations to the garden, and E. Law, in his *History of Hampton Court Palace*, tells us that it was laid out 'in accordance with the precepts of the day' to take into account our very variable weather. Alas, he does not tell us what those precepts were. However, we learn that for cold wet weather there were sheltered alleys (galleries?) and dry walks. These last were probably sanded or gravelled; indeed, John Lydgate (1370?-1457) says, in speaking of gardens in *The Chorle and the Bird*, 'all alleys were made playne with sand.' Then there were garden houses only slightly open to the fog and air and, Law says, walled 'parterres'. What is meant by this is difficult to decide, since the word 'parterre' does not seem to have come into use in England until the seventeenth century. A parterre, as defined by the Oxford English Dictionary, is 'a level space in a garden occupied by an ornamental arrangement of flower beds of various shapes and sizes'. It is just possible that by 'parterre', the knot-garden (of which more later) is meant.

For summer pleasure there were arbours, shady nooks, grass plots, bowers and banqueting-houses – banquets were then merely courses of sweet dishes and wine. Also dotted about were many sundials, and these were often very beautiful indeed. Then there were the ubiquitous 'king's beasts': dragons, lions, unicorns, greyhounds, harts, bulls, griffins, leopards, tigers and other animals which held the shields and vanes upon which the king's arms, and also those of the queen, were displayed. Whether the queen's arms were changed as occasion demanded I cannot say. Many of these beasts were made in stone as well as in wood, but all appear to have been brightly painted and gilded.

Arbours for summer were sometimes known as 'roosting-places', so this explains the allusion to such places in the orchard at Thornbury. On 17 March 1503, Henry VII paid an unnamed person 5s. 'For making an arber at Baynards Castle'.[4] A year before that, on 10 July 1502, he paid one Henry Smith, a clerk of Windsor Castle, 4s. 8d. for labour employed in making an arbour for the queen. About the gardens at Windsor Castle at this period we know virtually nothing, but an arbour could be of brick or stone – 'arbour' means 'harbour' – and built like a turret into the wall, or it could be made of trees with intertwined branches or of impermanent trellis-work covered with creeping plants and sweet-scented honeysuckle. 'In a harbour grene aslepe whereas I lay,'[5] runs the first line of a poem written about 1550, and the poet may have been lying asleep on a turf seat, for arbours often contained a turf seat on which to roost.

Arbours were not an innovation of the Tudor period. In fact we find mention of one, together with a turf seat, in Chaucer:

> Hoom to myn hous ful swiftly I me spedde
> To goon to reste, and erly for to ryse,
> To seen this flour to sprede, as I devyse.
> And, in a litel herber that I have,
> That benched was on turves fresshe y-grave [dug-out],
> I bad men sholde me my couche make;[6]

Turf seats were 'sometimes built against a wall, sometimes round a tree. The arms were brick or stone and the seat, though faced with stone, was of earth raised a foot or 18 inches from the ground and turfed over with ordinary turf or with sweet-smelling camomile, violets or penny royal.'[7] Together with banks of earth they provided the garden seats of the time and can have been useful only in dry weather. It is difficult not to think that Shakespeare magically transformed one of these garden banks into Titania's bed when Oberon said to Puck:

> I know a bank whereon the wild thyme blows,
> Where oxlips and the nodding violet grows
> Quite over-canopied with luscious woodbine,
> With sweet musk-roses, and with eglantine:[8]

This is enchanting and natural. Knot-gardens were not. The knot-garden, which probably came in with the first Tudor and went out with the last, obviously charmed the sixteenth-century eye but could hardly have been a more contrived or unnatural affair. When exactly it made its first appearance is not known, but by 1520 the knot-garden had become high fashion. We do know that Henry VII's garden at Richmond is described as being made with 'royal knots alleyed and herbed',[9] so possibly he set the fashion, and we do know that some of the gardens at Hampton Court were terribly knotted. We can be sure that where court or cardinal led, noblemen and rich men followed.

These tortured little plots could be either raised or on the level. If the earth were raised it was held in place by brick or tile borders; if level, low clipped box or thrift usually performed this service. The bed was in most instances square and, inside this enclosed square, patterns were made by using low clipped shrubs. The patterns were often geometrical, interlacing or in the shapes of animals, and the more intricate the design the better. In the interstices flowers were planted. Thus, the finished product must have looked like a piece of excessively coarse mosaic pavement.

Another relatively new idea was the railed garden. Here the bed was enclosed by trellis-work or fences, which were made very low to provide a decorative frame for the bed. The idea of railing beds seems to have made its appearance just prior to the Tudor century, but such beds soon became fashionable and when Henry VIII made his alterations to the garden at Hampton Court,

Railed garden beds and royal beasts

or at some other or possibly all of his palaces, he seems to have had railed oblong beds. The rails were painted the Tudor colours, green for eternity, white for purity – the colours of the leek, in fact.

There is a famous painting after Holbein in the Royal Collection at Hampton Court in which one catches a glimpse of railed beds. The king sits under a cloth of estate with Jane Seymour – long since dead, as the picture was painted around 1546 – standing on his left and his only legitimate son, Prince Edward, on the right. The Princesses Mary and Elizabeth stand apart on either side – in the wings, so to speak. Behind and to one side of each princess is a narrow arched opening which looks out into a garden, variously identified as Hampton Court or Whitehall. Behind the Princess Elizabeth in the arched opening stands a man with a monkey on his back, who is reputed to be Simon, the king's fool; just beyond him lies the garden. In the arch behind the Princess Mary is a woman wearing a close-fitting striped cap; she may be the princess's 'Jane the Fole'. It would seem so because of the colour and the type of cap, which fits her head tightly – we know from the Privy Purse accounts of the princess that she frequently paid a barber to shave her fool's (Jane's) head. Here, despite Jane – who seems rather agitated – one sees much more clearly that part of the garden with the beds railed in green and white, and here too are some of the king's banners or escutcheons raised on ornamental poles.

The flowers which grew in such railed beds and in knot-gardens were by our standards woefully limited in number, kind and variety. The great days of exploring new countries, discovering new lands, had only just begun and we had not yet imported many plants from 'outlandish' places. We know from Richard Hakluyt (1552?–1616) that Dr Linacre is said to be responsible for introducing the damask rose into this country, for he says: 'And in time of memory things have been brought in that were not here before, as the Damaske rose by Doctour Linaker king Henry the seventh and king Henrie the eights Physician.'[10] Although Hakluyt is writing in the time of Queen Elizabeth, he also tells us that Edmund Grindal (1519?–83), one of Edward VI's chaplains, prebendary of Westminster and, later, Archbishop of Canterbury, brought the tamarisk back to England from Germany, a country to which he had prudently retired during Queen Mary's reign. Here it should be remembered that after the Reformation in England Protestant refugees from the continent must have brought with them new plants and new skills, and thus enriched our gardens.

Hakluyt also tells us that the 'Artichowe' was introduced during the reign of Henry VIII, and also the 'Abricot' – this last by a French priest, Wolfe Gardiner, which sounds rather an odd name for a priest and a Frenchman. But he adds, rather sadly – and we can well believe him – 'many other things have been brought in that have degenerated by reason of the colde climat', while others had 'by negligence bene lost'.[11]

But, to return to roses, it seems hardly necessary to say they were, as they still are, the favourite flowers, and the damask rose was merely a new variety of an old favourite. Poetry of the day is full of roses: 'I love the rose both red and white,'[12] sings Sir Thomas Philipps, who may thus be intimating to King Henry VII his strict impartiality, for he continues, 'to hear talk of them is my delight' and, further, ends this particular verse on what might be considered a slightly sycophantic note with:

> Joyed may we be
> Our prince to see
> And roses three.

It is thought these lines refer to the birth in 1486 of Prince Arthur, who through his parents combined in himself the virtues of those two noble houses whose badges were the white rose and the red rose.* The baby prince is therefore likened to a

* The white rose had been the hereditary cognizance of the House of York ever since its beginning (Edward III) and was not just adopted, as Shakespeare says, at the time of the Wars of the Roses. The red rose was the badge of Edmund Plantagenet (1245–96), second son of Henry III, and Earl of Lancaster. It was also the badge of John of Gaunt (1340–99), fourth son of Edward III, and Duke of Lancaster, who was created Earl of Richmond in 1342. Edmund Tudor, father of Henry VII, was created Earl of Richmond in 1453.

third rose – possibly the striped 'Tudor rose'. In any case, it was in the time of Henry VII that the rose was first adopted as the badge of England.

Although poets were always singing, as they had been for centuries, about roses, at this time they also make frequent mention of lilies, violets and primroses. It is probable that these were the favourite flowers of the era, although it is equally probable that such mention was a poetic convention. Edmund Spenser (1532–99), admittedly not an early Tudor poet (though the flowers he names obviously existed before he did), speaks in his *Prothalamion* of 'the Violet, pallid Blew' and of 'vermeil Roses', as well as 'The little Daizie'. In his *Epithalamion* he also mentions lilies and roses, which were 'Bound truelove wize, with a blew silke riband'. Earlier, John Skelton, in his *Garlande of Laurell*, tells us of 'the ruddy rosary', as well as 'sourayne rosemary', and when, in the same poem, he addresses 'Mastres Margery Wentworthe' he speaks of 'marjoram gentle, the flowre of goodlyheed [head]', and refers to her as the 'praty primrose' and the 'goodly columbyne'. Who copied whom we cannot say, but Sir Thomas Philipps, in the poem cited above, also refers to 'marjoram gentle'. Possibly that was the usual epithet for marjoram, like Homer's repetitive 'wine-dark sea' and 'Ox-eyed Hera', although an early use of the word 'gentle' meant cultivated as opposed to wild. Philipps also refers to 'Columbine golds' and mentions as well daisies, gilliflowers, camomile, borage, savory, lavender, primroses and violets.

'The violets, cowslips and the prime roses/Bear to my closet,'[13] Cymbeline's queen orders Pisanio and her ladies, while in *The Winter's Tale* Autolycus begins his song, 'When daffodils begin to peer . . . Why then comes in the sweet o' the year',[14] although, rather unromantically, his 'pugging tooth' is set on edge (for a quart of ale) by the sight of 'a white sheet bleaching on the hedge'.[15] But this, at least, tells us of a common way of bleaching linen, while the upthrusting daffodils were probably wild ones.

'Wild bulbs,' says Pliny, 'compounded with silphium* and swallowed in pills, relieve intestinal wounds and affections.'[16] It is likely that Pliny may be referring here to wild onion or garlic, but he may equally well have meant the wild daffodil or narcissus, both of which grew around the Mediterranean and were known to ancient authors. They were known to William Turner too. The narcissus, he says, in *The Names of Herbes*, 'is of diuerse sortes'. One, which he says he has never seen, has a purple flower, and there is another 'wyth a white floure which groweth plentuously in my Lordes gardine in Syon'.[17] ('My Lord' was Protector Somerset.) 'It may be called also,' he continues, 'the whyte daffydyl.' He also specifically states that Pliny mentions another kind which, in his judgement, is our yellow daffodil, although he may have meant afadille or asphodel, one of the old names for daffodil. Just how he arrives at this conclusion is not clear from Pliny's own words,† 'Narcissi duo genera . . . purpureo flore et alterum herbaceum', which is all he says about the actual flower. He then gives the medicinal properties of the 'root' and says that oil from the flower is good for soothing 'callosities' and for the ears, but it produces headaches.

Wild flowers had been used medicinally for thousands of years and had also been especially grown, particularly in monastic times, in the physic gardens of monasteries. From here they probably crept into ordinary lay gardens, both into the physic plot and the ornamental plot. This dual function – medicinal and ornamental – domesticated certain wild flowers and, due to cultivation, they must have altered in size and colour, although these features can also vary greatly with the type of soil. The flower Chaucer's 'hero' was hurrying home to his arbour to see was the one he loved most:

* A plant, variously identified, which yielded gum-resin, anciently much used in medicine.

† Turner does not state from which book of the Natural History he takes this observation. But I can find no relevant reference other than Book XXI, section lxxv.

The 'dayeseye' or elles the 'ye of day,'
The emperice and flour of floures alle.[18]

Although this was the meadow daisy, 'whyte and rede',[19] we know from Thomas Tusser (1524?–80) that daisies were also cultivated in gardens for 'strewing' even if the famous song,

When daisies pied and violets blue
And lady-smocks all silver-white
And cuckoo-buds of yellow hue
Do paint the meadows with delight,[20]

continues to suggest that daisies as well as violets were meadow flowers only.

What cuckoo-buds were we do not know but, though yellow, they cannot have been buttercups, since the buttercup was commonly known as 'crow-flower' and also as 'crow foot', names in use until the nineteenth century and still used in parts of northern England today. Just to complicate matters, however, John Gerard, in his *Great Herbal* (1597), gives the name 'crow-foo' to the ragged robin. But many flowers seem to have borne this name; the word 'crow' appears to allude to the shape of the leaves, which suggests a crow's foot.

We can, however, piece together from various sources* other flowers grown in Tudor gardens, although it is difficult to differentiate between those grown purely for pleasure and those grown for their medicinal or other properties. Thomas Tusser gives a list of 'Herbs, branches and flowers for windows and pots',[21] which includes bay, bachelor's buttons, cornflowers (known as 'bottles') – 'blue, red and tawny',[22] columbine, campion, cowslips, 'daffadown dillies', eglantine, flower amour, feather few, double marigolds, 'Paggles' (primula), rosemary, roses, snap-dragon, sops-in-wine, sweet John, Star of Bethlehem,

---

* I have used, in addition to poetic references, Thomas Tusser's *500 Poyntes*, William Turner's *The Names of Herbes* and *Libellus de re herbaria novus*, Sanders' *Encyclopaedia of Gardening* and the OED. This last, of course, gives only the first mention in print of any flower, but obviously plants existed before the written word.

Sweet briar, garden tools and watering pot

Star of Jerusalem, violets (yellow and white) and wall gillyflowers of all sorts. Obviously some of these are more suited to an open garden than to a window-box – and there were window-boxes – or a pot; often flowers were set out in the garden in pots.

Then there were pinks – tradition has it they came to England with the Conqueror; sweet William, the scent of which gladdened the brain; heartsease, the name speaks for itself. There were irises, better known by the name 'Floure delyce', as William Turner, who was Dean of Wells, a physician and our first scientific botanist, points out in his *Herbaria*. He also notes in his *The Names of Herbes* that 'Fluellyng' is the English name for Veronica. This is included in his list of thirty-seven 'newe founde Herbes, whereof is no mention in any olde auncient wryter'. Perhaps, too, there were cyclamen. Turner speaks of them as 'cyclaminus', and has seen them abroad. 'I heare say,' he tells us, 'that it groweth also in the west countrey of England but I have not hearde yet the englishe name of it. Me thynke that it might wel be called in englishe Rape Violet because it hath a root like a Rape & floores like a Violet or sow-brede.' Such cyclamen must have been the small, wild, outdoor variety.

There were lilies of the valley and, of course, broome. The paeony was grown, perhaps only for physic. It had been known here for at least five hundred years and its healing powers much extolled by Arnold of Villanova* (1235–1312). Roots, flowers and seeds of the paeony continued to be used medicinally until the seventeenth century. Poppies too had medicinal properties, as did, amongst others, dittany, saxifrage, valerian and woodbine. Turner is careful to say in what degree heat, cold, moisture and dryness lie in a number of herbs, so that 'Poticaries should be excuseless when as the ryghte herbes are required'.[23]

William Turner (15??–1568) is rightly called the father of scientific botany in this country. He wrote two books on the subject which still make fascinating reading, *Libellus de re herbaria novus* (1538) and *The Names of Herbes* (1548). A Northumbrian

---

* His commentary on the *Regimen Sanitatis Salernitanum* gives the most authentic account of that verse ms.

by birth, he went to Cambridge and then to the continent to study medicine and botany. He took his M.D. at either Ferrara or Bologna and later incorporated it at Oxford. In 1543, when living in Basle, he wrote religious books which were so eagerly read in England that they were prohibited in 1547. Returning to England in the time of Edward VI, he became physician to the Lord Protector but, wisely, fled the country when Mary became queen and did not return until after her death, when he was made Dean of Wells. His two books on botany, one in Latin, the other in English, are the very first attempts made in this country to catalogue plants in alphabetical order and to give some of their uses. Unlike Thomas Tusser he gives no practical hints on gardening although, as we know, he does give advice on the use of herbs in physic.

Many kinds of herbs and plants were grown for other specific purposes and, although gardens for physic and pot herbs were, it seems, kept in separate plots, some of these other plants with special uses may equally well have been grown in what might be called the non-utilitarian pleasure garden. For example, there were strewing herbs, including lavender (relatively new), lavender cotton, marjoram, roses, basil, balm, cowslips, daisies, sweet fennel, germander, hyssop, pennyroyal, tansy, violets, camomile and other sweet-smelling flowers and shrubs, some of which must also have been grown in the pleasure garden. The same could apply to those plants used for distilling sweet or medicinal waters: blessed thistle, betony, dill, eyebright, endive, fumitory, hyssop, mint, roses, saxifrage, woodruff and succory.

Nicholas Grimald (1519–62), chaplain to Bishop Ridley, and the poet so given to Poulter's Measure, has a poem about a garden which sums up its purposes. It reads, in part, as follows:

The garden gives good food, and ayd for leaches cure:
The garden, full of great delite, his master dothe allure.
Sweet sallet herbs bee here, and herbs of every kinde;
The ruddy grapes, the seemly fruites bee here at hand to
   finde ...

Beholde with lively heew, fayr flowrs that shine so bright:
With riches, like the orient gems, they paint the molde in
   sight ...

From heavy hartes and doolfull dumps the garden chaseth
   quite.

The poem ends, 'Seed, leaf, flowr, frute, herbe, bee and tree
are more than I can sing.'[24] It does seem rather fortunate that his
voice gave out.

It is difficult to imagine what great parks or large gardens or,
even more, the whole countryside were like without the variety
of trees which now grow in this country. There were, for
example, no horse-chestnuts, no plane, no silver fir, no Lombardy
poplar. There were oak, ash, lime, alder, wych-elm, birch and,
in certain parts of the country, beech, Scots pine – called 'pyn-
apple' – sycamore, the sweet chestnut, possibly introduced by
the Romans, and the larch – a newcomer to the century – were
our chief trees. 'Though we had a predominately wooded
landscape, the number of species that composed it was very few.'[25]

We cannot accept that all trees mentioned by Chaucer in his
Parlement of Foules grew in England, for some, such as 'the
olyve of pees' and the 'victor palm', belong to a different climate,
but he does refer to a number which did.

> The bilder ook, and eek the hardy asshe;
> The pilar elm, the corfe unto careyne;
> The boxtree piper; holm to whippes lasshe;
> The sayling firr, the sipres, deth to pleyne,
> The sheter ew, the asp for shaftes pleyne.*[26]

Spenser, in Canto I of the *Faerie Queen* – this is two hundred
years later than Chaucer – also mentions the elm, oak, ash,
poplar, pine, aspen, laurel, fir, yew, birch, sallow, beech and
holm-oak, and adds the maple and the weeping willow. He too

---

* Corfe – *coffin*; careyne – *corpse*; pleyne – *lament*; pleyne – *smooth*.

speaks of the olive and the cedar; these two must have been a poetic convention. Cedars, at least, the cedar of Lebanon, did not make their appearance here until the seventeenth century. Cypress trees, we know from Turner, certainly grew in great plenty in the Protector's garden.

We do know that certain types of trees and shrubs, such as the myrtle, box, bay and laurel, and possibly berberis and hornbeam, began to be used ornamentally in gardens in a new way. This novelty was topiary work, an art which had been well-known to the Romans, but if they introduced it into this country when it was a Roman colony the art, like that of brickmaking, seems to have been lost after their withdrawal. How or from where it was re-introduced I cannot say, but just before mid century John Leland notes topiary work in several places in England.

The castle of Wressel in the East Riding of Yorkshire, one of the finest beyond the river Trent, was stone-built and had a great gate-house. Although it was 'old', having been built in the time of Richard II, it looked as new. At the time of Leland's visit it belonged to the Earl of Northumberland. Leland gives a brief description of its plan and some of its furnishings, noting the 'garde-robe' was 'exceeding fair' – which is hardly usual for the time – and so 'wer the gardeins withyn the mote, an yn the orchards wer mountes *opere topario*, writhen about like turnings of cockilshilles to come to the top without payne.'[27] These mounts with spiral paths bordered by fancifully clipped trees or shrubs must have been fairly large affairs, particularly if to climb one without winding one's way up would have caused the climber discomfort.

Also in Yorkshire, at Ulleskelf near Towton in the West Riding, Leland says, 'there is a goodly house longing to a prebend in York, and a goodly orchard with walkes *opere topario*.'[28] Topiary walks through orchards sound as strange to us as does an orchard containing mounts. At Little Haseley, Oxfordshire, 'Master Barentine' (perhaps Sir William Barantyne or Balantyne) had 'a right fair mansion place and marvelous fair walkes of *toparii operis*',* plus 'orchardes and pooles'.[29] It would be useful to know just what trees were used for topiary work, but Leland does not say. What is interesting is that topiary is usually mentioned in connection with orchards, which suggests that owners of 'fair' houses treated an orchard as part of the pleasure garden. And although Leland does not specifically say so, it is perhaps possible to assume that the pools at Little Haseley were, in part at least, ornamental.

We do know that at Hampton Court there was a garden called the 'Pond Garden' but this, it would seem, was ornamented only by the king's beasts. There were, however, fountains in royal gardens; one in the second court of Henry VII's palace at Richmond was embellished with dragons and other animals as well as with roses which spouted water. And there must have been fountains at Greenwich, Beaulieu, Wanstead, Woodstock and Oatlands. A late-century visitor describes one at Hampton Court. In the centre of the 'chief area', which was paved with stone, there was 'a fountain that throws up water, covered with a gilt crown, on the top of which is a statue of Justice, supported by columns of black and white marble'.[30] About Windsor Castle we know only that it had a vineyard, which was producing in the time of Edward IV and might well have still been doing so, and some walks. Cardinal Wolsey laid out a handsome garden at York Place and this too, when he fell, became a royal garden.

In later life Henry VIII laid out gardens around his now-vanished palace of Nonsuch, near Ewell, Surrey. In 1538 he had enlarged the property by adding to it the lands of Cuddington, so that the palace was 'so encompassed with parks full of deer, delicious gardens, groves ornamented with trellis-work, cabinets of verdure, and walks so embrowned by trees, that it seems to be a place pitched upon by *Pleasure* herself, to dwell in along with *Health*'.[31] Here were 'two fountains that spout water one round

* Haseley Court Gardens, Little Haseley, are on the same site today. These famous gardens with their topiary work belong to Viscount Hereford and are open to the public at certain times of the year.

the other like a pyramid', which is a rather confusing description, particularly as the writer then adds, 'upon which' were perched small birds 'that stream water out of their bills'.[32] Another fountain in 'the grove of Diana' was 'very agreeable', as it showed the goddess in her bath whilst her nymphs splashed water over the wretched Actaeon, already transformed into a stag. Admittedly this description was not written until 1598, but the fountains in the garden may have been there or been installed during the time of Henry VIII.

Unfortunately, this account lists the contents of the garden in no great detail and, more infuriatingly, gives no inkling of the plan or layout, but we can be sure that the gardens, like the palace, were on a magnificent scale. But the king did not live to complete the palace and we may assume that the gardens were also incomplete at the time of his death, because Henry FitzAlan (1511?–80), Twelfth Earl of Arundel and a godson of the king, who held the palace for a time after the monarch's death, continued to carry out the royal plans. As the palace was not restored to the crown until 1591, the original plan may well have continued to exist in 1598. Succeeding sovereigns stayed there occasionally. It was finally given by Charles II to his mistress, the Duchess of Cleveland. This rapacious woman had it torn down for the value of its stone and wood.

That the royal gardens supplied the sovereign with pleasure and also with seasonal delicacies is illustrated by various items contained in Privy Purse Accounts. A rather laconic entry in the spring of 1493, 'To the gardiner at Shene for sedes 6s. 8d.',[33] must have brought King Henry VII some later-in-the-year pleasure in flowers and herbs, while on 17 February 1496 the same gardener was paid £2 for 'grafts', which suggests an orchard of some size. On 17 March of this same year one Bayley was paid 13s. 4d. 'for watching crows'. He must have played scarecrow for some time to earn that amount of money, as such labour received 2d. or 3d. a day. An unusual entry for 26 January 1498 reads, 'to the gardiner for sope hashes 10s.'. So ashes from burned wood or green stuff must have been supplied by the gardens to the royal household as an ingredient for soap – most great households made their own soap in those days. Soap, however, was in infrequent use even in noble families, but good quality soap was imported by the rich from Venice and Spain or perhaps bought at Bristol, where there was now a soap works.

More unusual is an entry in 1530, when Henry VIII paid out 10s. 8d. to 'laborers that made clean the Aleys in the parke at Wyndesor'.[34] And on 22 April of that year the gardener at Greenwich – his name was Walshe and his salary £3 10s. a quarter – received 20s. for 'weding, delving and for laborers'.[35] Jasper, the gardener at 'Beaulie', frequently figures in the accounts of Henry VIII for bringing herbs to wherever the king happened to be, and was usually rewarded 6s. 8d. for this service. He received this sum on 25 May 1530, 'for bringing streberyes to the king'. Jasper too received £3 10s. a quarter as well as his 'rewards'.

On 4 June 1530, an entry appears which is of more than passing interest. It reads, 'paied in rewarde to a servant of the Mayer of London for bringing Cherys to my lady Anne vi s viij.' My lady Anne was the king's new love, Anne Boleyn, and doubtless the Mayor was quietly currying favour. Later, on the 27th and 30th of the month, the gardener at York Place was rewarded 4s. 8d. for taking cherries and also herbs to the king at Hampton Court. On 1 July he brought 'lettuze and cherys',[36] and on 10 August the gardener at Hampton Court took 'peres and damsons' to the king. On 16 August the gardener at Richmond received 4s. for bringing 'philberts and damsons'[37] – although it sounds a bit early for filberts – to the king, who was then at Easthampton, while the gardener at Whitehall brought him some unspecified fruit.

By September, when the king was at Hartford, one James Hobart was tipped 20s. 'for bringing Oranges and lymmons'[38] and on the 7th Jasper journeyed down from Beaulieu with 'Artichokes and Cocoms and other herbs'.[39] In June 1531 strawberries were received from Hampton Court 'diuerse times',[40] and on the 28th cherries were brought. The Tudors appear to have had a penchant for cherries, perhaps because, as Pliny says, they 'relax the bowels', although 'injurious to the stomach'.[41]

The year 1532 was a busy one in the gardens at Greenwich. On 8 April the keeper of the park, Edward Astell, paid £3 17s. 6d. 'for thornes and for laborers work'.[42] The thorns may have been quick-thorn used for hedging. On the 10th he was paid £3 10s. for keeping the fowl in the garden and also for keeping the house – presumably the fowl-house – clean for a year. Much weeding and digging went on during the ensuing months; the park was refurbished, rats were taken, the brake was mowed – that is, it was scythed – ditches were dug in new ground, and Astell received 3s. 4d. 'for scowring the new pale of the parke there'.[43] 'Scowring' is interesting, for here, as the park pale is described as new, it can hardly mean 'cleansing' – if indeed pales were ever cleaned. But 'scow' is an old word meaning 'strips of wood' or 'lathes', so it is very possible that the 'scowring' done by Edward Astell was the nailing of strips of wood vertically or horizontally to the paling in order to reinforce it. In any event, Greenwich park and gardens were obviously being put in good order.

The king then set off in October with the newly created Marquis of Pembroke* – more usually known as Anne Boleyn – for Calais, to meet Francis I and to sign the Treaty of Boulogne for an Anglo–French alliance. Whilst there he spent £3,592 12s. on jewels, and the whole expedition is said to have cost £11,033 10s. 11d. In fairness, it should be said that the English king lavished gifts upon his French brother, and when Francis returned the compliment he had to borrow money to do so.

Sir Thomas More had a famous garden which sloped down to the river at Chelsea, where he and the king would often walk. Although its beauty is spoken of by contemporary writers, no detailed description has come down to us. John Heywood (1497–1580), who married Sir Thomas's niece, Elizabeth Raskell, says it was 'Wonderfully charming . . . both from the advantage

* Marquis, not Marchioness, because she held the title, conferred on 1 September 1532, in her own right.

of its site . . . and also for its own beauty: it was crowned with almost perpetual verdure; it had flowering shrubs; and the branches of fruit trees interwoven in so beautiful a manner that it appeared like a tapestry woven by Nature herself.'[44]

When Sir Thomas was so shamefully confined to the Tower, on one occasion when his wife visited him she urged him to get out of 'this filthy prison' by conforming to the king's will as others had done, and she reinforced her argument by saying, 'at Chelsea you had a right fair house, your library, your books, your gallery, your garden and your orchard.'[45] And when Sir Thomas asked, 'Is not this house . . . as nigh heaven as my own?' Lady Alice in her 'accustomed, homely fashion . . . answered "Tilly-vally, tilly-vally".'[46]

Chelsea was then rural, but there were gardens in towns and cities too. In the City of London, close-packed as it was, there were many small private gardens, while the great houses along the Thames to Westminster had larger gardens. Within the city, in Broad Street, Sir William Paulet, who had built himself a new house there during the reigns of Henry VIII and Edward VI, had a large walled garden attached to his house. Thomas Cromwell, as we already know, also had a garden, as did Stow's father, a far 'lesser' man than Cromwell in the worldly sense of the word. In Red Cross Street behind 'fair houses' was a large plot of ground called the 'Jew's garden', as it had once been the only place in which the Jews were allowed to bury their dead, but this had been 'turned into fair garden plots and summer-houses for pleasure',[47] Stow tells us. But by Stow's time the garden at Northumberland House had been made into 'bowling alleys' and 'dicing houses',[48] and this sort of thing was happening elsewhere too.

In Worcester, for example, 'The number of gardens scattered about the city was large', although 'Many inventories suggest that they were not cultivated at all, but were used to keep horses or pigs, and for the storage or disposal of unwanted objects',[49] and 'these garden areas were gradually built over during the late sixteenth and earlier seventeenth centuries'.[50] This building-

over of gardens happened in expanding cities and towns, more
so in the south than in the as yet more scantily populated north.

Apart from gardens proper, orchards were very popular with
those who had enough land. At Hampton Court the Great
Orchard and the King's Private Orchard were separated by a
moat which was spanned by a decorative drawbridge. An
orchard then, however, did not consist entirely of fruit trees.
There is a record extant of the purchase of 200 young trees of
oak and elm for the Great Orchard at Hampton Court, and this
orchard also contained apple, pear and service-berry trees. One
item in this record reads, '600 chery trees at 6d. the hundred',[51]
which sounds an incredibly low price but supports the view that
the Tudors must have had a passion for cherries.

When we consider that at this time 500 red rose 'trees' – not
rose trees as we know them but, rather, bushes – were also
bought and that the orchard contained as well all those oaks and
elms, it is reasonable enough to conclude that market gardeners
and nurserymen must have existed as a source of supply. On this
point we have a little evidence from John Stow who, when telling
what happened to the poor cottagers in Portsoken Ward, East
Smithfield, during the latter part of the reign of Henry VIII,
remarks that the 'residue of the field was for the most part made
into a garden by a gardener named Cawsway, one that served the
market with herbs and roots'.[52] It can hardly be supposed that
Mr Cawsway was the only market gardener in London or in
England. His garden was in the city, and there must have been
others outside the city walls and in southern counties.

This is borne out by a pamphlet entitled *The Husbandman's
Fruitful Orchard*, published in 1609 and written by one 'N.H.',
which is hardly illuminating as to authorship. The relevant
extract from the pamphlet is as follows:

One Richard Harris of London, borne in Ireland, Fruiterer
to King Henry the eighth, fetched out of Fraunce a great store
of graftes especially pippins before which time there were
no pippins in England. He fetched also out of the Lowe

Countries, cherrie grafts and Peare grafts of diuers sorts: Then took a pees of ground belonging to the king in the Parrish of Tenham in Kent about the quantitie of seauen score of acres, whereof he made an orchard planting therein all these foraigne grafts. Which orchard is and hath been from time to time the chiefe mother of all other orchards for those kinds of fruit in Kent and diuers other places. And afore that these said grafts were fetched out of Fraunce and the Lowe Countries although there was some store of fruite in England. Yet there wanted thereof both rare fruite and lasting fine fruite. The Dutch and French finding it to be so scarce especially in those counties nere London, commonly plyed Billingsgate and diuers other places with such kinde of fruite, but now (thanks bee to God) diuers gentlemen and others taking a delight in grafting ... have planted many orchards fetching their grafts out of the orchard which Harris planted called the New Garden.[53]

It is interesting to note that both the French and the Dutch brought fruit into the country and sold it at Billingsgate, which was, even then, more noted for fish than fruit. But the pippins mentioned must have been a new variety, since pippins, as such, were known here as early as the fifteenth century at least; Lydgate mentions them, and the monks had been great grafters. We also had pears in fair quantity, grafted ones too, for grafting was also perfectly familiar to country folk. There is a charming, amusing and simple poem, written long before Mr Harris set up in business, in which two verses illustrate this:

> In the middle of my garden,
> is a pear tree set.
> and will no pear bear
> but a pear Jenet [early] ...
>
> The fairest maid in town
> prayed me

to engraft with a graft
of my pear tree[54]

The remaining verses, as can be imagined, have a double meaning and the fairest maid, the appropriate time later, finds herself not with a pear Jenet but with a 'pear Robert'.

Thomas Tusser, born at Witham, Essex, bred to music at Cambridge and holder of some minor office at court at the end of Henry VIII's and the beginning of Edward VI's reigns, gave up his job to become a farmer in Sussex. Here he wrote a book, *A Hundreth Poyntes of Good Husbandrie*, first published in 1557[*] and later enlarged and reissued as *Five hundreth pointes of good husbandry united to as many of good huswifery*. The book, written in doggerel, is a compendium of all tasks a farmer and his wife must undertake throughout the year.

In his *January Abstract* 'Of Trees of fruits to be set or remoued' at this time of year, he lists twenty-seven varieties: apples, apricocks, barberries, bullace, cherries, chestnuts, cornet plums, damsons, filberts, gooseberries, grapes, green plums, hurtle-berries, medlars, mulberries, peaches, pears, pear-plums, quinces, 'respis', 'reisons', strawberries (red and white), service trees, small nuts, walnuts and wheat-plums.

Some of these are nut trees, some are bushes, and when he mentions 'reisons' we can, I think, assume that he means some kind of currant. Wheat-plums were apparently a wax-coloured plum and 'respis' are raspberries. Of raspberries Turner says, 'Raspeses', or Rubus ideus, 'growe most plentuously in the woddes of East Friselande besyde Aurik, and in the mountaynes besyde Bon, they growe also in certayne gardines of Englande.'[55] Tusser, writing later, seems to regard them as a necessary fruit for the garden.

The gooseberry, or 'Groserbush', which, it seems, was not known in earlier gardens, was now fairly common and goose-berries are found in Henry VIII's garden as early as 1516. The

[*] It ran into many editions and was in use until the eighteenth century. I have used the editions of 1573, 1580 and 1585, as collated and edited by W. Mavor, 1812.

bush may have come to England from Germany where, Turner says, it grew in fields. All in all, the Tudor century was fairly fruitful, although the taste, size, colour and quality of the fruit must have been very different from those of our modern kinds.

Only great land-owners can have had large pleasure orchards as well as other kinds of gardens – flowers, herbs, physic – but manor houses, doubtless, imitated these on a much smaller scale, and in the country all farms and cottages must have had gardens. But gardening, like keeping the fowl and pigs and seeing to the production of butter, cheese and milk, was specifically woman's work. Fitzherbert, in his *Boke of Husbandrie* (1523), sets out the duties of a husband and wife and does not forget that she is the gardener. He recommends that her garden should be made ready by the end of February or the beginning of March and that she should get as many 'good sedes and herbes as be good for the potte and to eate, and as oft as may need shal require it must be weded, for els wedes wyl ouergrow the herbes'. Herbs, as we know, included vegetables, but a few herbs now appear which were not previously known, such as asparagus, melons, tarragon, horse-radish and artichoke. How melons were managed in this climate without benefit of glass is not easy to understand – it may be that summers were hotter then – but it is almost impossible to visualize such exotics being grown in farm or cottage garden even though, as we shall see, they were re-commended to farmers.

Tusser, who is far more notable for his good sense than for the verse in which he clothes it, also admonishes the housewife to begin her garden:

> In March and in April, from morning to night
> In sowing and setting, good huswives delight;
> To have in her garden, or other like plot,
> To trim up their house, and to furnish their pot.[56]

He also lists 'Herbs or roots to boil or butter'. These are beans, cabbage, citrons, gourds, nawes, pompions, parsnips, runceval peas, rapes and turnips; whereas herbs and roots to be used for salads and sauces are alexanders, artichokes, blessed thistle, cucumbers, cresses, endive, mustard seed, 'Musk Millions', mints, purslane, radish, rampion, rocket, sage, sorrel, spinach, sea-holly, 'Sparage', skirrets, succory, tarragon and, oddly, violets of all colours.

There were also lettuce, beet, colewort, fennel, leeks, onions, orach, parsley and thyme – Pliny held this brightened the vision and was of great use in chronic coughs – to be grown, and the garden plot, which sounds as if it would have had to have been on the large side, was to be 'well trenched and muckt'.[57] No doubt the housewife did both trenching and mucking.

What is puzzling is the mention of 'citron', an old name for citrus fruits. These can never have been grown save in specially built houses which farmer or cottager was unlikely to have. But oranges were grown by the rich in Elizabethan times and Tusser, due to his period at court, must have known rich people. 'Nawes' is probably *Brassica nepus*, and 'pompions' are unlikely to be the pumpkins we know but may have been some sort of gourd or melon, since 'Musk Millions' (musk melons) are mentioned. Melons may possibly have been grown in frames, but hardly by cottagers. The Elizabethans had wheeled frames which could be trundled about to catch the sun, but I can find no sure evidence of their existence in earlier Tudor times.

It is very probable that only a few of the vegetables listed by Tusser were grown at any one time in any one garden. Here William Harrison makes a relevant comment when he maintains that vegetables were grown plentifully until the reign of Edward I (1239–1307) and a bit later, 'but in the process of time they grew also to be neglected so that from Henry the Fourth to the latter end of Henry the Seventh and the beginning of Henry the Eighth there was little or no use of them in England.'[58] This statement is reinforced by the fact that vegetables are rarely mentioned, as such, in contemporary bills of fare for various feasts or dinners.

Seed was saved each year for next year's sowing and neighbours exchanged seeds. Thus if one person had, by chance or good fortune, a new kind of flower or vegetable not possessed by her neighbour she would, were she kind – and gardeners generally are – give her neighbour a bit of this seed or a slip of the plant, or exchange seed or plant for something she did not have. Originally the new seed or plant had probably been given to – or taken by – a workman on the manor farm, or a tenant farmer or a gardener at the manor house. In this way the rarer kinds of vegetables and flowers were gradually spread throughout the country and cottages were trimmed with hitherto unknown flowers and plots filled with new herbs to boil and butter.

If, in the absence of any plan, we attempt to picture a Tudor garden as opposed to an Elizabethan one, for which plans do exist, we can only generalize. As far as we can tell most great gardens were square or oblong, enclosed by outer walls of brick or stone. A door from the house opened into it and probably a door in the outer wall gave into the orchard or meadows beyond. The outer walls were often ornamented on the inner side with galleries, or banks held in place by brick or stone and planted with flowers. Such raised beds must have made weeder's lumbago relatively uncommon. Within the large square or oblong, divisions were made by low walls or hedges and each division may have held a different type of garden – one, a knot-garden, another with railed beds, a third, perhaps, with topiary work, a fourth with a scythed lawn, an arbour and turf seat. Walks, shaded or open, led through the garden, and in great gardens there were fountains, some perhaps as elaborate as that at Nonsuch. Mounts, trellis-work, sundials, banqueting-houses, summer-houses, all played their several or combined parts to make it a pleasure garden, whilst orchards with their mixed trees must have been a pure delight.

Outdoor entertainments often took place in gardens, and the banqueting-house played an important part here. But such entertainments were neither so sophisticated nor so elaborate as they were to become from mid century on. When Gaveston hears that Prince Edward has become King Edward II and he can therefore return to England, he thinks at once of the entertainment he will give the king:

Garden Tools

And in the day, when he shall walk abroad,
Like sylvan nymphs my pages shall be clad;
My men, like satyrs grazing on the lawns,
Shall with their goat-feet dance the antic hay.
Sometime a lovely boy in Dian's shape,
  With hair that gilds the water as he glides ...

Shall bathe him in a spring; and there hard by,
One like Actaeon peeping through the grove,
  Shall by the angry goddess be transformed ...

Such things as these best please his majesty.[59]

These words were put into Gaveston's mouth by Christopher Marlowe (1564–93), and although Edward II had been dead for more than two centuries the setting and description of the garden is Elizabethan, and the touch about Actaeon sounds as if Marlowe were familiar with the gardens at Nonsuch.

Marlowe was writing in the time of Queen Elizabeth when garden revels, with costumed nymphs, shepherds, elves, water sprites and nereids all taking part, were special entertainments given for the Queen. Yet such lavish, pastoral diversions could not have sprung up overnight, as it were, any more than could the gardens. Both must have begun prior to 1558.

But gardens as a setting for palace, house or even cottage, gardens for pleasure divorced from utility and, more, gardening as an art, began in England in earlier Tudor times.

CHAPTER EIGHT

The Queen is Dead –
Long Live the Queen

When the only half-foreign grandchild of Henry VII died the Tudors had ruled England for seventy-three years; and Tudor government was, as all governments had been before, monarchical. It centred on the king. The crown possessed a magic, no matter who wore it, and upon this age-old magic the new dynasty to a certain extent relied. But the monarchy was by no means absolute. Whatever the faults of the first two Tudors, they did not try to become absolute monarchs as their European counterparts did. On the contrary, they and their ministers overhauled and modernized the old machinery of government and used it. That there were flaws is obvious – there always are – but good government did grow under the Tudors and they were responsible for many useful modifications and changes in administration.

Henry VII, a man of fixed purpose, strong and able, rebuilt his government on the foundations of the Yorkist kings. Undoubtedly sound finance was one of the keys to his success; Edward IV was not impoverished when he died, but Henry VII became rich and the country, peaceful and ordered, prospered with him. His government was not only strong, it was, quaint though it may sound to us, solvent. The king also chose men for their ability, not for their nobility, to advise him. Ability and nobility are not mutually exclusive, but at this point in our history the noble followers of the houses of Lancaster and York had for the most part behaved like the old robber barons, intent only upon self-aggrandizement and power. Now there was to be no place in the kingdom for the over-mighty subject who could threaten both the king and ordinary people. The state was kept well under the eye of the first Tudor and his hard-working Councillors. That largely indefinable thing, the 'common law', which was in some degree independent of the crown, was by no means abrogated. It was strengthened and integrated with the crown. No Tudor was ever silly enough to do away with or try to defy any of those elements of common law which were a part of our tradition. They were wise enough to use them and incorporate them into the royal administration.

The immensely powerful and popular Henry VIII has been called 'a despot under the law'. Even so, the important word is 'law'. Undoubtedly certain laws were tailor-made either for or by the king to suit his wishes, but he could not have taken action by himself alone, for by about 1530 the Privy Council had already become an executive body with a direct function. It could act in its own right and in its own name and issue orders over the signature of its members. Although Henry could and did chop off members' heads rather freely he did it 'legally' according to the standards of the day. On the other hand, in Europe Councils were merely advisory bodies to be disregarded at the king's will or pleasure; action could be taken by the king alone, whereas in England laws could only be made by the king-in-parliament, although parliament was summoned only by the king's will or pleasure and the king's will also commanded obedience. Nevertheless, parliament was not solely an instrument of the crown, nor was it without power to oppose or resist. It was, in fact, becoming a fundamental part of the mechanism of government, and in this we led the way.

There were, of course, other changes too. In seventy-three years of any period changes are inevitable, no matter what the dynasty, but the socio-economic changes of this period must have been as great, proportionately speaking, as they have been in our own time. For one thing there was an almost steady inflation, with levelling-off periods between bumps and slumps. Between 1500 and, say, 1560, the prices of everything doubled, whilst food prices, despite government attempts to fix them, trebled. Bad harvests meant rising food prices, and hunger and ruin for many. The rise in the price of all goods meant that landlords had to raise rents and this led to great hardship amongst those tenant farmers and copyholders (probably about fifty per cent) who were not protected by long leases, and in consequence there was misery and unemployment amongst agricultural labourers. Many different theories have been propounded as to the cause of this inflation, not the least the influx of silver into Europe, chiefly from Peru. In England an over-production of sheep and an increase in population are considered to be among the causes – bad harvests were but a sporadic contributory factor. But, no matter what the causes, the results were the same and the spiralling circle as vicious as it always is. Better times came later because Mary's financial policy laid the foundation for Elizabeth's re-coinage and Elizabeth had also inherited her grandfather's financial acumen and ability to choose the right advisers. The two were in many respects very alike.

Inflation was a destructive force; so, culturally, was the Dissolution. Beautiful medieval buildings decayed; the exquisite objects they contained were carted off by vandals. Priceless manuscripts vanished from monastic libraries. These things happened as lands passed from Church to lay hands. And another socio-economic (and religious) factor operates here too. Such lands gave the layman – whether they came by purchase or by gift – a solid reason for maintaining the Reformation settlement. When Mary tried to restore Church lands, her faithful and tractable Commons informed her they would agree to the restoration of the Papacy and the return to Roman Catholicism – Protestant theology could go hang or, rather, burn – but Church lands would not be returned.

Despite these and other difficulties, trade increased steadily over the whole period, particularly the cloth trade. Henry VII, 'who could not endure to see trade sick',[1] confirmed and extended the privileges of English merchants in the Netherlands, for Antwerp was a great market for cloth, and as Antwerp's trade grew so did London's. Cloth was usually exported 'white'; finishing and dyeing were done abroad. Raw wool, declining as an export, continued to be channelled through Calais until Calais fell. Henry also encouraged English merchants to break the Venetian mono-poly of trade in the Mediterranean and, when Venice imposed heavy duties on our trade with Crete, he persuaded Florence, Venice's rival, to set up a wool staple at Pisa – for Venice imported our wool to feed the looms of the Republic. William Hawkins (d. 1554), sea-captain, father of John Hawkins and, later, Mayor of Plymouth, traded for ivory on the Guinea Coast, and West African trade – but not in flesh – developed under Edward VI and Mary.

Hawkins also touched at Brazil, made a second voyage there in 1532 and returned bringing one of the 'savage kings' with him, whom he presented to 'K. Henry 8 . . . at the sight of whom the king and all his Nobilitie did not a little marvaile.' Not surpris-ingly, for this king had holes in his cheeks 'wherein small bones were planted', and another hole in his lower lip set with a precious stone the size of a pea, while his clothing, behaviour and gestures 'were very strange to the beholders'.[2] But the North Atlantic was ignored, save for cod-fishing in the coastal waters off Newfound-land. This appears only to have become 'common . . . about the beginning of the raigne of Edward the 6 . . . and it is much to be marveiled, that by the negligence of our men, the countrey in all this time hath bene no better searched.'[3]

The treaty with Spain had early on brought us important trade concessions, and a treaty with Denmark opened up Icelandic trade and fisheries. The first Henry had also insisted that as much trade as possible, export and import, should be carried in English bottoms. Thus England began to oust Venice, and to become the greatest trading nation in the world, but we imported only those luxuries which the rich could afford as we were still self-sufficient. Although internal trade was still greater than external trade, after a slack period in the previous century it was cloth, cloth and more cloth upon which we mainly depended. The Tudors encouraged this industry by all possible means.

There were no cloth factories; the industry was carried out in cottages, and this meant prosperity for many villages and areas around York, Bristol, Ipswich, Beverley, Coventry, Winchester, Northampton and Norwich, which had their own separate cloth markets. Cloth was also sent in quantity from the country to the great market in London. Carding, spinning and weaving were carried out with wool supplied by large and small middlemen or 'capitalist' employers. Clothers (clothiers), in particular, prospered. These were the large-scale producers of woollen cloth who employed many men, women and children in all the process of cloth-making. Although all operations were, in the main, carried out in cottages, fulling mills had been known since the thirteenth century and there were a number of these. The clothier John Winchcombe (d. 1520) of Newbury owned one and his business made him so immensely rich that his lavish exploits and extravagances inspired many legends and chap-book stories, as well as the famous narrative prose piece by Thomas Deloney (1543?–1600?), *Jack of Newbury*. 'Jack's' son John (1487?–1555) carried on the business and became M.P. for West Bedwin and later for Reading. This was another step up. His father, who had begun life as a weaver and ended as a clothier, had founded a fortune; he himself founded a solid country family.

Many men other than rich merchants, who had always had power, and successful 'industrialists' like Jack of Newbury were now also able to take a step up or even climb a whole flight of steps. The upper servants of the nobility and gentry found a greater scope for their abilities and more lucrative employment in the service of the crown. So did lawyers, and law was a profession into which the younger sons of the nobility and gentry were put to make their own way in the world. Many went into trade, for there was no stigma attached to trade as there was in the nineteenth century. Small merchants found initiative and enterprise worthwhile in a well-ordered society where wrongs could be righted – not that they always were. It was, in fact, an age of economic individualism and men of middling fortune, whose influence increased over the period, were forming a healthy and rising middle class. Upon this class the Tudors depended a good deal.

Henry VIII was our first Renaissance prince and was educated in the 'humanities'. The High Renaissance was not to flower until the Elizabethan era. Nevertheless, its roots grew and remained firm in the soil provided by the earlier Tudors. For, without a united country, without peace and order, and despite sundry rebellions, uprisings, opposition, and religious changes, there was yet no great slaughter and no civil war. Had there been, the country could not have become united, could not have become a nation-state as it did. And it was the earlier Tudors who created this nation-state and, more, gave the country a sense of nationhood. Although after this great dynasty the crown went to two 'foreign' houses – Stuart and Hanover – this sense of nationhood never deserted us. It preserved and strengthened us in many troubles to come. This, then, was perhaps the greatest achievement of the early Tudors.

When the last grand-daughter of Henry VII ascended the throne she rejoiced in the fact that she was 'mere English'. So did her people.

Selected Bibliography

Amherst, the Hon. A., *A History of Gardening in England*
Anon. (Italian), *A Relation of the Island of England*, ed. and trans. C. A. Sneyd
Antiquitatis Culinaria, ed. the Rev. R. Warner (1791)

Bacon, Francis, *History of the Reign of King Henry VII*, ed. J. Rawson Lumby (1881)
Bickerdyke, S., *Curiosities of English Beer and Ale*
Bindoff, S. T., *Tudor England*
Boorde, Andrew, *The Brevyary of Helthe*
   The Dyetary of Helthe, ed. J. Furnivall (1870)
Bridges Adams, W., *The Irresistible Theatre*, Vol I
Burton Adams, G., *The Constitutional History of England*

Calendar of State Papers, Domestic, Vols III and IV, ed. M. A. E. Green
Calendar of State Papers, Foreign, Edward VI and Mary I, ed. W. B. D. D. Turnbull
Campbell, Lord John, *Lives of the Lord Chancellors*, Vols I and II (1846)
Chapman, H., *The Last Tudor King*
Chaucer, Geoffrey, *The Complete Works*, ed. W. W. Skeat (O.U.P.)
Cholmeley, W., *The Request and Suite of a True Harted Englyshman* (1553), ed.
   W. J. Thoms (Camden Miscellany Vol II)
Chrimes, S. B., *Henry VII*
Copeman, W. S., *Doctors and Diseases in Tudor Times*
Crowley, R., *The Way to Wealth* (1550), ed. R. H. Tawney and E. Power

Davey, R., *The Nine Days' Queen*
Drummond, Sir J., and Wilbraham, A., *The Englishman's Food*
Dyer, A. D., *The City of Worcester in the Sixteenth Century*

Elton, G. R., *England Under the Tudors*
   Henry VIII (Historical Association Publication No. 51)
   The Tudor Constitution
   The Tudor Revolution in Government

Elyot, Sir T., *The Book Named the Governor* (Everyman)

Fitzherbert, ?Anthony, *The Boke of Husbandrie*
Forbes, T. R., *The Midwife and the Witch* (Yale, 1966)
French, R. V., *Nineteen Centuries of Drink in England*
Fuller, T., *Worthies of England*, ed. P. Austin Nuttall (3 vols, 1860)

Guthrie, D., *A History of Medicine*

Hadfield, M., *Gardening in Britain*
Hakluyt, R., *Voyages* (8 vols, Everyman)
Hall, E., *Union of the Noble Families of Lancastre and York* (Henry VIII), ed.
    C. Whibley (2 vols, 1904)
Halstead, C. A., *A Life of Lady Margaret Beaufort*
Harrison, W., *A Description of England*, ed. F. J. Furnival
Hazlitt, W. Carew., *Old Cookery Books*
Hentzner, P., *Travels in England in the Reign of Queen Elizabeth*, ed. and trans.
    the Hon. H. Walpole (1797)
Holinshed, R., *Chronicles*, Vols III and IV (1806)
Hollis, C., *St. Thomas More*
Holmes, G., *The Middle Ages*
Household Books of John, Duke of Norfolk and Thomas, Earl of Surrey (*1481–90*),
    ed. J. Payne Collier (Roxburgh Club, 1844)
Howard, L. (ed.), *A Collection of Letters*, Vol I (1753)

Jacob, E. F., *The Fifteenth Century 1399–1485*
Jeaffreson, J. C., *A Book about the Table* (2 vols)
Jordan, W. K., *Edward VI* (2 vols)

King Edward VI, *Literary Remains*, ed. J. G. Nichols (2 vols)
King Henry VIII, *Miscellaneous Writings*, ed. F. Macnamara
    Songs, Ballads and Instrumental Pieces, collected and ed. Lady Mary Trefusis

Law, E., *History of Hampton Court Palace* (3 vols)
Leland, J., *Collectanea*, Vols IV and V, ed. T. Hearne (1770)
    Itinerary, ed. L. Toulmin Smith (5 vols)
Loseley MSS, ed. A. J. Kempe

Machyn, H., *Diary*, ed. J. G. Nichols
Mackie, J. D., *The Earlier Tudors – 1485–1558*
MacNalty, Sir A. S., *Henry VIII – A Difficult Patient*

Neill, the Rt Rev. S., *Anglicanism*
Nichols, J., ed. and printer, *Illustrations of the Manners and Expences of Ancient
    Times in England in the 15th, 16th and 17th Centuries* (Society of Antiquaries,
    1797)

Selected Bibliography

Nicoll, Allardyce, *British Drama*

Platt, Sir Hugh, *The Jewel House of Art and Nature* (1653)
Pollard, A. F., *Henry VIII*
Prescott, H. F. M., *Mary Tudor*
Privy Purse Expenses of King Henry VII, in *Excerpta Historica*, ed. S. Bentley
    (1830)
Privy Purse Expences of King Henry VIII, introd. and ed. Sir N. H. Nicolas (1827)
Privy Purse Expenses of Princess Elizabeth, ed. Sir N. H. Nicolas (1827)
Privy Purse Expenses of Princess Mary, ed. F. Madden (1831)
Pullar, P., *Consuming Passions*

Regimen Sanitatis Salernitatum, ed. Sir A. Croke (1830)
Rhode, E. S., *The Story of the Garden*
Rutland Papers, ed. W. Jerden (Camden Society, 1842)

Salzman, L. F., *Building in England down to 1540*
Samuelson, J., *The History of Drink*
Scarisbrick, J. J., *Henry VIII*
Singer, C., *A Short History of Anatomy and Physiology from the Greeks to Harvey*
    A Short History of Medicine
    A Short History of Scientific Ideas to 1900
Stevens, J. E., *Music and Poetry in the Early Tudor Court*
Stone, L., *The Tudor Age*
Stow, John, *The Survey of London* (Everyman)
Strutt, J., and Horn, W., *Sports and Pastimes in England* (1830)

Tottel, R., *Tottel's Miscellany*, ed. E. Arber (English Reprints No. 11)
Trevelyan, G. M., *English Social H.story*
    History of England
Turner, W., *Libellus de re herbaria novus* (1538) (facsimile reprint of 1882 ed.,
    Ray Society, 1965)
    The Names of Herbes (1548) (facsimile reprint)
Tusser, T., *Five hundreth poyntes of good husbandrie*, ed. W. Mavor (1812)

Vergil, Polydore, *Anglica Historia*, ed. Denys Hay (Camden Society, 1950)

Watkin, E. I., *Roman Catholicism in England from the Reformation until 1950*
Wilkie, W. E., *The Cardinal Protectors of England*
Williams, N., *The Royal Residences of Great Britain*
Williamson, J. A., *The Tudor Age*
Wilson, C. A., *Food and Drink in Britain*

Sources

CHAPTER I

1. Howard, L. ed., *A Collection of Letters*, Vol. I (1753)
2. Bacon, Francis, *History of the Reign of Henry VII*
3. *Ibid.*
4. Trevelyan, G. M., *History of England*
5. Bacon, Francis, *op. cit.*
6. Elton, G. R., *The Tudor Constitution*
7. *Ibid.*
8. *Ibid.* (Introduction)
9. Vergil, Polydore, *Anglica Historia*
10. Mackie, J. D., *The Earlier Tudors*
11. Elton, G. R., *England Under the Tudors*
12. *Ibid.*
13. *Ibid.*
14. Wilkie, W. E., *The Cardinal Protectors of England*
15. Bacon, Francis, *op. cit.*
16. *Ibid.*
17. Elton, G. R., *England Under the Tudors*
18. Vergil, Polydore, *op. cit.*
19. Bacon, Francis, *op. cit.*
20. *Ibid.*
21. *Ibid.*
22. Hakluyt, R., *Voyages*, Vol. V
23. Bentley, S., ed., *Privy Purse Expenses of Henry VII*, Item, 10 August 1497
24. Sneyd, C. A., ed. and trans., *A Relation of the Island of England* (Anon., Italian)
25. *Ibid.*
26. Trevelyan, G. M., *English Social History*
27. Baker, R., *Chronicle*
28. Sneyd, C. A., *op. cit.*

29. *Ibid.*
30. Bacon, Francis, *op. cit.*
31. Sneyd, C. A., *op. cit.*
32. *Ibid.*
33. Bacon, Francis, *op. cit.*
34. Leland, J., *Collectanea*, ed. T. Hearne, Vol. IV (1715)
35. Sneyd, C. A., *op. cit.*
36. Bacon, Francis, *op. cit.*
37. Elton, G. R., *England Under the Tudors* (Revisions, 1972)
38. *Ibid.*
39. Vergil, Polydore, *op. cit.*
40. Scarisbrick, J. J., *Henry VIII*
41. Roper, W., *The Life of Sir Thomas More, Knight*
42. Skelton, John, *Poems Against Garnesche*
43. Vergil, Polydore, *op. cit.*
44. Roper, W., *op. cit.*
45. Elton, G. R., *The Tudor Revolution in Government*
46. Mackie, J. D., *op. cit.*
47. Elton, G. R., *England Under the Tudors*
48. Hall, E., *Chronicles* (Henry VIII), ed. C. Whibley, Vol. I
49. Neill, S., *Anglicanism*
50. *Ibid.*
51. Campbell, J., *Lives of the Lord Chancellors*, Vol. I (1846)
52. Dunbar, W., *Lament for the Makers*, v.2
53. Trevelyan, G. M., *English Social History*
54. Neill, S., *op. cit.*
55. *Ibid.*
56. Mackie, J. D., *op. cit.*
57. *Ibid.*
58. Dickens, Charles, *A Child's History of England*
59. Nichols, J. G., ed., *Literary Remains of Edward VI*, Vol. I
60. *Ibid.*, Vol. II
61. *Ibid.*, Vol. I, Journal, entry for 12 May 1546
62. Elton, G. R., *England Under the Tudors*
63. *Ibid.*
64. Campbell, J., *op. cit.*, Vol. I
65. Nichols, J. G., *op. cit.*, Vol. II, Journal, entry for 22 January 1552
66. Mackie, J. D., *op. cit.*
67. Nichols, J. G., *op. cit.* Vol. II, Journal, entry for 2 April 1552
68. Machyn, H., *Diary*, entry for 6 July 1552
69. *Ibid.*, entry for 1 July 1553
70. Holinshed, R., *Chronicles*, Vol. IV

71. *Ibid.*
72. *Ibid.*
73. Machyn, H., *op. cit.*, entry for 30 September 1553
74. *Ibid.*
75. Holinshed, R., *op. cit.*, Vol. IV
76. Mackie, J. D., *op. cit.*
77. Hakluyt, R., *op. cit.*, Vol. I
78. *Ibid.*
79. *Ibid.*
80. Bentley, S., ed., *Excerpta Historica*

CHAPTER 2

1. Bentley, S., ed., *Privy Purse Expenses of Henry VII*, date as in text
2. *Ibid.* (date as in text)
3. Pevsner, N., *An Outline of European Architecture*
4. Leland, J., *Itinerary*, Vol. I, Pt I
5. *Ibid.*, Pt II
6. *Ibid.*, Pt I
7. *Ibid.*
8. *Ibid.*
9. *Ibid.*
10. *Ibid.*
11. *Ibid.*
12. *Ibid.*
13. *Ibid.*
14. Nichols, J. G., ed., *Literary Remains of Edward VI*, Vol. II, Journal
15. *Ibid.*
16. Summerson, J., *The Book of Architecture of John Thorpe* (Walpole Society Publication XL, 1964–66)
17. Stow, J., *The Survey of London*
18. *Ibid.*
19. Harrison, W., *A Description of England*
20. *Ibid.*
21. *Ibid.*
22. Shakespeare, William, *King Henry VIII*, Act IV, sc. i
23. Holinshed, R., *Chronicles*, Vol. III
24. Salzman, L. F., *Building in England down to 1540*
25. Shakespeare, William, *King Henry IV*, Pt II, Act II, sc. iii
26. Boorde, A., *Dyetary of Helthe*
27. *Ibid.*
28. *Ibid.*

29. Salzman, L. F., *op, cit.* (citing Hope's *Windsor Castle*)
30. Law, E., *Hampton Court Palace*, Vol. I (citing *The Fortnightly Review*, 1879)
31. Bacon, Francis, *Essayes . . . Civill and Morall*, XLV
32. Nicolas, N. H., ed., *Privy Purse Expences of King Henry VIII*, Item, 19 February 1531
33. Leland, J., *op. cit.*, Vol. 1, Pt I
34. *Ibid.*, Vol. 2, Pt V
35. More, T., *Utopia*
36. Holinshed, R., *op. cit.*
37. Stow, J., *op. cit.*
38. *Ibid.*
39. *Ibid.*
40. *Ibid.*
41. *Ibid.*
42. Nichols, J. G., *op. cit.*
43. Kempe, A. J., ed., *Loseley Manuscripts*
44. Hall, E., *Chronicles* (Henry VIII), ed. C. Whibley, Vol. I
45. Shakespeare, William, *King Henry VIII*, Act I, sc. i
46. Hall, E., *op. cit.*, Vol. I

CHAPTER 3

1. Havinden, M. A., ed., *Household and Farm Inventories*, 1550–1590 (Oxfordshire Record Society, 1965)
2. *Ibid.*
3. Sneyd, C. A., ed. and trans., *A Relation of the Island of Britain* (Anon., Italian; authors' translation here)
4. Havinden, M. A., *op. cit.*
5. Gloag, J., *The English Tradition in Design*
6. *Ibid.*
7. Vergil, Polydore, *Anglica Historia*, XXV
8. Nichols, J., ed. and printer, *Illustrations of the Manners and Expences of Ancient Times*, etc. (Society of Antiquaries, 1797)
9. Edwards, R., *The English Chair* (HMSO, 1951)
10. Harris, M., *The English Chair* (1937)
11. Society of Antiquaries, *op. cit.*
12. *Ibid.*
13. *Ibid.*
14. *Ibid.*
15. Boorde, A., *Dyetary of Helthe*
16. Leland, J., Itinerary, Vol. I, Pt II
17. Haward, J. F., and Blair, C., *The Connoisseur* (June 1962)

18. Bentley, S., ed., *Privy Purse Expenses of Henry VII*
19. *Ibid.*
20. Payne Collier, J., ed., *Household Books of John, Duke of Norfolk*, etc
21. Harrison, W., *A Description of England*
22. Leland. J., *op. cit.*, Vol. 5, Pt XI
23. Burton, E., *The Elizabethans at Home*
24. Bentley, S., ed., *op. cit.*
25. Shakespeare, William, *Timon of Athens*, Act III, sc. vi
26. Nicolas, H., ed., *The Privy Purse Expences of King Henry VIII*, Item, 7 December 1530
27. Bentley, S., ed., *op. cit.*
28. Weaver, J. R. H., *Some Oxfordshire Wills* (Oxfordshire Record Society, 1958)
29. Harrison, W., *op. cit.*
30. Boorde, A., *op. cit.*
31. *Ibid.*
32. Wright, L., *Clean and Decent*
33. Leland, J., *Collectanea*, ed. T. Hearne, Vol. IV
34. *Ibid.*
35. *Ibid.*
36. *Ibid.*
37. *Ibid.*

CHAPTER 4

1. Leland, J., *Collectanea*, ed. T. Hearne, Vol. IV
2. *Ibid.*
3. *Ibid.*
4. Langland, William, *Piers the Ploughman* (trans. J. F. Goodridge)
5. Chaucer, Geoffrey, *The Nonne Preestes Tale*, ll.4025–8
6. Virgil, *Georgics*, Bk 1, ll.80–81 (trans. C. Day Lewis)
7. Pliny, *Natural History*, Bk. XVII
8. Fitzherbert, ?Anthony, *The Boke of Husbandrie*
9. Hales, J., 'A Discourse of the Common Weal', etc., in *Tudor Economic Documents*, ed. R. H. Tawney and E. Power
10. 'The Decaye of England by the Great Multitude of Shepe', in *Tudor Economic Documents*, ed. R. H. Tawney and E. Power
11. Harrison, W., *A Description of England*
12. Wilson, C. A., *Food and Drink in Britain*
13. Chaucer, Geoffrey, *Canterbury Tales*, Prologue, l.389
14. *Ibid.* l.384
15. Anderson, J. L., *A Fifteenth Century Cookry Boke*

16. Boorde, A., *Dyetary of Helthe*
17. Machyn, H., *Diary*, entry for 1 July 1552
18. Kempe, A J., ed., *Loseley Manuscripts*
19. Robbins, R. H., ed., *Secular Lyrics of the XIVth and XVth Centuries*
20. Boorde, A., *op. cit.*
21. Bentley, S., ed., *Privy Purse Expenses of Henry VII*, Item, 12 February 1496
22. Nicolas, N. H., ed., *Privy Purse Expences of Henry VIII*, Item, 26 November 1530
23. Machyn, H., *op. cit.*, entry for 12 December 1555
24. *Ibid.*, entry for 20 July 1557
25. Vergil, Polydore, *Anglica Historia*
26. Clair, C., *Kitchen and Table* (citing *A Book in English Metre*, etc.)
27. Taylor, G., *Silver*
28. Nichols, J., ed. and printer, *Illustrations of the Manners and Expences of Ancient Times*, etc. (Society of Antiquaries, 1797)
29. *Ibid.*
30. Jeaffreson, J. C., *A Book about the Table*, Vol. II
31. *Ibid.*
32. *Ibid.*

CHAPTER 5

1. Holinshed, R., *Chronicles*, Vol. III
2. Vergil, Polydore, *Anglica Historia*, XXIV
3. Boorde, A., *The Brevyary of Helthe* (1647 edn)
4. Singer, C., *A Short Story of Medicine*
5. Graham, H., *Surgeons All*
6. Chaucer, Geoffrey, *The Canterbury Tales*: Prologue, ll.411-14, 421-4, 431-5
7. Coke, A., ed., *Regimen Sanitatis Salernitatum* (1830, with introduction and notes)
8. Boorde, A., *Dyetary of Helthe*
9. *Ibid.*
10. *Ibid.*
11. *Ibid.*
12. *The Englishman's Doctor or the School of Salernie* (anonymous translation printed for J. Helm and J. Burby, 1607)
13. *Ibid.*
14. Boorde, A., *The Brevyary of Helthe*
15. *Ibid.*
16. *Ibid.*
17. *Ibid.*

18. *Ibid.*
19. *Ibid.*
20. *Ibid.*
21. *Ibid.*
22. *Ibid.*
23. Forbes, T. R., *The Midwife and the Witch* (Yale, 1966)
24. Boorde, A., *The Brevyary of Helthe*
25. *Ibid.*
26. *Ibid.*
27. MacNalty, A. S., *Henry VIII – a Difficult Patient*
28. Heywood, J., *The Playe called the Foure PP*, ll.615–18
29. Madden, F., ed., *Privy Purse Expenses of Princess Mary*, Item, November 1537
30. Boorde, A., *The Brevyary of Helthe*
31. Fuller, T., *Worthies of England*, Vol II
32. *Ibid.* Vol. I
33. *Ibid.*

CHAPTER 6

1. Hall, E., *The Union of the Noble and Illustre Famelies of Lancastre and York* (Henry VIII), ed. C. Whibley, Vol. I
2. *Ibid.*
3. Stow, J., *The Survey of London*
4. *Ibid.*
5. *Ibid.*
6. *Ibid.*
7. Machyn, H., *Diary*, entry for 26 May 1554
8. Stow, J., *op. cit.*
9. Bentley, S., ed., *Privy Purse Expenses of Henry VII*, Item, 10 November 1497
10. Holinshed, R., *Chronicles*, Vol. III
11. *Ibid.*
12. Chaucer, Geoffrey, *The Pardoner's Tale*, l.623
13. Shakespeare, William, *Much Ado About Nothing*, Act II, sc. i
14. Strutt, J., *Sports and Pastimes of the People of England*, ed. W. Home (1830)
15. Chaucer, Geoffrey, *op. cit.*, l.591
16. Chaucer, Geoffrey, *The Man of Law's Tale*, Prologue, ll.124–5
17. Anon., *Thinterlude of Youth*
18. Shakespeare, William., *Henry VIII*, Act V, sc. i
19. Shakespeare, William, *The Merry Wives of Windsor*, Act IV, sc. v
20. 'Mr. S.', *Gammer Gurton's Needle*, Act II, sc. ii
21. Boas, F. S., ed., *Five Pre-Shakespearian Comedies* (Introduction)
22. Nichols, J. G., ed., *Literary Remains of Edward VI*, Vol. II, entry for 1 April 1550

23. Surrey, Earl of, *Poems*, ed. E. Jones, No. 27, v.4, ll. 13–15
24. Bentley, S., ed., *op. cit.* (date as in text)
25. Nicolas, N. H., *Privy Purse Expences of Henry VIII*, Item, 22 October 1532
26. Elyot, T., *The Book Named the Governor*, Bk I, xxvii
27. Strutt, J., *op. cit.*
28. Stow, J., *op. cit.*
29. *Ibid.*
30. Elyot, T., *op. cit.*, Bk I, x
31. Hall, E., *op. cit.*, Vol. I
32. Bentley, S., ed., *op. cit.*, Item, 4 June 1492
33. Scarisbrick, J. J., *Henry VIII*
34. Elyot, T., *op. cit.*, Bk I, xxvii
35. *Ibid.*
36. *Ibid.*, Bk I, xviii
37. Shakespeare, William, *Romeo and Juliet*, Act II, sc. i
38. Wyatt, Thomas, *Collected Poems*, ed. K. Muir, No. 170
39. Shakespeare, William, *Hamlet*, Act V, sc. i
40. Hall, E., *op. cit.*, Vol. I
41. Stow, J., *op. cit.*
42. Machyn, H., *op. cit.*, entry for 9 December 1554
43. Wardroper, J., ed., *Demaundes Joyous*
44. *Ibid.*
45. Bentley, S., ed., *op. cit.*, Item, 28 December 1495
46. Udall, N., *Ralph Roister Doister*, Prologue
47. Heywood, J., *The Playe Called the Foure PP*, ll.509–13
48. Singer, C., *A Short History of Scientific Ideas*
49. Steinberg, S. H., *Five Hundred Years of Printing*
50. Mackie, J. D., *The Earlier Tudors*
51. *Ibid.*
52. *Ibid.*
53. Strickland, A., *Lives of the Queens of England*, Vol. II, Elizabeth of York (1851 ed.)
54. Puttenham, G., *The Art of English Poesy* (1584)
55. Shakespeare, William, *The Merry Wives of Windsor*, Act I, sc.i
56. Elyot, T., *op. cit.*, Bk I, vii
57. *Ibid.*
58. Bentley, S., ed., *op. cit.*, Item, 1 February 1500
59. *Ibid.*, Item, 3 November 1493
60. *Ibid.*, Item, 6 January 1493
61. *Ibid.*, Item, 7 January 1502
62. Chaucer, Geoffrey, *Canterbury Tales*, Prologue, l.95
63. Stevens, J., *Music and Poetry in the Early Tudor Court*

64. Blom, E., *Music in England*
65. Stevens, J., *op. cit.*
66. Elyot, T., *op. cit.*, Bk I, xx
67. Hall, E., *op. cit.*, Vol. I
68. Stevens, J., *op. cit.*
69. Udall, N., *op. cit.*, Act II, sc. i
70. Trefusis, Lady M. ed., *Songs and Ballads and Instrumental Pieces Composed by King Henry the Eighth*
71. Baines, A., *Victoria and Albert Museum Catalogue of Musical Instruments*, Vol. II
72. Redford, J. and Happé, P., eds., *Wit and Science*

CHAPTER 7

1. Hadfield, M., *Gardening in Britain*
2. Amherst, A., *A History of Gardening in England* (citing unspecified State Papers)
3. Hadfield, M., *op. cit.*
4. Bentley, S., ed., *Privy Purse Expenses of Henry VII* (date as in text)
5. Weaver, R., *In Youth is Pleasure*
6. Chaucer, Geoffrey, *The Legend of Good Women*, Prologue (later version) ll.200–205
7. Burton, E., *The Elizabethans at Home*
8. Shakespeare, William, *A Midsummer Night's Dream*, Act II, sc i
9. Prescott, H. F. M., *Mary Tudor* (citing Antiquarian Repertory II, 1809)
10. Hakluyt, R., *Voyages*, Vol. III
11. *Ibid.*
12. Philipps, T., 'I Love a Flower' in *Treasury of Unfamiliar Lyrics*, ed. N. Ault
13. Shakespeare, William, *Cymbeline*, Act I, sc. vi
14. Shakespeare, William, *The Winter's Tale*, Act IV, sc. ii
15. *Ibid.*
16. Pliny, *Natural History*, Bk XX
17. Turner, W., *The Names of Herbes*
18. Chaucer, Geoffrey, *op. cit.*, ll.184–5
19. *Ibid.*, l.42
20. Shakespeare, William, *Love's Labour's Lost*, Act V, sc. ii
21. Tusser, T., *Five hundreth poyntes of good husbandrie*
22. *Ibid.*
23. Turner, W., *op. cit.*, Preface
24. Grimald, N., poems in *Tottel's Miscellany*
25. Hadfield, M., 'Britain, Land of Exotic Trees', *Country Life*, 23 December 1971

26. Chaucer, Geoffrey, *The Parlement of Foules*, ll.176–80
27. Leland, J., *Itinerary*, Vol. 1, Pt I
28. *Ibid.*, Vol. 1, Pt II
29. *Ibid.*, Vol. 1, Pt II
30. Hentzner, P., *Travels in England*, ed. trans. H. Walpole
31. *Ibid.*
32. *Ibid.*
33. Bentley, S., ed., *Privy Purse Expenses of Henry VII*, Item, 13 March 1493
34. Nicolas, N. H., ed., *Privy Purse Expences of Henry VIII*, Item, 20 March 1530
35. *Ibid.* (date as in text)
36. *Ibid.* (date as in text)
37. *Ibid.* (date as in text)
38. *Ibid.*, Item, 5 September 1530
39. *Ibid.* (date as in text)
40. *Ibid.*, Item, 27 June 1531
41. Pliny, *op. cit.*, Bk XXIII
42. Nicolas, N. H., ed., *op. cit.* (date as in text)
43. *Ibid.*, Item, 14 July 1532
44. Rhode, E. S., *The Story of the Garden* (citing J. Heywood)
45. Roper, J., *The Life of Sir Thomas More, Knight*
46. *Ibid.*
47. Stow, J., *The Survey of London*
48. *Ibid.*
49. Dyer, A. D., *The City of Worcester in the Sixteenth Century*
50. *Ibid.*
51. Law, E., *History of Hampton Court Palace*, Vol. I, Appendix H
52. Stow, J., *op. cit.*
53. Amherst, A., *op. cit.* (citing Johnson, *History of English Gardening*, 1829, and Philips, *Companion to the Orchard*, 1821)
54. Sloan MS 2593 (British Museum), in *Lyrics of the XIVth and XVth Centuries*, ed. R. H. Robbins (author's translation)
55. Turner, W., *The Names of Herbes*
56. Tusser, T., *op. cit.*
57. *Ibid.*
58. Harrison, W., *A Description of England*
59. Marlowe, Christopher, *Edward II*, Act I, sc. i

CHAPTER 8
1. Bacon, Francis, *History of the Reign of Henry VII*
2. Hakluyt, R., *Voyages*, Vol. VIII
3. *Ibid.*, Vol. V

Index